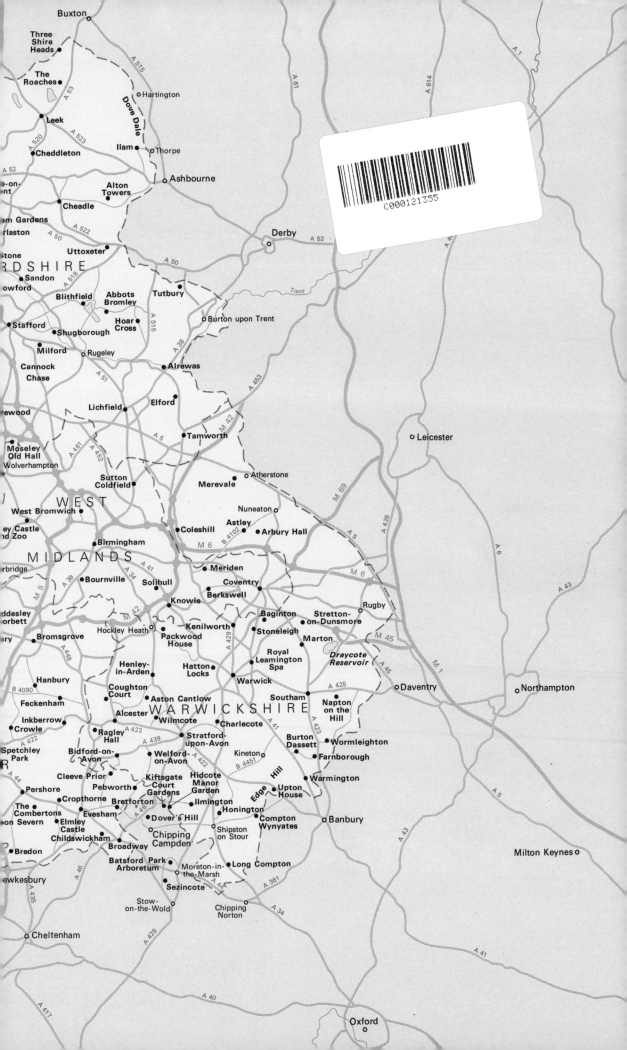

HEART OF ENGLAND

BEAUTIFUL BRITAIN

HEART
OF
ENGLAND

Published by the Reader's Digest Association Limited, London for the Automobile Association,
Fanum House, Basingstoke, Hampshire RG21 2EA

HEART OF ENGLAND
was edited and designed by
The Reader's Digest Association Limited
for the Automobile Association,
Fanum House, Basingstoke, Hampshire, RG21 2EA.

This book contains material from
the following titles originally
published by Drive Publications Limited:
*Treasures of Britain, Discovering Britain,
Hand-picked Tours in Britain, No Through Road,
Book of the British Countryside, Book of
British Towns, Illustrated Guide to Britain,
Book of British Villages, Illustrated Guide
to Country Towns and Villages of Britain,
250 Tours of Britain, Book of British Coasts,*
and from the following titles published by
The Reader's Digest Association Limited:
*Folklore, Myths and Legends of Britain,
The Past All Around Us, Nature Lover's Library,
Food From Your Garden, The Cookery Year.*

ISBN 0-86145-723-4

Filmset by MS Filmsetting Limited, Frome, Somerset.
Separations by Scantrans Pte Ltd, Singapore.
Printed and bound by C & C Joint Printing Co. (HK) Ltd, Hong Kong.

Printed in Hong Kong

Cartography by Thames Cartographic Services, Maidenhead
and the Automobile Association, Basingstoke based on
mapping by John Bartholomew & Son Ltd, Edinburgh.

A name printed in bold type on the endpapers map
or underlined and printed in capital letters on
the tours maps indicates that the place is featured
in this book.

Cover photographs: Malvern by *Patrick Thurston* (top);
Mary Arden's House, Stratford-upon-Avon by *Patrick Thurston* (bottom left);
Introduction (pages 6–7) Flowers in a garden near Bosbury by *Richard Dudley-Smith*.

CONTENTS

Introduction | 6–7

Gazetteer | 8–155

Tour around Coventry | 45

Tour around Hereford | 59

Tour around Lichfield | 75

Tour around Ludlow | 84

Tour around Newport | 95

Tour around Shrewsbury | 113

Tour around Worcester | 153

Index | 156–159

Acknowledgments | 160

HEART OF ENGLAND

No better name could be given to these
central shires. Not only do they include the
country's geographical centre – the
Warwickshire village of Meriden – but also
its quiet, unchanging, rural heart, beloved
of the poet Housman, and its throbbing
industrial heart which first began to beat in
Coalbrookdale, beside the Severn.

Not that it was always quiet or industrious:
the western border is lined with castles,
busy for centuries keeping the warlike
Welsh at bay. It also saw one of the
last battles on English soil, when
Cromwell's army defeated Charles II at
Worcester in 1651.

Outside the busy industrial centres of
Birmingham and the West Midlands, these
shires retain the appearance and values of
the traditional English countryside.

Idyllic towns and villages with timber-
framed houses built from the oaks of long
vanished forests stand amid still-hedged
fields and form a backdrop for a scattering
of old cathedral cities – Hereford, Lichfield,
Worcester. It has its wild places too, the
lonely tops of the Malverns, the Wrekin
and The Long Mynd, formed of the rocks
that are the very heart of England.

ABBERLEY
Hereford and Worcester
8 miles southwest of Bewdley

In the 16th century, Abberley's rector was a saintly man named John Blamyre. He came from an old Cumberland family and had been the abbot of a monastery in the north of England. But when he was deprived of his position, at the Dissolution of the Monasteries, such was the unquestionable uprightness of his life amid the general corruption rife in many monasteries that Henry VIII was obliged to give him some compensation. This the king did by appointing Blamyre rector of the parish of Abberley, which lies at the southern end of a lush, undulating valley. A large bell, now cracked, stands in a corner of the Church of St Michael to remind us of the former abbot. He had brought it from his monastery in the north.

The fine Rectory where Blamyre lived may date partly from the 14th century and, together with the 12th-century church beside it, stands on a little knoll in the centre of the old part of the village. Of the church, only the chancel is still intact, but the ruins of the nave have been well preserved and form part of a charming little garden overlooking the village square. Opposite the garden, on the other side of the square, is the imposing red-brick, 18th-century Jaylands, and a Dutch gabled, partly 16th-century building, which is now the village shop. Nearby is the superb, timber-framed Town Farmhouse, probably 17th century.

Just behind the square rises the rich green Abberley Hill. Near the top is Abberley Hall, now a private school for boys – which includes among its former pupils the politician Sir Geoffrey Howe and the actor Anthony Quayle. The present house was built in the mid-19th century for the Moilliets, an Anglo-Swiss banking family. Later owners of Abberley Hall were the Jones family, who had made a fortune in the Lancashire cotton industry. They built the tall Gothic-style clock tower at the top of the hill.

Abberley's second church, dedicated to St Mary, was built by James Moilliet. It stands near the early 18th-century Tump House, across a small valley from the old church and the village square.

ABBEY DORE
Hereford and Worcester
2 miles north of Pontrilas

A forest of gravestones witnesses the past importance of Dore Abbey, a Cistercian foundation built on a terrace on the west bank of the River Dore in 1147. Virtually derelict after its suppression in the 1530s, the truncated remains of the abbey church were restored in the 1630s. The lavishly vaulted superstructure shelters 17th-century wall paintings, a minstrels' gallery, richly carved side aisles, monumental tombs and well preserved 13th-century tiles. The magnificent oak chancel screen was designed in the 17th century by John Abel. The stonework of the choir and 13th-century presbytery are also impressive. Nearby is a 14th-century farmhouse, The Grange.

The wide, flat Dore valley provided excellent agricultural land around the abbey. One of the valley farms, Abbey Dore Court, has a walled garden which is open from March to October, except Wednesdays.

At Bacton, 1 mile north of Abbey Dore, the Church of St Faith dates from the 13th century. The west tower was added in the 16th century. Some of the stalls are ornamented with poppy-head carving. The most important monument is to Blanche Perry, a local girl who was Queen Elizabeth's maid of honour. She is shown kneeling before the Queen; the inscription to her ends: 'Allwaye wythe maeden queene a maede did ende my liffe.'

ABBOTS BROMLEY
Staffordshire
6 miles south of Uttoxeter

A Butter Cross on the village green is a reminder of the days when Abbots Bromley was a market town. The six-sided timber building marks the spot where, as far back as the 14th century, local people did their trading in butter and other produce. There are several fine half-timbered and Georgian brick houses in the village, particularly in Bagot Street where the Bagot Almshouses date from 1705.

THE MYSTERIOUS HORN DANCE

The Abbot's Bromley horn dance is so ancient that its origins are shrouded in mystery. Most people believe that it was originally a pagan ritual used to bring fertility and good luck.

ROMANTIC RUIN *A cedar stands in front of Acton Burnell's ruined castle which in spite of its name was only ever a fortified manor.*

Abbots Bromley was in the Forest of Needwood in medieval times, and continues traditions associated with the forest. The Horn Dance is performed on the Monday after the first Sunday in September and starts at 8 a.m. outside the vicarage. The horns are kept in the church throughout the rest of the year. The six sets of reindeer horns are of Saxon origin, but the dancers wear Tudor dress as they dance their way around an 8 mile circuit of local farms. The deer-men carry the horns on their shoulders and are accompanied by a Fool, a Hobby Horse, Maid Marian and a Bowman. The Horn Dance is probably an ancient version of a hunting or fertility ceremony.

Richard II hunted in the forest, and was often the guest of the Bagot family. As a reward for providing him with good hunting, Richard gave the Bagots a herd of goats whose descendants, a horned, hardy breed known as Bagot goats, were in a special park at Blithfield Hall until the 1970s. The house was built by the Bagot family in Elizabethan times.

The Church of St Nicholas stands slightly downhill from the village, and although of medieval origin has a Queen Anne tower with a balustraded top. The ceremonial reindeer horns are kept at the east end of the north aisle.

Near the church is the school of St Mary and St Anne, a public school for girls. It was founded in 1874, and became part of the Woodard Foundation in 1921.

ACTON BURNELL
Shropshire
7 miles south of Shrewsbury

Timber-framed black-and-white cottages and buildings of grey-green stone stand side by side in Acton Burnell, a small village which lies close to a ruined castle of red sandstone. The second half of the name comes from William Burnell, who held the manor in 1183. Robert Burnell – Lord Chancellor of England and Bishop of Bath and Wells in the reign of Edward I – built the castle about 1284. It was originally regarded as a fortified manor house. It is open to the public and overlooks the grounds of Acton Burnell Hall, built early in the 19th century and now a college.

The Church of St Mary stands nearby and, apart from its Victorian tower, is almost entirely 13th century. It contains ornate memorials of the Burnell family, including one to Sir Nicholas Burnell, showing him in 14th-century armour, and of the Lees, who owned the village in the 17th century. The Lees were ancestors of the American statesman Richard Henry Lee, one of the signatories in 1776 of the Declaration of Independence, and also of General Robert E. Lee (1807–70), who was chief commander of the Southern forces during the American Civil War.

ACTON SCOTT
Shropshire
3 miles south of Church Stretton

The farming clock has been turned back a century at Acton Scott Farm Museum, where superbly groomed Shire horses plough the upland soil, russet-coloured Tamworth piglets squeak among their straw, and Norfolk black turkeys strut round the farmyard. Far from being just a show place, it is a working mixed farm of 22 acres, within sight of Wenlock Edge, using 19th-century techniques which can still teach the modern farmer valuable lessons. Displays of traditional crafts include regular demonstrations of butter-making in a churn.

Apart from the barns and other farm buildings, Acton Scott has a fishpool, paddocks and meadows, a waymarked nature trail, café and picnic tables. Warm clothing and strong shoes or boots are recommended, as this is an outdoor site and conditions are often wet and muddy. The farm is open daily from mid spring through the summer and near the entrance there is a large picnic site.

ALCESTER
Warwickshire
7 miles west of Stratford-upon-Avon

An old market town, Alcester stands at the junction of two Roman roads where two rivers, the Alne and the Arrow, meet. Little remains of the Roman camp near the Roman Ryknild Street, but the town was a market centre in the Middle Ages and still keeps its old-world look with timber-fronted houses, old windows, its Old

Malt House and its 17th-century, timber-topped town hall. Alcester, once famous for iron-working, has long been known for its cabinet making.

ALMELEY
Hereford and Worcester
4 miles southeast of Kington

The tiny village of Almeley, hidden down quiet twisting back roads, once boasted two castles and a railway station. None survives intact, although the solid conical earth mound of one of the castles still stands next to the mainly 14th-century Church of St Mary.

Completing the traditional medieval threesome of castle, church and manor is the seat of the local landowner, the timber-framed Almeley House, opposite the churchyard. A small area of commonland still survives behind the main street.

ALREWAS
Staffordshire
5 miles northeast of Lichfield

Pretty gardens surround many of the half-timbered, thatched cottages that line the main street of Alrewas and the narrow lanes that adjoin it.

The parish church of All Saints was built in the 13th century, and some of the original work remains. It was later enlarged with lofty arcades and good 16th-century roofs. The grotesquely carved font is 15th century, the pulpit 17th century.

A rough road starting beside the canal bridge at Fradley leads to Fradley Junction, where the Coventry Canal joins the Trent and Mersey Canal. Locks and bridges evoke the atmosphere of the canal's heydays.

ALTON TOWERS
Staffordshire
5 miles east of Cheadle

The great garden at Alton Towers is one of the largest and most fantastic landscape creations in Europe. It was the brainchild of Charles Talbot, 15th Earl of Shrewsbury, a nobleman of immense wealth whose mania for building and landscape is said to have matched in extent that of 'mad' King Ludwig of Bavaria who decorated his kingdom with fairy-tale castles. It is now, appropriately, the site of one of the most extraordinary leisure parks in Europe.

At Alton Towers the earl built an incredible variety of temples, pagodas, grottos and fountains, as well as

TAMWORTH PIGS

The Acton Scott Farm Museum is one of the few places where the ancient breed of Tamworth pig can still be seen. Its long snout is inherited from the wild pig and it gets its colouring from an imported West Indian pig.

planting thousands of trees and shrubs. Entire dead trees were even planted for dramatic effect.

With the passing of time the woods and shrubs have ripened to full-blown maturity, diminishing the shock of the architectural fantasies. Softened by the shade of foliage, the follies no longer intrude.

Especially delightful is the Pagoda Fountain, designed by Robert Abraham (1774–1850) and completed in 1826. It is situated on an island in a chain of small lakes, an airy, three-storey structure from the top of which a fountain spurts a further 70ft into the air. Tinkling bells hang from upcurving extremities of each octagonal roof – the effect is enchanting.

Other notable structures include a fine, seven-domed conservatory, also designed by Robert Abraham, the Corkscrew Fountain and a hilltop Chinese temple. The most fanciful creations, though, remain gloriously bizarre. There is, for example, an imitation Stonehenge, bearing little resemblance to the famous circle on Salisbury Plain since it is constructed in a straight line. In addition, the garden is graced by a Swiss cottage, the size of a warehouse, in which lived a blind Welsh harper who used to play music for the benefit of the earl's strolling guests.

The 15th Earl of Shrewsbury died in 1827, but the house and garden were extended and further embellished by his nephew, John, the 16th Earl. It was he who gave the name Alton Towers to the mansion and its grounds, and he also erected the Corinthian-style memorial to his uncle, which crowns a knoll above the chain of small lakes. On its walls, the 16th Earl caused a noble inscription to be placed, in tribute to the founder: 'He made the desert smile.'

Yet there is much more to admire at Alton Towers than the unique collection of ornamental follies. The lawns are interspersed with well-planted rosebeds, and the garden is renowned for its rhododendrons which bloom in vivid masses in mid-June. From the memorial, a splendid rock garden, probably the finest in Britain, tumbles down the hillside, crowded with dwarf conifers and spiraeas.

Backing the central chain of lakes are beautiful woods where many miles of winding pathway lead among oaks, cedars, sycamores, horse chestnuts and Wellingtonias. The many ornamental specimens include the fern-leafed beech (*Fagus sylvatica* 'Laciniata') and the magnificent tulip-tree (*Liriodendron tulipifera*) whose large leaves, turning bright butter yellow, contribute to the autumn mosaic of tones.

Today, the garden is well maintained as a showpiece, secluded from the other enterprises at Alton Towers, which include some of the most ingeniously engineered man-made attractions in the world, including the Corkscrew rollercoaster and the Black Hole 'space ride in the dark'. The 15th earl would undoubtedly have approved.

At Croxden, about 5 miles south, there are the remains of a 12th-century abbey. The west front is particularly impressive, pierced by lancet windows.

Shropshire 'magpie'. The dominant building is the elm-shaded Church of St Mary which is also built of sandstone and is mottled with moss. It dates from the 12th century, but its exterior was restored in 1878–9.

Inside the church, a brass commemorates John Grove, a native of Alveley who became a Freeman of the Grocers' Company in London. The memorial records how Grove, who died in 1616, left two annual gifts of £10 to the village. One was to employ a schoolmaster; the other was to help 'five poore aged ... labouring men'.

There are several pleasant walks down to the River Severn, where steam-trains of the Severn Valley Railway run along the far bank.

GOLDEN TREE

A lofty tulip-tree lights up a corner of the gardens at Alton Towers. In summer its tall frame is speckled with cup-shaped flowers. But its brightest show comes in autumn when the four-lobed leaves turn a rich yellow or russet. The slightest breeze sets the leaves shimmering on their long slender stems.

ALVELEY
Shropshire
6 miles southeast of Bridgnorth

One long street on the crest of a hill, lined by sturdy sandstone cottages, forms the central part of Alveley village. In contrast to these are other buildings whose black-and-white fronts add a dash of traditional

ARBURY HALL
Warwickshire
3 miles southwest of Nuneaton

The seat of the Newdegate family since the 16th century, Arbury Hall was built on the site of an Augustinian priory. It was originally Elizabethan, but in the 18th century was transformed into a castellated Gothic-style mansion by Sir Roger Newdegate, who also founded the Newdegate Poetry Prize at Oxford University. It has large grounds and a landscaped garden. The novelist George Eliot (1819–80) was born at South Farm on the estate.

ASTLEY
Warwickshire
4 miles southwest of Nuneaton

The Collegiate Church of St Mary the Virgin at Astley was built about 1340. It has a central tower and spire. After the Reformation, the building fell into disrepair until the tower collapsed around 1600. A few years later the old chancel became the nave of a restored parish church, and a new chancel and west tower were built. The choir stalls, about 1400, have painted figures and misericords. There are brasses and monuments.

ASTON CANTLOW
Warwickshire
4 miles northeast of Alcester

The Norman family of de Cantelupe acquired the manor at Aston in 1205, when it was known as Estone, and gave the village its name. They built a castle on the banks of the River Alne, but within two centuries it had fallen into ruin and today nothing remains.

The village is grouped around a small green and has some fine old buildings, including the 17th-century King's Head Inn and the black-and-white timbered Guild House. In the early 16th century the Guild House was the centre for Aston Cantlow's weekly market and annual fair. The building, restored by local funds, now serves as the village hall.

The Church of St John the Baptist dates mainly from the 13th century, and one of its early rectors, Thomas de Cantelupe, became Bishop of Hereford and Chancellor of England. He was made St Thomas de Cantelupe in 1320. The church is also said to be where William Shakespeare's parents were married in 1557.

ASTON MUNSLOW
Shropshire
14 miles north of Ludlow

Overlooking the village, medieval, Elizabethan and Georgian building styles amalgamate in a fascinating architectural jumble known as the White House. In Saxon times there was a manor here known as Estune, held by Lord Edmund in 1042, but the earliest part of the present house dates from the 11th century. The vast beams of the original medieval hall are still visible in places. The outbuildings now form part of a Museum of Buildings and Country Life.

ASTON ON CLUN
Shropshire
10 miles northeast of Ludlow

In the centre of Aston on Clun stands an ancient black poplar, known as the Arbor Tree, which is ceremonially decorated with flags and bunting each May 29 –

Royal Oak Day. The custom celebrates the marriage of a local landowner on May 29, 1786. Many of the decorations remain throughout the year, and the tree is a popular centrepiece for weddings.

From the hedged and narrow-laned western foot of Hopesay Common, about 2 miles northeast of Aston on Clun and just north of the village of Hopesay, a path climbs steeply up to the sparse pines on the crest of Hopesay Hill. Another track east of the hamlet of Round Oak makes a wide grassy swathe southwards through bracken along the lofty summit of the hill, with its grazing sheep and ponies, and its crystalline views on a clear day.

Nowhere is so airy and peaceful as Hopesay in the early morning in late summer, when mists hang in the valleys all the way to The Wrekin in the northeast. Yet this is the edge of the border country, with Wales only 7 miles away. It has been fought over for centuries. To the north the bare peak of Wart Hill rises above dark Forestry Commission conifers. It is capped by an Iron Age hill-fort. So, too, is the green cone of Burrow, 2 miles to the southwest, its centuries-old fortifications sharply defined in the morning sun. On Hopesay it is possible to see how these hill-forts mark a clear line across Shropshire, each one backed up by the next. Caer Caradoc's ramparts stand out crisp against the sky. There is a sense of watchfulness here, and of great age. Below, sheltered farms waken for the day, to follow the age-old pattern of the harvest. Even the trees that brood over the scene are old: ancient hollies, hawthorn, ash and thin Scots pine.

ATCHAM
Shropshire
4 miles southeast of Shrewsbury

On the main road into Atcham village a tiny thatched cottage – like an outsized dolls' house – contrasts with the elegantly Classical lodge and gateway to Attingham Hall. Set in wooded parkland through which deer roam, the 18th-century mansion is now owned by the National Trust. Built in 1783 for Lord Berwick, the house contains a fine collection of early 19th-century English and Italian furniture.

Facing the lodge is a charming Georgian inn, the red-brick Mytton and Mermaid. A large metal sculpture of a mermaid is in the adjacent stable-yard; and the name 'Mytton' refers to 'Mad Jack' Mytton, an early-19th-century squire and MP, whose wild exploits and eccentric behaviour made him a local legend. On one occasion he alarmed his guests by entering a room astride a bear. The joke misfired when the bear bit him in the leg.

Atcham is set on a bend of the River Severn, which is crossed by two bridges. The older bridge has five arches, and was built in 1769–71 by a founder member of the Royal Academy, John Gwynne of Shrewsbury. The modern road bridge dates from 1929.

Behind the inn is the red-sandstone 13th-century church dedicated to St Eata, a 7th-century Celtic bishop. It is the only church in England dedicated to him, and he is commemorated in stained glass.

PEACEFUL HILLS *The poet A. E. Housman described the country-side surrounding Hopesay Hill as 'the quietest under the sun'. In the tranquillity, sheep graze on a patchwork of fields that climbs the hill's broad back.*

B

BAGINTON
Warwickshire
3 miles south of Coventry

The runways and buildings of Coventry airport lie close to the village of Baginton, and the tower blocks and church spires of the city itself punctuate the horizon to the north. Inside the airfield grounds is the Midland Air Museum, with exhibits of jet fighters and rare historic aircraft. There is an exhibition dedicated to Sir Frank Whittle, pioneer of the jet engine, who was born in Coventry.

Near the airport is 'The Lunt', a turf-and-timber reconstruction of a Roman fort. The fort was built after Boudicca's uprising in AD 60 and includes a stockade thought to have been a training ground for military horses, a granary, the east gate and a portion of the eastern defences.

BARLASTON
Staffordshire
3 miles north of Stone

In 1906, many documents and wares were discovered at the Etruria factory, which had been built for Josiah Wedgwood in 1769. The discovery led to the foundation of the Wedgwood Museum Trust at Barlaston, which displays only Wedgwood wares and associated documents.

Exhibits include three copies of Wedgwood's first edition Portland Vases, as well as two of the six 'First Day Vases' thrown by Wedgwood himself on the opening day of the Etruria factory. Also on show are pieces from the Queen's Ware service made for Catherine of Russia. The museum complex includes a demonstration area, in which visitors can see the arts of pottery practised in a manner almost unchanged since the days of the first Josiah Wedgwood.

BATSFORD PARK ARBORETUM
Gloucestershire
1½ miles northwest of Moreton-in-Marsh

In the totally English and rustic setting of the Cotswolds, with the Vale of Evesham spreading out below, Batsford Park unfolds like a sequence from some oriental dream. Over 1000 species of trees and shrubs create a panorama of ever-changing shapes and hues. Many were brought here in the late 19th century by Lord Redesdale, former British Ambassador to Japan. His zeal as a collector embraced ornamental statuary as well – a pair of bronze deer step shyly from a dark copse, and a Buddha contemplates the peace of an English wood.

BAYTON
Hereford and Worcester
6 miles west of Bewdley

Because of its isolation among rolling hills on the Shropshire border, Bayton has retained much of its traditional charm.

The narrow lanes present unexpectedly picturesque vistas as they meander through the village. Cosy mellow brick and half-timbered cottages look out over their creeper-clad garden walls, and the whole village has an air of serenity.

Not far from the Wheatsheaf pub, which has been

WINDMILLS CHANGING THROUGH THE YEARS

Britain has had windmills since the 12th century and had 10,000 windmills before the steam engines of the Industrial Revolution began to replace them. Now Berkswell's tower mill is a rare example of a windmill which is still in good order.

POST MILL *The whole mill is turned to face the wind.*

TOWER MILL *Invented in 1520, only the cap needs to be turned.*

SMOCK MILL *A wooden version of a tower mill was named after a countryman's smock.*

an inn since 1825, stone steps lead to the door of the village store and the post office, an attractive red-brick building looking like a large dolls' house.

At the other end of the village the parish church of St Bartholomew stands on a bluff of high ground. Its early-19th-century tower rises above Norman stonework, and inside is a drumshaped Norman font and a Jacobean pulpit. The church was extensively restored in 1905. Just below the church, to the north, is the rectory, a red-brick Georgian house approached by an avenue of elms. To the east of the church lies the early-19th-century village school, single-storeyed and now a private house.

From the high churchyard can be seen the parkland of the red-brick Georgian mansion of Shakenhurst, 1 mile or so to the west. This imposing house is approached by a long, narrow track which passes one of Bayton's many architectural gems, a small black-and-white lodge looking as though it had been lifted straight out of a picture-book.

MARKING TIME *Just off Windmill Lane, an old millstone is propped up outside Berkswell's beautiful tower mill, which was built in 1826 and has been recently restored.*

BERKSWELL
West Midlands
6 miles west of Coventry

Behind the red-brick Victorian almshouses facing on to Berkswell's green is a square stone well that belonged to a long-forgotten lord of the manor, called Bercul; which is how the village got its name. Opposite the almshouses is the bowfronted post office and shop, while nearby, beneath the trees on the green, is the old whipping post and stocks, the latter pierced by five holes. It is said that the fifth hole was put there to accommodate a persistent local villain with only one leg. The real explanation seems to be that there were originally six holes and the sixth one has rotted away.

Beside the well there is a handsome, stone-faced 17th-century house that was once the Rectory, and along the main street stands the 400-year-old partly timbered Bear Inn, whose leafy frontage is guarded by a Russian cannon captured during the Crimean War. A small agricultural museum nearby contains a collection of farm implements, Victorian domestic items and church and parish documents.

The Church of St John the Baptist is considered one of the finest Norman churches in the Midlands. Its pink stone is well set off by an unusual timbered porch of two storeys, of which the upper is the vestry. Its chief glory, perhaps, is the beautifully arched double crypt, dating from the 12th century.

Berkswell Mill stands in Windmill Lane at Balsall Common, some 1½ miles south of the village of Berkswell. The four-storey tower mill was built in 1826 and the sails, 60ft in diameter, drove two pairs of millstones. Most of the mill's machinery is intact and was driven by a diesel engine from 1933, when the sails were destroyed in a gale, to 1948 when it was last used for grinding corn. The mill has been fully restored and can be visited on Sundays in summer.

BERRINGTON HALL
Hereford and Worcester
4 miles north of Leominster

Thomas Harley, a banker and government contractor, bought the estate, with Capability Brown's advice, in 1775. Brown redesigned the 450 acre parkland, and his son-in-law, the architect Henry Holland, built the mansion between 1778 and 1781. The impressive front entrance is a portico with Ionic columns, while inside is elaborately decorated. Owned by the National Trust, it is open to the public from April to October.

Less than a mile to the southwest of Berrington Hall is Eye Manor, a 17th-century house, built by Ferdinando Gorges, a slave-trader of Barbados. Its fine plaster ceilings resemble those of the Palace of Holyroodhouse in Edinburgh.

BEWDLEY
Hereford and Worcester
4 miles west of Kidderminster

A handsome three-arched bridge designed by Thomas Telford in 1798 leads over the Severn to Bewdley, which clings to a hillside above the west bank of the river at the southeastern corner of the Wyre Forest.

In Elizabethan times Bewdley was a prosperous trading and woollen town, but its waterfront has long since been quiet. The town museum, housed in the Shambles – the former butchers' market – has displays devoted to local trades of the past, including charcoal-burning and ropemaking. Several craftsmen have studios in the museum and sometimes demonstrate their crafts.

The Church of St Leonard's, Ribbesford, has a carved early-Norman doorway and a bell that may date back to 1225. St Anne's parish church is a classical building of the 1740s. Several 18th-century houses line picturesque Load Street.

Tickenhill Manor, an 18th-century house with a brick façade on a hill above the town, contains 15th-century roof timbers. It replaces the Royal Manor where, in 1499, Prince Arthur, heir to Henry VII, was married by proxy to Catherine of Aragon. He died in 1502 and his widow married his brother, the future Henry VIII.

Bewdley is the southern terminus of the Severn Valley Railway, which operates a steam service to Bridgnorth during the summer. A 3½ mile nature trail, leading into the Wyre Forest starts near the Duke William Inn.

RIVERSIDE RAILWAY *Severn Valley steam trains link Bewdley to Bridgnorth and Kidderminster.*

BRIDGE WITH A BALUSTRADE *A pretty riverside street is reflected in the smooth waters of the Severn as it flows through the elegant arches of Bewdley's sandstone bridge, built by the great engineer Thomas Telford in 1798 for a cost of £9000.*

BIDDULPH

Staffordshire
9 miles north of Stoke-on-Trent

A small, well-planned industrial town, Biddulph is set in the heart of lonely moorland. The parish church contains beautiful Flemish stained glass. Biddulph Old Hall, dated 1558, was badly damaged by Parliamentary troops during the Civil War but has recently been restored.

On Biddulph Moor, rising to over 1000ft just east of the town, is the source of the 170 mile long River Trent, England's third-longest river after the Severn and the Thames. To the north are the Bridestones, a burial chamber in which it is said a Viking and his Anglo-Saxon wife were interred. The original barrow is thought to have been over 300ft in length.

To the west of Biddulph is the hill of Mow Cop which is crowned by a sham castle. It was built to enhance the landscape by Randle Wilbraham around 1750, and comprises a ruined round tower and a ragged curtain wall broken by archways. On the summit of the hill Hugh Bourne, a Staffordshire carpenter, began to hold open-air camp meetings in 1807 similar to the revivalist camp meetings then sweeping America, and out of these meetings Primitive Methodism was born.

BIRMINGHAM

West Midlands
100 miles northwest of London

Britain's second-largest city was spawned by the Industrial Revolution, and grew during the 19th century into one of the world's great workshops. Hundreds of trades flourished, especially in metalwork. Birmingham was noted for its large number of smiths who, using coal from the North Warwickshire mines as fuel, hammered out anything from door knockers to arms, buttons to steam engines. During the Civil War they made more than 15,000 swords for Cromwell and the Parliamentary forces.

The centre of old Birmingham is the Bull Ring where a market which has been held since the 12th century still thrives six days a week. Beside the traditional open-air market is a covered market hall, built on different levels.

Subways and an outdoor escalator connect the Bull Ring to the main shopping area, which includes an enclosed complex of shops built over the ultramodern New Street Station.

The Town Hall in Victoria Square was designed by Joseph Hansom (1803–82), inventor of the Hansom Cab. It was opened in 1834 and is modelled on the Temple of Castor and Pollux in Rome. The City of Birmingham Symphony Orchestra has made the Town Hall its home, and weekly organ recitals are given.

Across the square from the Town Hall stands the Council House, home of the city council, which was built in the 19th century in the Italian Renaissance style. The Central Museum and Art Gallery next to the Council House has an impressive collection of Pre-Raphaelite paintings and works by Van Gogh, Botticelli, Gainsborough and Constable.

The museum's collection of gold and silver is a reminder that Birmingham has been a centre for the precious-metals trade for nearly 200 years.

There are more fine paintings, including works by Rubens and Dégas, at Birmingham University's Barber Institute of Fine Arts. The institute, on the university campus at Edgbaston, about 3 miles from the city centre, also has medieval ivories and antique bronzes and furniture.

Birmingham's industrial history is recorded in the Museum of Science and Industry in Newhall Street. Its collections range from small arms to steam turbines. The museum building was once the premises of the Elkington brothers, electroplaters in the 19th century. The original façade of the building has been removed to accommodate a glass-fronted extension which houses the steam locomotive *City of Birmingham*. The engine stands on a section of track and can move, powered by an electric motor.

Sarehole Mill, an 18th-century water mill on the River Cole in the southern suburb of Hall Green, has been restored and is now a branch of the City Museum. The mill was once leased by the engineer Matthew Boulton for rolling sheet steel, before he opened his Soho foundry where he and James Watt perfected the steam engine.

Birmingham has more miles of waterways than Venice. Its canal system was built in the 18th and 19th centuries to provide water transport into the heart of the city, and consists of several converging waterways. The Birmingham Canal, built by James Brindley in 1769, brought coal from the Wednesbury coalfields and meets the Worcester-Birmingham Canal and the Birmingham-Fazeley Canal to the east of the city. The Grand Union runs up from London and connects with the Birmingham-Fazeley at Graveley Hill, while the Digbeth Branch Canal links the two waterways at Aston and Bordesley.

Much of this intricate network of canals has been preserved. The Gas Street Basin has moorings for narrowboats and modern cabin cruisers, and there are several canalside walks such as Brindley Walk, Summer Row and Kingston Row. Boat trips on the canals are run daily all year round from the Gas Street Basin and from Kingston Row.

Aston Hall, $2\frac{1}{2}$ miles north of the city centre, is a Jacobean house standing in pleasant parkland which remains almost exactly as it was when built between 1618 and 1635. It has fine carved fireplaces, and needlework hangings, and contains a magnificent balustraded staircase which still bears the scars of cannon shot from a three-day siege by Parliamentary troops during the Civil War. There is an elegant panelled gallery, and a kitchen set out with period cooking equipment. The rooms are furnished in 17th and 18th-century styles, and there are some good examples of English Japanwork, a form of lacquer-ware that was made in the Midlands during the late 17th and early 18th centuries.

Blakesley Hall, in the eastern suburb of Yardley, is a 16th-century, timber-framed yeoman's house with several rooms containing original wall-paintings and exhibited as period rooms. The rest of the house has displays of rural crafts, toys, kitchen utensils and domestic equipment. The garden has been set out with lawns, yew trees and fruit trees in the style common to a house of that period.

Birmingham has 6000 acres of parks and open spaces. Cannon Hill, the largest of the city's parks, includes a nature centre. The centre covers 5 acres in which plants and animals can be studied in their natural surroundings. There are also displays of farming activities.

VICTORIAN MASTERPIECE 'The Last of England' by Ford Madox Brown hangs in the Birmingham City Art Gallery. It depicts an emigrating couple's final glimpse of the English coast.

St Philip's, in Colmore Row, is Birmingham's Anglican cathedral. It was consecrated in 1715, but did not become a cathedral until 1905. The designer Thomas Archer had lived in Rome, and the Baroque style of the building reflects the Italian influence. Edward Burne-Jones (1833–98), the painter, was baptised in St Philip's for which he later designed four great stained-glass windows. The cathedral is surrounded by acres of well-kept gardens where city workers relax in summer.

The Roman Catholic cathedral, St Chad, was completed in 1841, making it the first Roman Catholic cathedral to be built in England since the Reformation. It was designed by Augustus Pugin, who helped to design the Houses of Parliament. But Birmingham's most famous church is St Martin's in the Bull Ring. It dates from the 13th century, though it was extensively restored in Victorian times.

Birmingham's newest venture, the giant National Exhibition Centre, is 8 miles east of the city centre on the M42, close to Birmingham Airport. The centre is a complex of halls, restaurants and hotels.

BISHOP'S CASTLE
Shropshire
8 miles northwest of Craven Arms

Bishop's Castle is a border town in rich sheep-farming country on the edge of Clun Forest. It lies 500ft above sea level and is ringed by hills rising to 1000ft and more. The origins of its name go back to the late 8th century, when Edwin Shakehead, lord of the manor at nearby Lydbury North, was cured of palsy at St Ethelbert's shrine – on the site of which Hereford Cathedral now stands. He bequeathed all his territory to St Ethelbert. Over 300 years later the Normans interpreted this as a bequest to the Bishop of Hereford, and in 1127 they built a fortified castle for the bishop near Lydbury North, to protect his land. Around this castle the present town grew up.

The bishop's successors, with their chief tenants, the Walcots and Plowdens, governed the town until 1570. A bowling green at the top of the town now stands on the castle's fragmentary remains. The 18th-century town hall, at the top of the steep High Street, contains two silver maces, hallmarked 1697.

The Three Tuns Inn, which dates back to 1642, serves beer brewed on the premises. There are three Tudor houses in Bishop's Castle: the Old Hall, the Old Market Hall and the House on Crutches, which was given its name because its overhanging upper storey is supported by posts.

ELEPHANT AND CASTLE *In Bishop's Castle, in front of the old Bull Inn, an elephant appears on the coat of arms belonging to Clive of India's son, the Earl of Powys.*

BLISTS HILL
Shropshire
2 miles east of Coalbrookdale
See Coalbrookdale, page 39.

BLITHFIELD
Staffordshire
4¼ miles north of Rugeley

Blithfield's Church of St Leonard dates from the 13th century, with Victorian restoration work by Pugin. There is some interesting medieval glass, and many monuments, one by William Stanton and another by Sir Richard Westmacott

Situated in an Elizabethan house nearby, which has been the home of the Bagot family for 600 years, is a museum of childhood. Two Victorian dolls' houses are on display with a collection of antique dolls, and children's toys, books, furniture and costumes. Also

shown are embroidered Georgian costumes and coronation robes, and uniforms of the Victorian Staffordshire Yeomanry and the royal household. The house contains a very fine carved oak staircase.

BOSBURY
Hereford and Worcester
4 miles north of Ledbury

Before mechanisation, the hop-gardens surrounding Bosbury echoed every September to the accents of the South Wales valleys and industrial Midlands, as the pickers and their families moved in by the hundred to help with the harvest. Now machines strip the green vines, and the autumn invasion is history.

The village, which probably derives its name from Bosa, a 9th-century local landlord, has seen invaders before – Saxons, Normans and marauding Celts. It is believed to have been a large town in pre-Saxon times, but it was destroyed by the Saxons and never regained its importance.

It is a traditional village, a pleasant mixture of half-timbered, stone and brick buildings. Dominating the whole village is the massive, detached stone tower of the 12th-century Church of the Holy Trinity. It is one of seven free-standing church towers in Herefordshire, and was built as a fortified refuge from the Welsh raiders who pillaged these border lands until the 15th century. Its six bells were installed in the 16th century.

In the churchyard stands a rare 14th-century preaching cross, one of the few to escape destruction by the Puritans, who regarded such medieval relics as symbols of Popery.

BOURNVILLE
West Midlands
4 miles southwest of Birmingham

In 1879 the chocolate manufacturers George and Richard Cadbury set up a factory on the southern outskirts of Birmingham, by a tiny stream, the Bournbrook. They called the factory Bournville, a name derived from this, and later the name was used for a blend of chocolate.

Around the factory the Cadburys built houses for their employees. Two 14th-century houses – Selly Manor and Minworth Greaves – were transported to the site to give it a rural atmosphere; they are now museums containing domestic equipment.

BREDON
Hereford and Worcester
3 miles northeast of Tewkesbury

High above the River Avon, a slender church spire rises from the meadows and acts as a landmark for Bredon. The main village street, with the church and its lych gate in the background, is lined with charming thatched black-and-white cottages, with here and there buildings of Cotswold stone or mellow brick.

Near the churchyard are some exceptionally fine buildings: the Elizabethan rectory; the Old Mansion, an outstanding example of 17th-century red brick with mullioned windows and dormers; and the elegant 18th-century Manor House.

To the west of the Manor House is the 600-year-old

Bredon Tithe Barn. It is 132ft long – one of the largest stone barns in England. In one of its two porches is an upper room with a fireplace. The property, owned by the National Trust, is open to the public.

Bredon has two inns, the 17th-century Royal Oak and the Fox and Hounds, a thatched, half-timbered building dating from the 16th century. The novelist John Moore, who died in 1967, was a frequent visitor to the Fox and Hounds.

Bredon Hill, 3 miles northeast, rises to more than 900ft. It has a Gothic folly on its slopes – known as Parson's Folly after its builder – and the remnants of prehistoric and Roman earthworks on its summit. From the folly there is a magnificent view of the Avon winding its way across the plain of Malvern.

How many counties can be seen from Bredon Hill depends on the weather and on the viewer's imagination; some say eight, some say 14. Rewarding hours can be spent motoring or walking along the ribbon of narrow lanes through attractive villages like Bredon's Norton, Beckford and Kemerton.

BREDWARDINE

Hereford and Worcester
11 miles west of Hereford

In the west of Herefordshire, near the Welsh border, the peaceful village of Bredwardine sprawls down a hillside to the church beside a wide meander of the River Wye. Its name comes from Old English, and, appropriately, means 'place on the slope of a hill'. In this quiet, rural setting the Reverend Francis Kilvert wrote his mid-Victorian diary of parish life.

Kilvert, son of a Wiltshire clergyman, became Vicar of Bredwardine in 1877, but already knew and loved the area, having spent several years at nearby Clyro. He died of peritonitis in 1879 at the age of 38, only a month after his marriage, and is buried in the church-yard. His marble cross bears the inscription 'He being dead yet speaketh'.

The church itself, on a knoll overlooking orchards and cattle pastures, goes back to the 11th century. It contains effigies of medieval knights. The south door-

A CHOCOLATE FACTORY IN A GARDEN

Michael Reilly.

The BOURNVILLE VILLAGE TRUST

In 1879 George Cadbury and his brother, Richard, set up a factory by Bournbrook stream and so the factory was called Bournville. Houses were built in tree-lined avenues amid lawns and gardens. The brothers even moved two 14th-century houses to help improve the surroundings.

Some of the domestic equipment, wrappers and tins used 100 years ago can be seen in Bournville's museums.

way and nave are original Norman, as is the huge font hewn from a single rock. The church has long outlasted the old Norman castle, whose mound, bailey, fishpond and ivy-covered walls survive just south of the churchyard.

Nearby, on Merbach Hill, 1045ft up, is an arrangement of enormous stones known as Arthur's Stone. Three legends surround the stones – that they mark the burial place of King Arthur, of a giant whom he slew, and that of a king who started a fight with Arthur. What is certain is that the stones are the entrance to a long barrow or grave, dating from around 2000 BC. From the hill there are views over the Golden Valley to the Black Mountains and it is claimed that in clear weather 11 counties can be seen.

BRETFORTON

Hereford and Worcester
4 miles east of Evesham

Hidden away in the Vale of Evesham lies the mellow village of Bretforton. Its documented history goes back more than 1200 years to a Saxon deed of 714. The Saxons called it Brotfortun – 'the ford with planks' – possibly a reference to a footbridge alongside the ford. The village is set in a rich patchwork of fields and orchards, halfway between Evesham and the steep western edge of the Cotswold Hills. These hills supplied the honey-coloured stone for many of Bretforton's buildings. One of its showpieces is the Fleece, a quaint old inn tucked in a corner of The Cross at the heart of the village. The inn was originally a farmhouse, believed to date from the 14th century, and is one of the few inns owned by the National Trust. Creepers ramble over its oak-beamed walls,

framing lead-lined windowpanes under a roof of mossy Cotswold stone. Inside, on the stone floor, there are 'witch marks' designed to keep out evil spirits – a reminder of the inn's medieval past. Among its antiques, is a 48-piece set of Stuart pewter.

St Leonard's Church has stood at the northern end of The Cross for nearly 800 years. Like the rest of the village, it was the property of Evesham Abbey until Henry VIII dissolved the monasteries in the 1530s. Elizabeth I later gave the manor to her favourite courtier, the Earl of Leicester. The church, part of whose decoration seems to have been inspired by that of Wells Cathedral, has round medieval piers with capitals carved in fantastical designs, and monuments to the Ashwin family, whose links with the village and Manor House go back to Tudor times.

An avenue dark with yews links the churchyard to the Manor House, a handsome gabled mansion which dates from the 14th century but was rebuilt in the early 1600s. The old village stocks stand in the grounds. Bretforton Hall, on the opposite side of the road, stands out against the village's mainly traditional architecture. Built in 1830, it is an elegantly eccentric stone house with a balcony, arched windows, ornate ironwork and a battlemented tower.

Bretforton's Main Street approaches the village square, known as The Cross, swinging right and left before opening out on to the square. Part of the area is now a car park, but the rest is still green, crossed by footpaths and roads. On one part of the green is a solitary tree ringed by an iron seat, from which the Fleece and the church can be admired at leisure.

OPEN ALL HOURS *In 1848 a 14th-century farmhouse became the Fleece Inn, serving Bretforton ale from 5.30 a.m. to 10.30 p.m.*

BRIDGNORTH

Shropshire
14 miles southwest of Wolverhampton

There are two towns at Bridgnorth – Low Town, which sits on the banks of the Severn, and High Town, perched on a sandstone cliff rising sheer from the opposite river bank. The two towns are connected by a six-arched road bridge, dating from 1823, a winding road and a cliff railway.

The 17th-century town hall stands solidly in the middle of High Town's High Street, and traffic passes through the arches on which it is built. The half-timbered top storey was originally part of another building. Close to the cliff edge are the remains of a castle whose ruined Norman keep leans at an angle of 17 degrees, twice that of the leaning tower of Pisa, the result of undermining by Parliamentarians after the Civil War. Nearby is the 'top' station of the cliff railway, said to be the steepest in Britain with a 1 in 1½ gradient. A walk along the cliff edge gives views across the Severn, with Low Town and the bridge looking like a miniature town far below.

Cartway leads down to the river from the High Street, and was once the only link between the two levels. In this road is Bridgnorth's oldest house, the timber-framed Bishop Percy's House built in 1580 and the birthplace in 1729 of Thomas Percy who became Bishop of Dromore.

Low Town also has its share of old buildings. They include Diamond Hall, built in the late 17th century by Colonel Roger Hall with the winnings of his racehorse Diamond, and a post office dating from 1700.

Looking up to High Town from the far bank of the river, the outstanding feature is the Church of St Mary Magdalene, a dignified classical building built in 1792 by Thomas Telford, better known for his roads, bridges and canals.

Bridgnorth is the northern terminus of the Severn Valley Railway, originally opened in 1862, which runs steam trains to Kidderminster, 16 miles away, during the summer. The society which runs the service owns more than 30 steam locomotives, and much of the rolling stock has been restored to its Great Western Railway livery.

BROAD DOWN AND CASTLEMORTON COMMON

Hereford and Worcester
½ mile south of Little Malvern

Below Herefordshire Beacon the Malvern Hills become gentler, and Broad Down immediately to the south-east is, as its name implies, a wide round hill with steep woods owned by the National Trust. There is a 19th-century reservoir at its northern edge, from which Turkey oaks, sweet chestnuts and rowan trees have spread uphill. Nightjars and rare red-backed shrikes were once known to nest here, but have not been recorded since 1969.

On the western side of Broad Down is a small man-made cave cut from the basalt rock called Giant's or Clutter's Cave. It is said that the cave was once occupied by a hermit. Legend also links it with the Welsh prince Owain Glyndwr, who hid in it after fleeing from a battle against the English on Herefordshire Beacon in about 1405. Another story claims that the fugitive Lollard leader, Sir John Oldcastle, sheltered here after plotting against Henry V. Once a boon companion of the king, Sir John was a model for Shakespeare's Falstaff in *Henry IV*. It is more likely that the small hollow – conveniently close to the ancient spring of Walm's Well – was probably carved out as a shelter by one of the lonely medieval shepherds or swineherds who had to spend weeks on the hills.

East of Broad Down, on the edge of the Severn plain below the Malvern escarpment, is Castlemorton Common. It is one of the many areas of commonland in the Malverns saved from enclosure at the turn of the 18th and beginning of the 19th centuries by the stubborn, sometimes riotous, resistance of local people. So valuable are Castlemorton's 600 acres of ancient and unimproved rough-grazing land that 200 acres have been designated by the Nature Conservancy Council as a Site of Special Scientific Interest, and the area is now protected.

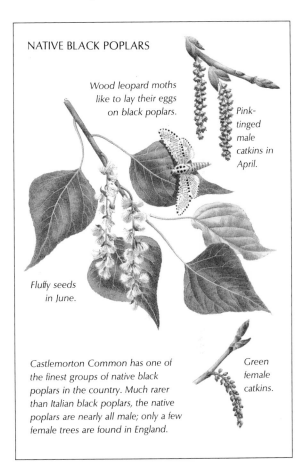

NATIVE BLACK POPLARS

Wood leopard moths like to lay their eggs on black poplars.

Pink-tinged male catkins in April.

Fluffy seeds in June.

Green female catkins.

Castlemorton Common has one of the finest groups of native black poplars in the country. Much rarer than Italian black poplars, the native poplars are nearly all male; only a few female trees are found in England.

Marshy, with streams and patches of gorse, Castlemorton Common supports at least 200 species of plants, including marsh marigolds, cowslips, harebells, marsh pennywort, ivy-leaved crowfoot, devil's-bit scabious and ragged-robin. It is well known for fungi, with almost 100 recorded species, and for the 60 pollarded native black poplars which are now rare in Britain.

Yellowhammers, linnets and stonechats flit through the gorse wilderness of Castlemorton, and even the sheep and cattle that graze unfenced along the single minor road that crosses the common have about them a rangy, untamed look.

BROADWAY

Hereford and Worcester
5 miles southeast of Evesham

Not without reason has Broadway been called 'the show village of England'. The long, broad main street is lined with gracious houses and cottages built of the honey-coloured Cotswold stone in the style of the 16th and 17th-century builders who knew best how to use this attractive material. There is a pleasant lack of uniformity in the houses that front the green-verged roads. Steep gables thrust their shoulders above the roofline of dormer-windowed cottages, bay windows peer out from under stone tiling, and here and there thatch and half-timbering soften the bluffness of weathered stone.

In the centre of the village is a wide green, overlooked by the Broadway Hotel. The Lygon Arms Hotel, which dates back to the 16th century, still looks like the large private house it once was. Both Charles I and Oliver Cromwell stayed there at different times.

Near to the Lygon Arms is the factory of Gordon Russell Ltd, the furniture manufacturer who began by repairing the furniture for the hotel in 1904 and went on to build up a business in hand-made furniture.

Broadway's High Street climbs gently from the green for almost 1 mile. Then it steepens at Fish Hill, topped by the odd-looking Fish Inn. The building was originally a summer-house built on the estate of a local landowner in the 18th century, and has a sun-dial on its roof. The inn stands at 800ft above sea level, but further on along Buckle Street the ground rises to

FOLLY VIEW *From Broadway Tower the views stretch over 100 miles to the Black Mountains of Wales.*

more than 1000ft to Broadway Beacon, the second-highest point in the Cotswolds, which is crowned by one of the best-known landmarks in the Midlands – Broadway Tower. It was built in 1800 by the Earl of Coventry as a glorious folly, with no other purpose than that it could be seen from his family seat at Worcester, almost 20 miles away.

There is a path to the top of the Beacon, which provides one of the finest viewpoints in the British Isles. At your feet, the whole Cotswold escarpment tumbles away into a vastness of unbounded space. Down

below is the great sweep of the Vale of Evesham with Bredon Hill rising like an empurpled island from the flat green farmlands. Beyond, the eye travels to the long blue crest of the Malverns.

Rising to 65ft above the hilltop, and so topping Cleeve Cloud (1083ft) the highest point in the Cotswolds, the tower presents a romantic silhouette from a distance; close up it is a glorious absurdity. Built in a mish-mash of styles combining Norman with Saxon influences, it is plonked on the summit like a piece from a giant's chess game. The architect James Wyatt (1747–1813) was responsible for the design, and deliberately chose a more sombre stone than the local yellow Cotswold for its construction. His aim was to create a 'dark tower' effect, which he completed with scowling gargoyles near the top.

The approach road to the site is Buckle Street, part of an ancient hill track extending between Bidford-on-Avon and Bourton-on-the-Water. And the tower has a fascinating history in itself. In 1827 it was bought by Sir Thomas Philipps, a famous collector of manuscripts and something of an eccentric besides. It was his declared wish to possess a copy of every book in the world, and he so crowded his home at Middle Hill nearby with volumes that, it is said, his wife could barely reach her dressing table. In the folly, then very dilapidated, Philipps set up a printing press from which transcribed manuscripts were published.

Later in the 19th century the tower came into the hands of an Oxford lecturer, Cornell Price, who had it repaired and redecorated. Price was a friend of William Morris, the artist-craftsman and socialist, who used to spend holidays in the folly in the company of the Pre-Raphaelite artists Dante Gabriel Rossetti and Edward Burne-Jones. Between them the group did much to promote the unspoiled charm of the Cotswolds, which had been little admired before. They must have gloried in the tower's tremendous views, though Rossetti is said to have grumbled about having to carry food all the way up from the village of Broadway below.

Later occupants included William Sherratt, who used the folly as a farmhouse. He was a renowned local storyteller, one of his yarns concerning a milk-maid blown off Fish Hill by a strong gust of wind and carried sailing away by her breeze-filled petticoats. No such fate befell a certain Mrs Hollingsworth. The last person to use the tower as a home, she lived in it for 40 years, as caretaker, without mains water, electricity or sewerage, managing to bring up a family in the turreted fantasy – and leaving as recently as 1972.

Broadway Tower stands today in a delightful country park where a small flock of the now rare Cotswold sheep are maintained. The heavily fleeced breed descends directly from the old Roman longwool breed, but had practically disappeared from the Cotswolds by the mid-20th century; it is now expanding again. On the first floor of the tower is a room illustrating the history of sheep-farming in the Cotswolds, while the second floor is maintained as a William Morris room. The third floor contains a relief model of the surrounding countryside, and six viewing porthole windows with 'keys' illustrating what may be seen through them.

APTLY NAMED *The wide main street that gave Broadway its name is lined with elegant 16th and 17th-century houses, each with its own individual charm and character.*

BROMFIELD

Shropshire
3 miles northwest of Ludlow

Tucked just off the main A49, Bromfield is almost on the site of one of the biggest Bronze Age settlements in the west of England. In the water meadows at this junction of the rivers Teme and Onny are the ruins of what was once an important Benedictine priory. All that remains is one of the finest medieval timber-framed gatehouses in England, stone-built in its lower portion. Next to its stands St Mary's Church, much reduced in size by Henry VIII at the Dissolution of the Monasteries but still impressive, with its strong 13th-century tower and magnificent timber roof.

Just west of Bromfield, a path from the south side of the A4113 leads to Bringewood Forge bridge and Downton Castle, built in the 19th century by the Knight family whose wealth came from the forge. The furnaces once smelted over 500 tons of iron a year.

BROMSGROVE

Hereford and Worcester
14 miles southwest of Birmingham

When nails were made by hand, Bromsgrove was the nail-making capital of the world. But when machines took over in the 19th century, the trade declined. The town was also – and still is – the market for the fruit farms and market gardens of the surrounding countryside. The 14th-century Church of St John the Baptist has fine medieval and Tudor tombs of the Talbot and Stafford families. In the tower is a carillon which plays a different tune every day of the week. Many other fine buildings deserve notice, including the grammar school, built in 1553, and several attractive Georgian houses in the High Street.

ANCIENT TIMBERS *The 16th-century cruck-framed barn at the Avoncroft Museum came from a Herefordshire farm.*

OLDEST HOUSE *The 15th-century timber-framed Bromsgrove House, oldest in the town, is now preserved at the Avoncroft Museum, which saves ancient buildings from destruction.*

GRANARY GUARD *Dogs were kept in kennels under the elm-framed building to keep thieves and vermin at bay.*

The Avoncroft Museum of Buildings was founded when Bromsgrove's oldest building – a 15th-century house – was threatened with demolition in 1962. It was dismantled and reassembled at the museum, where many other ancient buildings have since been brought for preservation.

Grafton Manor, 2 miles southwest, has a Tudor chapel and lake.

BROMYARD

Hereford and Worcester
12 miles west of Worcester

The market town of Bromyard is rich in old houses, notably the half-timbered Falcon Inn. The town was recorded in the Domesday Book of 1086 as one of the most important in the country, but now it slumbers contentedly among apple orchards and hopfields. Even today, its street pattern remains medieval.

Above the town to the east are Bromyard Downs, steep sheep-grazing commonland with clear views westwards to Wales and southeast to the Malverns. Delicate blue harebells grow there in summer, particularly on the crest of the Downs in Warren Wood, which is owned by the National Trust.

Deep in the heart of a secluded valley on the other side of the Downs is Lower Brockhampton Hall, one of the most perfect medieval manor houses in England. Built in about 1400 for a local squire, it has survived almost untouched, complete with silvery half-timbering, latticed windows, a picturesque buckled roof of fine old tiles, a gatehouse dating from the late 15th century and a moat fringed with pink-flowered water mint. It is also owned by the National Trust.

Nearby, in Brockhampton Park, is a nature trail of just over a mile which winds through one of Britain's finest mature oakwoods, planted about 200 years ago and rich in bird and plant life, as well as by ancient yews that are relics of the native woodland. There are fragrant larch and beech plantations, and stands of ash trees. Tits, willow warblers and woodpeckers nest in the woods, and sometimes ravens can be seen.

At Acton Beauchamp, 3 miles to the southeast, the Church of St Giles has an Anglo-Saxon carving of the 9th century used as a lintel to the tower doorway. The west tower and Norman south doorway remain from the original church.

BROWN CLEE HILL

Shropshire
9 miles southwest of Bridgnorth

Highest of the Shropshire hills is Brown Clee Hill at almost 1800ft. The name 'Clee' derives from the Old English for clay or clayey soil. The hill is lined with stone cottages and barns. Many people around the slopes of Brown Clee had common rights for grazing and gathering wood on the hill, and those who lived further away, 'the out-commoners', used old tracks called 'driftways', 'straker ways' or 'outracks' to climb to the grazing areas on the hillsides or carry iron ore and coal down. Many of the driftways still exist as sunken tracks, and the name Outrack is still given to a sunken road in Ditton Priors leading to Brown Clee.

Just above one of these 'squatter' villages, the hamlet of Cockshutford on the western slopes of Brown Clee, is Nordybank Iron Age hill-fort, one of

three. The other two are on Abdon Burf and Clee Burf summits on Brown Clee, but they have been much destroyed by quarrying. Nordybank is well preserved with clear ramparts and ditches, and provides a fine vantage point and wide grass rides and bracken-covered slopes.

On the eastern side of Brown Clee, just out of the village of Cleobury North, lies Brown Clee Forest Trail climbing up open sunny hillsides to private woodlands. Managed by the owner in conjunction with the Shropshire Trust for Nature Conservation, this trail winds through woodlands of Norway and Sitka spruce and pine, although there are some fine deciduous trees including sweet chestnuts, sycamore and birch.

THE EMPEROR DRAGONFLY

Britain's largest dragonfly can be seen patrolling ('hawking') by the lakes in Brockhampton Park. The emperor can fly at speeds of up to 18mph and has little difficulty catching insects, including smaller dragonflies. Adult emperors only live for about a month after spending two years in the underwater larval stage.

Contorted courtship.

A pair may fly off still coupled after mating.

On the western slope of Brown Clee Hill narrow, twisting lanes lead to Clee St Margaret. The village has two main buildings – Church House and the Norman Church of St Margaret.

The first is an ancient half-timbered building with a dovecote in the south gable-end. The second is enhanced by yews and has clear views of the surrounding beauty spots, such as Corve Dale and the wooded crest of Wenlock Edge. The Clee Brook coincides with 50yds of the main road through the village, providing motorists with an unexpectedly long ford.

BUCKNELL
Shropshire
4 miles east of Knighton

Steep, conifer-clad hills shelter the village of Bucknell. A cottage near the church has a thatched roof, and there are houses of pleasant, grey-green stone.

Bucknell is divided by a small, attractive river, the Redlake. It flows past the little Church of St Mary, which dates from Norman times.

From the church, a narrow lane follows the Redlake downstream. It passes farms and black-and-white cottages. Nearby is the station, built in 1860. With its freestone walls and Tudor-style chimneys it is a rich example of 19th-century railway Gothic.

BUILDWAS ABBEY
Shropshire
3 miles northeast of Much Wenlock

Only the main body of the once lovely abbey of Buildwas still stands, though roofless and without its aisle walls. It dates from the 12th century and was founded from Furness Abbey by Roger de Clinton, Bishop of Coventry and Lichfield. The setting and the abbey remains have a serene simplicity, particularly in the seven arched bays on each side of the nave and the tall, slender windows at the eastern end.

BURFORD
Shropshire
½ mile west of Tenbury Wells

A pretty cul-de-sac hamlet consisting of a fine, red-brick Georgian house, a fascinating church and a few cottages, Burford stands beside the gently flowing waters of the River Teme.

Burford House is a graceful, early 18th-century country mansion, built for a wealthy glass manu-facturer. It is surrounded by gardens which are a plantsman's delight, full of shrubs and flowers collec-ted over the years by John Treasure, a leading clematis specialist. The handsome stable block contains a small museum on the history and development of the clematis, from Elizabethan times. The gardens are open from April to October.

Across the lane is the little Church of St Mary, which has a 13th-century priest's doorway on the south side of its Norman chancel.

BURTON DASSETT
Warwickshire
4 miles east of Kineton

Local tradition records that Cromwell stabled his horse at Burton Dassett before the Battle of Edge Hill in 1642, and watched the struggle from the church tower. The circular building at the northern end of the hills was a look-out post where a beacon was lit to flash the signal, relayed via Ivinghoe and Harrow, that told Parliament the outcome of the battle.

MILE UPON MILE *Below Brown Clee Hill, Shropshire's green fields are dotted with trees and hedgerows as they stretch north towards the distant hump of The Wrekin.*

CANNOCK CHASE

Staffordshire
8 miles northeast of Wolverhampton

An oasis of forest land and heath on the doorstep of south Staffordshire's Black Country, Cannock Chase is the remnant of the vast hunting ground which covered much of Staffordshire in Norman times. There are miles of lovely walks through forest land, particularly glorious in spring and autumn. Brocton Coppice, to the northwest, still has some of the original great oaks remaining. Good viewpoints include the 600ft Coppice Hill, from which the Clee Hills, 30 miles to the southwest in Shropshire, are often visible. The Chase has a large herd of fallow deer, descendants of those which escaped the arrows of the Plantagenets. Foxes and badgers abound, and lizards slither over rocks on the heathlands. Birdlife ranges from meadow-pipits to buzzards, and woodpeckers and nuthatches are common.

During the First World War the Chase was used for military training and there was a camp for prisoners of war. The remains of the encampments can be followed by a car trail, with marked walks from six car parks. German and Commonwealth cemeteries commemorate the dead of two World Wars.

A road zigzags through pine plantations and emerges at the country park. At the northwest end, a small nature reserve has been created around a flooded quarry.

Guides to the walking trails on the Chase can be obtained from the information centres at Marquis Drive and Milford Common. Guides to the walks through Forestry Commission plantations are available at the Forest Centre at Ladyhill.

CARDINGMILL VALLEY
Shropshire
1 mile northwest of Church Stretton
See Church Stretton, page 34.

CARDINGTON

Shropshire
11 miles south of Shrewsbury

Three hills provide shelter and seclusion for Cardington which clusters around the trees, grass and gravestones of St James's churchyard. To the north stands The Barracks, a private house built of stone and timber, with tall, narrow brick chimneys. To the west is a neat row of cottages. Also in the area is the Royal Oak pub, a pleasing blend of whitewashed stone and timber-framed, black-and-white architecture. A short distance away is a fascinating group of ancient, weatherbeaten barns.

SHADY GLADE Sunlight filters through the slender pines and silver birches in Cannock Chase. Under the forest's thick canopy, foxes and badgers search for food amongst the bracken.

The Norman Church of St James is notable for its long timbered roof, medieval door and formidable tower. By the altar is the ornate tomb of Judge William Leighton, Chief Justice of North Wales, who died in 1607. His effigy lies on its side, head on hand, while his wife and six children are depicted, kneeling, on the side of the tomb.

Judge Leighton built and lived in nearby Plaish Hall. It was the earliest brick-constructed house of its size in Shropshire, and is complete with minstrels' gallery, ornate chimneystacks, and vast fireplaces.

CHADDESLEY CORBETT

Hereford and Worcester
4 miles southeast of Kidderminster

The village street at Chaddesley Corbett is a rare example of the harmonious blending of several architectural styles. Mellow Georgian brickwork and colour-washed rendering share the scene with black-and-white timbered buildings, the most notable of which is the 17th-century Talbot Inn.

The Norman church has an 18th-century tower surmounted by a recessed spire. Its dedication to St

FALLOW DEER

The doe has no antlers and often has a spotted coat.

Narrow hoof print.

A large herd of fallow deer live in Cannock Chase, where they can sometimes be seen grazing at dawn and dusk. During the day they rest up under the trees.

Cassian is unique in the Midlands, and probably in England. The saint was an early Christian school-teacher who is said to have been stabbed to death by his pagan pupils. A few yards away, in the churchyard, is an old brick school building which bears a plaque recalling its extension in 1809. The village street is among the finest in the area and contains several intriguing houses, including the early 19th-century Charity House, which consists of three matching brick cottages. A mile and a half to the east, in Chaddesley Wood, is a 250 acre national nature reserve, which is a fine example of oak woodland.

ROSES AND ROPES

OIL LAMP *Narrowboats often travelled along the canals by night and needed a light on the bow to warn oncoming craft.*

WATER CAN *Usually decorated with painted flowers*

RAM'S HEAD *The rudder, or 'ram's head' was usually decorated with ropework in a 'turk's head' pattern. A beribboned 'horse's tail' and a rope fender would often be fixed to the rudder as well.*

CHARLECOTE

Warwickshire
4 miles east of Stratford-upon-Avon

Charlecote is a village of pleasing old cottages. The church was rebuilt in 1851, and in it can be found the Lucy family monuments, taken from the old church, the oldest dating from 1600.

An avenue of limes leads to Charlecote Park, a massive Elizabethan mansion set in fine, open park-land where deer roam. It was here that Shakespeare is said to have been caught poaching deer by the irate landlord. The story goes that he was birched and, in revenge, wrote lampoons on Sir Thomas Lucy, but when the authorship was discovered, fled to London, and so began his career. The red-brick house, built by

Sir Thomas Lucy in 1551–58, is now owned by the National Trust.

Charlecote stands on a terrace above the slow-flowing River Avon, overlooking the flat meadows where Charles I camped with his army in 1642 on the night before the Battle of Edge Hill. Although some of Sir Thomas Lucy's Great Hall survives, the house was largely remodelled in the 19th century, with heavy carved fireplaces, elaborate plasterwork and sombre decorations.

The beautiful pink-bricked Elizabethan gatehouse now houses a small museum of sporting life and the farm buildings opposite have been converted into a restaurant, which has a walled garden where water-fowl, budgerigars and other birds are kept.

CHARTLEY CASTLE

Staffordshire
6 miles southwest of Uttoxeter
See Weston Park, page 144.

CHASE END HILL

Hereford and Worcester
2 miles east of Eastnor

This is not only the southern tip of the Malvern Hills; Chase End Hill is the end of the chase, or hunting territory. It also marks the last spot where the Cambrian rocks of Wales appear in England. An Ordnance Survey triangulation stone stands like an isolated full stop on the bare summit of this beautiful bracken-covered hill. To the north the Malverns look like sleeping hounds, hunched against each other for warmth; to the west lie the blue hills of Wales. But south and east a pageant of plump and fruitful fields stretches across the Severn plain to the golden Cotswolds and the Vale of Evesham.

Yet Chase End Hill and the hamlet of Whiteleaved Oak at its foot form one of the most wild and romantic parts of the Malverns. A buzzard, wingtips curved and spread, can sometimes be seen circling the summit. Here grow the wild daffodil, heather, bracken and purple rosebay willowherb with sudden creamy-yellow spires of toadflax.

The tiny hamlet of Whiteleaved Oak, tucked into the narrow lonely pass between the hills of Ragged-stone and Chase End, is believed to have acquired its name from a variegated oak which once grew there. Sheltered in a green bowl of the wooded and bracken-covered hillsides, the perfect half-timbered cottages of this secluded place seem to belong to a past century. Some of them have working wells; while sheep wander over a tiny green and grassy verges.

CHEADLE

Staffordshire
8 miles northwest of Uttoxeter

An old market town set in the Staffordshire hills, Cheadle is a gateway to the wooded Churnet Valley. The 200ft steeple of Cheadle's Roman Catholic church, designed in 1846 by A. W. N. Pugin, one of the architects of the Houses of Parliament, is a distinctive landmark for miles around. There are several 16th-century, half-timbered houses in the High Street, and a 17th-century cross in the Market Place.

Hawksmoor, 2 miles east off the road to Oakamoor, is a 250 acre nature reserve and bird sanctuary now owned by the National Trust, where curlews nest and nature trails run through moor, marsh and woodlands. In the reserve is a hut once used by charcoal burners.

About 4 miles southeast of Cheadle is the little village of Checkley, notable for its impressive Norman Church of St Mary and All Saints. There is some medieval stained glass with heraldry and figures, as well as a screen, stalls and a Norman font.

CHEDDLETON

Staffordshire
3 miles south of Leek

For 200 years Cheddleton's water-driven mills ground the flint used to make earthenware in the potteries of

A TIGHT SHIP *The Vienna's highly decorated cabin illustrates how much the canal families valued their boats. Amazingly, children were often raised in these cramped and crowded conditions. The boat is 72ft long with only a 7ft beam.*

Staffordshire. North Mill and South Mill were linked to the canal system in 1777 so that the flint could be transported by boat. Both mills have been preserved in working order and millwright's tools are displayed.

Moored nearby, *Vienna* is typical of the many barges that worked the canals. Narrowboats were often the permanent homes of 'canal families' that vied with each other to decorate the boats lavishly.

The Church of St Edward the Confessor at Cheddleton was founded in about 1214 and restored in Elizabethan times, when the porch and part of the tower were added.

CHILDSWICKHAM
Hereford and Worcester
2 miles northwest of Broadway

Farms and market gardens surround Childswickham, an off-the-beaten-track village in the Vale of Evesham.

Although many new houses have sprung up in recent years, much of the village's old-world character has been preserved. Weathered red-brick cottages and others in honey-coloured stone contrast with those of black-and-white half-timbering and thatch to give a delightful visual variety to the place.

The old village cross lies to the south of the village. It is said to have been erected by the de Beauchamp family in the 15th century. The original cross at its summit was destroyed by Puritans and later replaced by an urn from the churchyard which is now preserved as an ancient monument. Nearby is the old Manor House. From there a peaceful lane leads to the Norman parish church of St Mary — with its oddly patterned font, and its slender 15th-century spire enhancing a charming village scene.

CHIRBURY
Shropshire
3 miles northeast of Montgomery

Houses of rustic brick and black-and-white cottages are speckled throughout Chirbury, which rests on a gentle green slope near the Welsh border. The spacious Church of St Michael stands in the north corner of the village. Its nave was originally part of a 13th-century Augustinian priory. Nearby is a timber-framed school of 1675, with a central gable and gabled porch. From the churchyard there is a fine view of Chirbury Hall, thought to be a 16th or 17th-century timber-framed house, with a stone façade added in 1736.

The Herbert Arms has a colourful heraldic sign paying tribute to Lord Herbert, the Shropshire-born writer and soldier who, in 1644, surrendered nearby Montgomery Castle — over the border in Wales — to Cromwell's troops in the Civil War.

CHURCH STRETTON
Shropshire
13½ miles south of Shrewsbury

The town of Church Stretton looks old — which it is. Its many black-and-white buildings look medieval, which most of them are not, having been built around the turn of the century when the town was enjoying a new vogue as a health resort.

Church Stretton is actually three settlements in one. Little Stretton stands 1½ miles south of the town and the village of All Stretton lies to the north. It is said that King James I distinguished between the three when he arrived first at Little Stretton, and gave it that name; then he went on to name Church Stretton because of its Norman church; and finally reaching the next village, he remarked: 'It's all Stretton about here.' An unlikely story, perhaps.

King John granted Church Stretton a Market Char-

HISTORIC HILL *Desolate Caer Caradoc is thought to be where the Romans finally defeated the British leader Caractacus, before taking him to Rome in AD 50.*

ter in 1214, and a small market is still held every Thursday in the square. Remains of the medieval town are in High Street, once part of the old Bristol to Chester road, an important coaching route. It is here that some genuinely old buildings are found. Most of the 18th and 19th-century buildings are also in High Street, both half-timbered and more conventionally Georgian and Victorian.

The Church of St Laurence, just behind High Street, was built on the site of a Saxon foundation. Its nave is Norman with a 14th-century roof, and the tower was built about 1200. Above the doorway in the north wall there is a well-worn medieval fertility figure. A poignant memorial to a tragic event of 1968 hangs over the aisle; it takes the form of a gridiron with twisted flakes of copper simulating flames, and is dedicated to three boys who died in a hotel fire. The gridiron is the symbol of St Laurence, who was burnt to death on one in AD 258.

In the south transept is a small memorial window to the Victorian novelist Sarah Smith. She was a constant visitor to All Stretton and wrote under the name of 'Hesba Stretton'. A figure in green on the window represents her book *Jessica's First Prayer*.

Victoriana at its most decorative can be seen along the wide and pleasant Sandford Avenue, which was created in 1884 by the Reverend Holland Sandford. At one end, The Hotel – originally an extension of The Crown inn – was where the boys died.

Shops, hotels and restaurants are reminders of the town's growth in the late 19th and early 20th centuries, when it was vigorously promoted as a 'health resort with natural springs of pure water second to none in the country'. However good the water, the Victorians came also to enjoy the 'very bracing and exhilarating surroundings', and for once the publicity men did not exaggerate. True, an old guidebook went a little over the top when it described Church Stretton's location as being within the 'Highlands of England', for the surrounding hills are barely 1700ft high. Yet what they lack in size they make up for in scenic grandeur. Cardingmill Valley between The Long Mynd to the west and Caer Caradoc, opposite, is particularly attractive. Cardingmill Valley belongs to the National Trust. It takes its name from an old mill, now demolished, and lies about a mile from the town centre. It is reached along a cul-de-sac road that winds its way up the hillside. The Trust has an information centre and shop, and further up the path from the car park is a peaceful little lake called the Devil's Mouth.

CLAVERLEY

Shropshire
5 miles east of Bridgnorth

Many of Claverley's charming black-and-white cottages have raised foundations to 'keep their feet dry' in the event of heavy rain. Their studded doors and diamond-leaded windows mingle with buildings made of weathered brick, red sandstone and ancient timber. Many houses are covered with creeping plants, which add to their attractiveness. One particular home, opposite the Plough Inn, has a beautiful sunken garden.

All Saints' Church is the centrepiece of Claverley, and was built 28 years after the Norman Conquest by the knight Roger de Montgomery, on the site of a Saxon church, which in turn stood on pre-Christian

foundations. The sandstone church contains a large and dramatic mural of armed knights fighting on horseback. Which battle they are fighting is not clear, but some of the knights are wearing French armour. It is thought by some to illustrate the allegorical Battle of the Virtues and the Vices. The mural dates from the 12th century, and was discovered during restoration work in 1902. The church also contains several fine crusader tombs decorated with sculptured scallop-shells, the emblem of medieval pilgrims who had visited the shrine of St Iago (James) of Compostella in Spain. The cross now in the churchyard was erected in 1349 as a memorial to victims of the Black Death.

To the north of the village a lane crosses a little trout stream, then passes between steep cliffs on its way to Ludstone, 1 mile northeast. Ludstone Hall, an early Jacobean manor house, stands on the site of an ancient monastery and is surrounded by a moat.

CLEE ST MARGARET
Shrophire
7 miles northeast of Ludlow
See Brown Clee Hill, page 27.

CLEEVE PRIOR

Hereford and Worcester
9 miles southwest of Stratford-upon-Avon

Cleeve Prior's fine manor house was the birthplace of an extraordinary man named Thomas Bushell. In 1609, at the tender age of 15, he joined the household of the philosopher and statesman Francis Bacon, and when Bacon became Lord Chancellor, Bushell went with him to court. There he ran up debts – which Bacon paid off for him – and attracted the notice of James I because of the richness of his dress. However, when Bacon died in 1626, Bushell elected to spend his next three years on a tiny Manx island, the Calf of Man, living austerely on herbs, oil, mustard, honey and water. This, he said, was 'such a repentance as my former debauchedness required.'

Returning to the mainland, he soon rose to prominence at the court of Charles I, and on a number of occasions entertained the king and queen at his house at Road Enstone, in Oxfordshire, with ingenious displays of fountains and other waterworks. In 1636 the king granted Bushell the right to exploit the royal silver mines in Wales. He was outstandingly successful, devising new methods of mining and ventilation, reclaiming flooded mines and extending others.

When the Civil War broke out, a few years later, Bushell supported the king. But following the Royalists' defeat he had to return to his family home in Cleeve Prior, where he hid from the victorious Parliamentarians in a secret chamber. However, he was later restored to his important positions, and when he died in 1674 he was buried in Westminster Abbey.

The manor, with its fine porch and avenue of yew trees representing the 12 apostles, stands on the northern edge of the village. Just south of it, the main road passes a charming row of stone houses set back on a green. Among them stands the King's Arms pub, built in 1542, with a large stone dovecote in its yard; and opposite is the fine Queen Anne Vicarage. At the back of the Vicarage is the Church of St Andrew, set secluded behind walls and poplars.

A yew tree outside the church porch probably

dates from the 14th century, and its wood was once used to make arrows. There are deep grooves in the southwest corner of the tower beside it, where archers are said to have sharpened the arrows. A tombstone nearby displays an intriguing slip of the carver's chisel. It commemorates Sara Charlett, who according to the stone died in 1693 at the age of 309.

Sara Charlett's family lived in Cleeve Prior from at least 1280. Their home latterly was Prior House, a Jacobean building now demolished. Opposite the present building named Prior House is Cleeve Barn, an interesting modern conversion.

CLEOBURY MORTIMER
Shropshire
10 miles east of Ludlow

The market town of Cleobury Mortimer derives its name from the great Norman family of Mortimer who established themselves here in 1086. Hugh de Mortimer built a fortress in 1160 which Henry II later demolished; the earthworks can still be seen near the church. In front of the mid-16th-century Talbot Hotel, once a coaching inn, are the remains of an ancient market cross, where the body of Henry VIII's brother Arthur was laid during the journey from Ludlow to Worcester Cathedral, where he is buried.

Half-timbered and 18th-century houses line the tree-shaded main street. It is believed that William Langland, author of *Piers Plowman*, was born here in the 14th century.

CLIFTON UPON TEME
Hereford and Worcester
6 miles northeast of Bromyard

How the River Teme got involved with Clifton is hard to see. The village stands on a hilltop nearly 650ft high and 1 mile away from the nearest point of the river. A sprinkling of modern houses has appeared in the village in recent years, but the main street retains considerable old-world charm. A seat girdles the trunk of a huge horse-chestnut tree beside a little green at the heart of the village. Generations of villagers have lingered in its shade for a gossip beside the village pump which stands there. Black-and-white cottages with dormer windows mingle with others of grey stone, timber and red brick. The occasional Georgian façade adds a touch of elegance, and the post office is a study of white rendering and black beams.

The 12th-century Lion Hotel, with its massive ivy-clad chimney, incorporates part of the original manor house, and next door is the 13th-century parish church of St Kenelm, named after the county's own boy saint, murdered at the age of seven in 819.

The door to the church has the largest drop handle in Hereford and Worcester (there is a smaller version on the door of the old brick forge opposite), and above the tower rises an octagonal spire clad in Canadian cedarwood shingles and topped by a golden cockerel weather vane. In the church is the effigy of a cross-legged knight of the 13th century, his feet resting on his dog. He is Ralph de Wysham, a crusader who once lived in nearby Woodmanton Manor.

Among the memorials to the Jeffreyes family on the nave wall, look out for the mis-carved stone that alleges that William died some nine months before he was born. The tablet is the work of Thomas White, who designed Worcester Guildhall. The adjacent memorial was carved by Grinling Gibbons, the 18th-century sculptor also famous for his wood carvings, and is of Italian marble.

From the main street of the village a footpath cuts between hedges beside Chapel House, and leads past the village football pitch into open fields from which there are magnificent views east to the Teme valley.

IRON-BOUND *Massive hinges and a huge drop handle augment the sturdy timbers of Clifton's church door.*

CLOWS TOP
Hereford and Worcester
4 miles southeast of Cleobury Mortimer

A hamlet at the peak of the long climb out of the Severn valley, Clows Top offers magnificent views in all directions. To the southeast, the Victorian clock tower of Abberley Hall school looks like Big Ben miraculously transported into the woody countryside. Eastwards lie the Clent Hills near Birmingham, and to the west are the hills of the Welsh Border. Southwards the Malverns may be seen in the distance.

CLUN

Shropshire
5 miles north of Knighton

People have lived in Clun since prehistoric times, and it has had an eventful past. But the village today matches its description in the poet A. E. Housman's verse from *A Shropshire Lad*:

Clunton and Clunbury,
Clungunford and Clun
Are the quietest places
Under the sun.

Locals have been known to change the word 'quietest' to 'prettiest', 'drunkenest' or 'wickedest'.

Clun is one of those character-packed settlements that grew around the Norman fortresses built along the border of England and Wales. But Clun is much older than its castle. In the Town Hall's small museum are flint and stone tools and weapons found in the area, the partly cremated remains of a Bronze Age inhabitant, and the plans of nearby Iron Age forts.

The village had manorial status from Norman times until the late 19th century, and silver maces from 1580 and 1614 are preserved by the Town Trust. The small Town Hall in Market Square is an attractive building of 1780, with cream roughcast above lower walls of natural stone, and an iron-studded front door.

The main part of the village, on a slope above the River Clun, is laid out like a gridiron, with streets running north-south and east-west. Many of its most interesting houses date from the 17th century. Down a lane off High Street is the Hospital of the Holy and Undivided Trinity, founded in 1614 by Henry Howard, Earl of Northampton, for '12 poor men'.

The gauntly impressive castle ruins are set among grassy earthworks above the point where the River Unk flows into the River Clun. On summer evenings,

games of bowls are played on the green beneath the castle walls. The castle was built around 1100 by Picot de Say, who was granted the lordship by one of the Conqueror's most powerful barons, Roger de Montgomery.

A print in St George's Church shows that the castle was in ruins by 1731, and it is said to be the 'Garde Doloureuse' in Sir Walter Scott's novel *The Betrothed*. Scott certainly visited Clun while gathering material for the book, staying at the Buffalo, an inn that stands in a corner of Market Square. Buffalo Lane and Bridge Street form two sides of a triangle running down to the river, and in Bridge Street is the old stone-and-timber smithy. A narrow, medieval bridge crosses the river at the bottom of Church Street, which is dominated by the massive, pyramid-roofed tower of St George's. The tower is Norman, but the roof is a 17th-century addition. It is believed to stand on Saxon foundations and to have been a place of refuge from marauders before the castle was built.

Great tracts of what was probably once royal hunting forest surround Clun, though much has been recently replanted. The main woods lie to the east of Clun, now one of the most remote parts of Shropshire. Studded with lonely farms and bracken-covered uplands where buzzards and ravens sweep, it has a turbulent history. The hills are full of Bronze and Iron Age remains – stone circles, forts, hilltop settlements and buried weapons and tools. Offa's Dyke strides north and south, marking that Saxon king's boundary.

Between Clun and Bishop's Castle are wood-capped hills and swathes of valleys, golden with corn in late summer. A solitary and beautiful walk over these upland fields starts from Clun, near the youth hostel on a minor road northeast of the town. The path heads northeast between Radnor Wood and Stepple Knoll to skirt Bury Ditches, an Iron-Age hill-fort.

AGEING RUINS *A dead tree's twisted branches reflect the state of Clun Castle's crumbling walls, which date from the beginning of the 12th century.*

CLUNGUNFORD

Shropshire
8 miles west of Ludlow

Clungunford, mentioned in A. E. Housman's *A Shropshire Lad*, was once known as and is still sometimes called by its Saxon name of Gunnas. It takes its present name from the Saxon lord, Gunna or Gunward, and his 'ford over the river Clun'. From the small village centre, on the slopes above the church, you can see the river meandering among rolling hill country close to the English-Welsh border.

Red-brick houses and older, more traditional cottages are scattered around the village. Clungunford House, a fine Georgian mansion, is hidden among trees and gardens. Splendid though it may be, however, its desirability as a residence is today matched by what was once a far humbler home – The Thatched Cottage on Beckjay Lane, built probably in the 14th century as a farm labourer's home.

Skilfully restored with an eye to authenticity, the timber-framed cottage even retains some of the original wattle-and-daub (woven twigs plastered with mud) filling between the timbers.

Clungunford's Church of St Cuthbert is an interesting mixture of styles, from the mid-13th century onwards. The tower looks Norman, but in fact was built in 1895, at the same time as the splendid timber porch. Near the porch are the remnants of an ancient preaching cross.

COALBROOKDALE

Shropshire
9 miles north of Bridgnorth

The world's first iron bridge spans the River Severn at Coalbrookdale. It is Britain's most famous industrial monument, for it was here in 1709 that the Industrial Revolution can truly be said to have begun.

Natural resources and the genius of a single family provide the key to why this part of Britain became the cradle of the Industrial Revolution. It had an immense wealth of raw materials – coal, iron ore, water for both power and transport, sand ideal for moulding cast iron, limestone to flux the slag in the blast-furnaces, and clay for bricks and tiles.

CLOCK-TOWER
In 1843 an elaborate and beautiful clock-tower, made of cast iron, was added to The Great Warehouse of the Coalbrookdale Company.

NAMESAKE *The world's first iron bridge, which gave the town its name, was built in 1777.*

It was this abundance that helped to attract Abraham Darby to Coalbrookdale in 1708 – the first of three generations whose achievements were to win them the title of founding fathers of the Industrial Revolution.

Darby was a Quaker ironmaster who came from Bristol to take over a blast-furnace at Coalbrookdale. In 1709 he became the first man to smelt iron by using coke as a fuel instead of the traditional charcoal.

This was a breakthrough of great importance. At this time, Britain was in the grip of fuel crisis. Charcoal, made from timber, was the sole source of fuel for the iron industry, whose demands were rapidly stripping the countryside of its woodlands. A single blast-furnace producing only a few tons of iron a week devoured several tons of timber a day.

A new fuel was urgently needed. Darby found it in the coal of the gorge. Having perfected the technique of converting it to coke, by separating out the gases, he launched the entire industry on a process of breakneck expansion. High-quality iron now became available in quantities undreamt of in the days of charcoal smelting.

Darby's iron, together with the new techniques that evolved around it, provided the basis for the Industrial Revolution that transformed Britain in the 18th and 19th centuries. Among the customers who came to his works was Richard Trevithick, the pioneer of the steam-engine. Coalbrookdale and what came to be known as the Ironbridge Gorge became a centre of innovation and new-found knowledge that attracted people from all over the civilised world. Engineers and industrialists from Sweden, Germany, France, North America and many other countries flocked there to look, learn and marvel.

But the greatest memorial to the Darby family is the iron bridge upstream on the Severn from Blists Hill.

The idea came about in 1775, when a group of local businessmen met to discuss improving communications between the industries established on both sides of the river. They included Abraham Darby III, who became the project's treasurer; John Wilkinson, a

EARLY IRON WORK *When Abraham Darby, the first to discover how to cast iron pots in sand, launched his new business, he produced vast pots, decorative plates and flowers.*

fellow ironmaster; and Thomas Farnolls Pritchard, an architect from Shrewsbury. Up to that time, the nearest bridges were at Buildwas and Bridgnorth.

Because of the great number of trading vessels using the Severn, a bridge with a single arch was essential. Pritchard proposed a revolutionary iron structure spanning 120ft at an estimated cost of £3200, and Darby agreed to build it.

Darby and his craftsmen needed all their hard-won experience, for they were entering a totally new field. They had no idea of the structural properties of cast iron. Casting and transporting the main ribs of the bridge must also have posed formidable problems, for each of the ribs weighed 5 tons 15cwt. The parts were assembled using carpentry joints, since bolts and

rivets were inventions of the future. The bridge's actual span is 100ft 6in and its total weight is 378 tons 10cwt.

A footpath on the river bank below the bridge affords a good view of the bridge's unique construction, particularly the five ribs which are secured to the uprights by wedges, and the baseplates held together by dovetail joints.

The builders obviously opted for wide safety margins, and the graceful arch has stood the test of time remarkably well. It was not closed to traffic until 1931, and pedestrians continued to use it for another 19 years on payment of a penny toll.

As industry expanded elsewhere in the 19th century, Coalbrookdale and the Ironbridge Gorge went into decline. But, unlike other areas, no new industries sprang up to replace the old ones. Thus, many of the earliest relics of the Industrial Revolution survive there today.

Darby's original furnaces still stand in the grounds of the Coalbrookdale Company, where iron castings of one sort or another have been made since the 1630s. The site is dominated by the Great Warehouse, built in the 1830s, which has window lintels, frames and sills all made of cast iron. Iron was also used for the arch over the loading bay and for the ornate clock-tower added in 1843. In the 1760s, the Darbys were making the world's first iron rails for wagons to run on. Later, the works made the cylinders and the boiler for Trevithick's first steam locomotive.

The exhibits at Coalbrookdale are now in the care of the Ironbridge Gorge Museum Trust. The Blists Hill section of the museum has become an 'orphanage' for important buildings and machines that would otherwise have been destroyed. But the 42 acre site has an industrial history of its own.

Blast furnaces operated there from the 1830s until 1912; brickworks, tileworks and a coalmine were in use until 1941. The site also has the track of a railway, opened in 1861, and the remains of a tramway – including an iron bridge – that was used by horses hauling trucks laden with coal.

There is also another legacy from the past. Part of the Shropshire Canal – inspired by William Reynolds, Abraham Darby II's grandson, and opened in 1793 – runs across Blists Hill. It ends at the top of the Hay Inclined Plane. This provided a very efficient means of moving tub boats to and from the Severn more than 200ft below.

Secured to cradles that ran on rails, the boats went up or down the incline in three and a half minutes. The alternative method, involving a long staircase of conventional locks, would have taken three or four hours.

At the foot of the slope, the boats were floated off into the short final section of canal that runs parallel to, but slightly above, the river. It ends at the wharf by Coalport Bridge. This section passes the old Coalport china works, with its distinctive bottle ovens. Beside the still, weed-covered water of the canal stand the abandoned buildings and kilns which together formed one of the foremost names in fine porcelain for 200 years.

The Coalport Company occupied this site from the mid-18th century until 1926, when it moved to Staffordshire; the buildings now form a museum showing the history of the porcelain china industry, and of Coalport in particular. The old kilns and workshops can be visited, and one kiln now houses a dazzling display of Coalport china.

Though now part of the Wedgwood Company, Coalport still retains its name, and in the entrance hall of the museum are displays of present-day products ranging from elegant tableware to the delicate flower-design ornaments for which Coalport is noted. The museum is open daily.

Many of the most interesting exhibits at Blists Hill come from elsewhere. These include *David* and *Sampson*, a pair of double-beam steam engines built in 1851; a tollhouse, designed by the great 18th-century engineer Thomas Telford, that previously stood on the A5 near Shrewsbury; a Victorian printing shop; and an iron tub boat. The candle factory, blacksmith's and plasterer's premises, sawmill and printer's workshop are all staffed by people in period costume.

Another remarkable feature is the Tar Tunnel, which starts near the foot of the Hay Inclined Plane and runs under the hill for at least 1000yds. It was driven into the hillside in 1787 – probably in connection with the nearby coal workings – but the miners struck a source of thick, black, treacle-like bitumen that still oozes from the walls. It was mainly used for treating ropes and caulking ships, but small amounts were processed, bottled and sold as 'Betton's British Oil', a remedy for 'rheumatic and scorbutic affections'.

To visit Coalbrookdale and the Ironbridge Museum is to step back to a time when a revolution that was to transform the world was being forged.

ANTIQUE POTTERY *Two of the Coalport China Works' bottle-shaped kilns survive at the Ironbridge Museum, beside a disused stretch of the Shropshire Canal.*

TSAR'S PLATE *Coalport made a dessert service for the Tsar of Russia in 1850.*

COALPORT
Shropshire
2 miles southeast of Coalbrookdale
See Coalbrookdale, page 39.

COLWALL
Hereford and Worcester
4 miles northeast of Ledbury

Colwall Stone, a large piece of limestone, stands in the centre of this big and sprawling village set on the wooded western slopes of the Malvern Hills. According to one legend a giant who lived in a cave beneath the nearby Herefordshire Beacon hurled the stone at his beautiful but faithless wife, killing her on the spot. Another version says that the stone was put there by the Devil, and that each midnight the stone turns around. No one, however, has seen this happen.

Just outside the present village is the Church of St James the Great. It was built in the 13th century as a chapel for the manor of Colwall. Close by is Park Farm, a mainly 16th-century timber-framed building.

Colwall is one of several Herefordshire villages near which the Holy Thorn grows – blossoming, it is said, at midnight on Twelfth Night. The story goes that it was grown from cuttings from the Glastonbury Thorn, itself supposed to have budded from the staff of Joseph of Arimathea.

THE COMBERTONS
Hereford and Worcester
3 miles south of Pershore

When Bredon Hill is shrouded in cloud, the people of the Combertons are reminded of a traditional Vale of Evesham saying:

> *When Bredon's got on his hat,*
> *Men of the Vale beware that.*
> *When Bredon Hill doth clear appear,*
> *The men of the Vale have nought to fear.*

Both Great and Little Comberton, about 1 mile apart, are among the most attractive of the Bredon villages. Great Comberton lies on the northern slopes, its narrow leafy lanes encircling the yellow-stone Norman Church of St Michael, with its unadorned, 16th-century benches and stalls with Jacobean panels. The neat churchyard shelters beneath the spreading branches of a giant yew tree.

In the summer this is a place of blossom, colourful gardens and a rare tranquillity. There is not even a post office; the villagers have to go to Little Comberton which, despite its name, is larger and busier than its neighbour but no less enchanting.

Little Comberton's church is dedicated to St Peter, and its 500-year-old tower looks down on a rustic scene of yet more timber-framed thatched cottages, mellow red brick and gardens walled with stone lining both sides of Manor Lane. The Manor House, close to the church, dates from the early 18th century and has a 17th-century dovecote in the grounds and a 16th-century timbered barn.

A circular stone-built dovecote in the gardens of Nash's Farm is one of the largest in England, and is thought to be medieval. The 17th-century timber-framed farmhouse stands almost opposite Old House, which was part of Henry VIII's provision for his sixth wife Catherine, who survived the king.

COMPTON WYNYATES
Warwickshire
5 miles east of Shipston on Stour

Compton Wynyates was one of the first of the great houses of England to be built for comfort rather than defence. It was built in the 1480s, as peace settled on Britain after the Wars of the Roses.

Amid the prosperity of the Tudor years the house was enlarged in the 1520s by William Compton, a courtier to Henry VIII. Tall decorated chimneys rose from numerous fireplaces to give extra warmth; mullioned windows admitted more light, at the expense of security. Henry VIII himself stayed here with the first of his six wives, Catherine of Aragon, and their emblems are painted on glass in the room where they slept.

War came to the great house in 1644 when it was attacked by Parliamentarian troops. The house was protected by a moat and drawbridge, but after two days it was captured. The Parliamentarians filled in the moat so the house could never be defended again.

The Church of St Mary in the village was built in 1665, after its predecessor was destroyed in the Civil War. Inside there is a magnificent set of heraldic hatchments, depicting the armorial bearings, crests and mottoes of the Compton family.

CONDOVER
Shropshire
4 miles south of Shrewsbury

A quiet country road snakes through the pretty village of Condover, its houses tucked away behind neat hedgerows, grassy banks and red-sandstone walls. There are several attractive old brick and timber-framed houses, a post office, a shop and a church which, standing back from the road, harmonises well with its surroundings. This handsome building of creamy-red sandstone is dedicated to St Andrew and St Mary.

A church has stood here for more than 1000 years, from the times when Condover was a Saxon settlement. The present building dates from Norman times, though much was rebuilt after a disaster in 1660 when, as the parish records have it, 'the steeple and church came all down and fell on heaps'. It has no steeple now, but the simple buttressed and castellated tower has a black-and-gold clock face.

Inside, instead of the usual nave and two aisles, there is one enormous nave, spanned by a magnificent, 17th-century hammerbeam roof.

In complete contrast to the rural simplicity of the village is Condover Hall, a magnificent Elizabethan house which is now a school run by the Royal National Institute for the Blind.

The hall was built for a wealthy merchant, Judge Thomas Owen, who died in 1598 before it was completed. It is not open to the public, but can be seen, framed by its stone archway, at the edge of the village. Made of the same creamy sandstone as the church, it is a perfect blend of gables, windows, bays and towers, topped by groups of tall chimneys.

Condover has another Elizabethan connection, for here lived Richard Tarlton who was jester to Elizabeth I. It is said that he was Shakespeare's inspiration for the character of Yorick, the 'fellow of infinite jest, of most excellent fancy', whose skull features in the graveyard scene in *Hamlet*.

COUGHTON COURT

Warwickshire
2 miles north of Alcester

In 1605, wives of several conspirators engaged in the Gunpowder Plot waited for news of the enterprise in a room of the great central gatehouse of this house, the home of the Throckmorton family from 1409 to 1946. The battlemented gatehouse dates from 1509 and there are two half-timbered Elizabethan wings and Georgian Gothic additions.

The gatehouse endured Royalist bombardment during the Civil War. The mansion contains some fine furniture and a collection of Jacobite relics.

ETERNAL PRAYERS *Foremost amongst the statues in Condover's church is the kneeling effigy of Sir Thomas Cholmondeley.*

COVENTRY

West Midlands
17 miles east of Birmingham

The modern cathedral beside the ruins of its medieval predecessor is the symbol of Coventry's resilience. In 1940, a single air-raid levelled 40 acres of the city centre, but now only the newness of most of its buildings hints at the scale of that night's destruction. Coventry has been skilful in keeping its many industries at a distance. The central area, much of it closed to cars, is dotted with parks. Green open spaces ring the suburbs, and southwards there are the meadows and woods of Warwickshire and the Shakespeare country.

Leofric, Earl of Mercia, started Coventry's development as a centre of commerce and industry in 1043, when he chose the small Saxon township as the site for a Benedictine monastery to replace a nunnery destroyed by the Danes. He gave the monks land on which to raise sheep, laying the basis for the wool trade which made Coventry prosperous for 500 years.

Yet the earl is cast as the villain in the city's best-known legend, that of Lady Godiva's naked ride. The story, in which Godiva pleaded with Leofric, her husband, to cut the taxes on the people of Coventry, was first recorded a century after her death.

Leofric told Godiva she could ride naked through the streets before he would grant her request. She did so, having sent messengers to tell people to stay indoors with their shutters closed, and the earl relented. Peeping Tom, who peered through a window at Godiva and was struck blind, was added to the tale in the 18th century. Figures of Godiva and Tom re-enact the legend hourly on the clock in the arch over Hertford Street. There is a modern statue of Godiva on horseback in Broadgate.

By 1400, Coventry ranked with Bristol, York and Plymouth as one of the four leading provincial centres of England. Part of its wealth came from cloth and thread, dyed blue by a special process which kept the colour from fading. 'True as Coventry blue', later 'true blue', entered the language as a byword for reliability.

In 1642 the city refused admission to Charles I, and throughout the Civil War it was a Parliamentary stronghold. Royalists captured in the Midlands were imprisoned in the 14th-century Church of St John in the Bablake area – 'sent to Coventry', in the words of an account written in 1647. The phrase came to mean 'banned from society', and is still in use today.

After the restoration of the monarchy in 1660, Coventry was ordered to knock down its city walls. The citizens left the 12 gates, two of which still stand at either end of Lady Herbert's Garden.

Over the next 200 years, clockmaking and silk-weaving became Coventry's main industries, but in the 19th century imports of silk from France and watches from Switzerland brought a slump in both. As a result, hundreds of local families emigrated to America.

Those who stayed turned to new occupations – cycle-making and engineering. In 1896, Daimler and Humber opened the city's first car factories, and other motor firms soon joined them.

In 1914, and again in 1939, the engineering skills which Coventry had developed were applied to the machinery of war. Its factories were an inevitable target for enemy bombers in the Second World War.

The bombing raid of November 14, 1940, was the most concentrated ever suffered by a British city. Out of 1000 buildings in the central area only 30 were undamaged, and most were devastated. St Michael's Cathedral was destroyed, apart from its spire and outer walls. These are now linked to the new cathedral. A wooden cross made from two charred roof timbers has been placed on the original altar with the inscription 'Father Forgive' carved behind it.

The new cathedral, designed by Sir Basil Spence, is an exciting example of modern architecture. The exterior is of pink-grey sandstone in a series of massive vertical structures, stark and Gothic in their effect. Graham Sutherland's vast tapestry of 'Christ in Glory' dominates the nave, which is lit by slanted stained-glass windows, including the great Baptistry window designed by John Piper, throwing strips of light towards the altar.

Some of Coventry's other historic buildings fared better. The 14th-century Guildhall of St Mary, with its minstrel galleries and tapestries, is still used for civic banquets. Whitefriars, part of a 600-year old Carmelite monastery, now contains the archaeological section of Coventry's Herbert Museum. Medieval

A LEGEND IN SILK A clothed Lady Godiva rides her white horse through Coventry in a 19th-century picture woven by the Coventry silk weavers. Such pictures were called Stevengraphs after Thomas Stevens, who was one of the first to make them.

Canal, castles and a glorious cathedral at England's centre

A short drive from the cathedral city of Coventry leads to a village at the centre of England, and then on to the attractive villages of Berkswell and Knowle. A few miles to the south is Packwood House, noted for its clipped yews, and then the tour continues to Hatton Locks, where 21 lock gates control the water flow on the Grand Union Canal. Queen Elizabeth I may have passed this way on her visits to Kenilworth Castle, which the tour visits next. Standing on its bluff on the outskirts of the town, the castle still dominates the landscape.

CHRIST IN GLORY *Graham Sutherland's tapestry looks down on the altar in Coventry Cathedral, designed by Sir Basil Spence to replace the medieval cathedral destroyed by German bombs during an air raid in November 1940.*

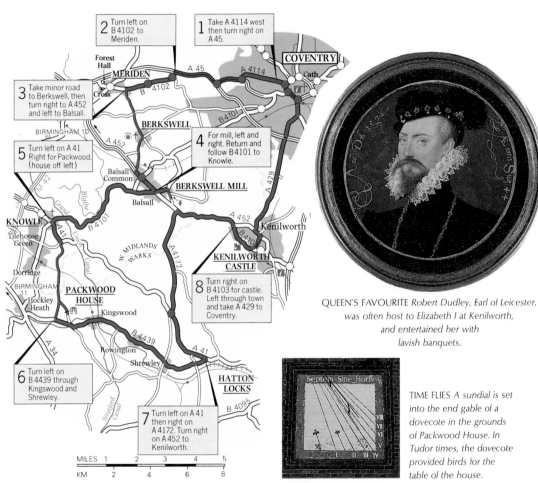

1 Take A 4114 west then turn right on A 45.

2 Turn left on B 4102 to Meriden.

3 Take minor road to Berkswell, then turn right to A 452 and left to Balsall.

4 For mill, left and right. Return and follow B 4101 to Knowle.

5 Turn left on A 41. Right for Packwood. (house off left)

6 Turn left on B 4439 through Kingswood and Shrewley.

7 Turn left on A 41 then right on A 4172. Turn right on A 452 to Kenilworth.

8 Turn right on B 4103 for castle. Left through town and take A 429 to Coventry.

MILES 1   2   3   4   5
KM   2   4   6   8

QUEEN'S FAVOURITE *Robert Dudley, Earl of Leicester, was often host to Elizabeth I at Kenilworth, and entertained her with lavish banquets.*

TIME FLIES *A sundial is set into the end gable of a dovecote in the grounds of Packwood House. In Tudor times, the dovecote provided birds for the table of the house.*

WORSHIPPERS' WAY *Churchgoers at Berkswell enter their church by this fine, two-storey porch, of which the upper storey is the vestry. The church, dedicated to St John the Baptist, is one of the finest Norman churches in the Midlands, and has a beautifully arched double crypt dating from the 12th century.*

BOATMAN'S BOGEY *It can take two hours to climb Hatton Locks, which raise the Grand Union Canal 150ft.*

buildings from various parts of the city have been reassembled in Spon Street, and Coventry has two fine Tudor almshouses – Bond's Hospital and Ford's Hospital – as well as lovely timbered houses in Priory Row.

At Binley, about 3 miles to the east of Coventry centre, is the Church of St Bartholomew, built about 1773 by Lord Craven and said to be the design of the Scottish architect Robert Adam. Certainly it is a beautiful classical edifice, with a western octagonal cupola, Tuscan columns and a shallow apsed chancel with plasterwork decoration.

CROFT CASTLE
Hereford and Worcester
5 miles northwest of Leominster

Owned by the Croft family from Domesday until 1957, except for the years 1750–1923, this Welsh Border castle served as a meeting place for Yorkist leaders in the Wars of the Roses (1455–85). The ancient walls and four round corner-towers of pink stone, dating from the 14th or 15th century, survive, in spite of modifications made to the castle in the 16th and 17th centuries and in the mid-18th century, when the Georgian-Gothic staircase and ceilings were installed.

Above the castle is Croft Ambrey, an Iron Age hillfort with multiple banks and ditches. An early rampart, of around 550 BC, was built just inside the present defences, which were erected around 400 BC. The site was occupied continuously until the Roman Conquest, as shown by the frequent replacement of postholes for the huts and gates (east, west and southwest). The population of about 500–1000 lived in small square huts arranged in streets, and obtained their pottery from manufacturers in the Malvern Hills area.

CROPTHORNE
Hereford and Worcester
3 miles west of Evesham

Cropthorne's tiny Church of St Michael contains two large 17th-century tombs. On one, the figure of Edward Dingley, who died in 1646, kneels facing his wife. His parents lie side by side on the other under an inscription that boasts their noble descent from the kings of England and Scotland and many ancient families. All four figures have a reposed and noble dignity. Nothing in them suggests the history of violence and insanity that brought their line to an end within three generations, after Edward's daughter Eleanor, who married Sir Edward Goodere, inherited estates in Cropthorne and neighbouring Charlton.

Of Eleanor's five sons, two died young and the others all came to violent ends, starting with Francis who was killed in a duel. His death left only John and Samuel, and these brothers were deadly rivals. In 1733 they both stood for election as mayor of Evesham. When both received exactly the same number of votes, Samuel, the younger, had his brother forcibly thrown out of the church where the investing ceremony took place. Eight years later, when John was threatening to cut Samuel out of the inheritance, the younger brother, by then a captain in the Royal Navy, took more effective action in Bristol where he was based in his ship, the *Ruby*. There, a friend, hoping to reconcile the brothers, had invited them both to dinner. All seemed to go well at the meal, but afterwards, as John was walking back through the streets of Bristol, he was seized and dragged on board the *Ruby*, where Samuel had three hired accomplices ready to strangle him.

But the foul murder came to light, and, a few months later, Samuel and the three assassins were hanged. Samuel left two sons. The elder boy, Edward, was 12 at his father's death and died insane in 1761. Samuel's younger son John then ran through the entire fortune within a few years of inheriting it, and spent the rest of his life as a poor knight at Windsor. There he became well known for presenting rich heiresses with written marriage proposals. He died in 1809, aged 80.

Cropthorne today is a quiet village of mostly thatched and timber-framed cottages stretched out along a ridge above the River Avon. At the centre is St Michael's, which is partly 12th century. Apart from the Dingley tombs, it also houses the magnificently carved head of a Saxon cross, decorated with delightful scenes of birds and animals. On either side of the church are the Manor and the Court, both dating from the 18th century. The Court stands on the site of a summer palace of Offa, an 8th-century king of Mercia. Beyond it is the long thatched and timber-framed Holland House, converted from a row of cottages. Its gardens were laid out by the early 20th-century architect Sir Edwin Lutyens.

At the north end of the village, the road forks at an attractively shady green, overlooked by a timber-framed cottage. One branch of the road leads to Charlton, once the home of the Dingleys, a mile northeast. Today, Charlton is a group of houses around a charming green with a brook running through it. The other branch of the road leads across Jubilee Bridge – built in 1933 to replace a 19th-century bridge which marked Queen Victoria's Jubilee – to Fladbury, a mile northwest. This large village has a number of fine buildings. On its southern edge, by the Avon, is the well-preserved, red-brick Fladbury Mill. In the centre, the Church of St John the Baptist has some good 15th-century brasses to the Throckmorton family. Standing nearby is the Manor, which was built in the early 18th century.

CROWLE
Hereford and Worcester
5 miles east of Worcester

A pleasant mixture of architectural styles borders Crowle's long main street: black-and-white half-timbering, the occasional thatched roof, Georgian and Victorian red brick and modern houses.

Just off the village street, at the end of a cul-de-sac, stands the mellow stone parish church of St John the Baptist, approached through yew trees in a neat churchyard. It was largely rebuilt between 1881 and 1885, but its history goes back to at least medieval times. Inside is a stone lectern incorporating the figure of a kneeling man, which is believed to have been made for Evesham Abbey in the 12th century.

Near the church is another reminder of Crowle's past, the stone remains of a medieval manor house, still clearly visible among the brickwork of Crowle Court Farm. Another farm, near the Victorian village school, has a stud with riding stables. The old Chequers Inn, a few hundred yards north of Crowle, has an attractive façade of bow windows and gables.

DORSTONE

Hereford and Worcester
6 miles east of Hay-on-Wye

Nestling under the Welsh hills at the head of the Golden Valley is a small package of history called Dorstone, which links the Stone Age with the present. Above the village, on Dorstone Hill, stands Arthur's Stone. A great slab set on upright stones, it was the entrance to a collective burial chamber around 3000 BC, and later a landmark for travellers. There are commanding views down the Golden Valley and across to Waun Fach, at 2600ft the highest of the Black Mountains.

In the village below, trim stone cottages stand around a small green, and spread out into a network of lanes. St Faith's Church, with its squat tower, can be reached across a small stream. It was rebuilt twice during the 19th century, but retains evidence of much earlier churches. It has a link with a murder which shocked England, for Richard de Brito, one of the four knights who killed Thomas Becket in 1170, founded a chapel there after serving 15 years' penance in the Holy Land. Inside the church is a superb late-19th-century pulpit in stone, which bears representations of the four Evangelists.

Even in the pub, the Pandy Inn ('Pandy' is Welsh for mill), the past lingers on in a history going back more than 500 years. Oliver Cromwell is listed among past guests. The cottages and houses nearby span the years, sharing an atmosphere of pride and care rewarded by a plaque on the green which reads: 'Best-kept Village'.

Standing sentinel at the northern end of the valley is Merbach Hill, swelling steeply to 1044ft. The river rises on its southern slope, and from the tranquil charm of Dorstone glides through Peterchurch, Vowchurch and Abbey Dore. It mingles with the Monnow at Pontrilas. All the way down, the dramatic natural rampart of the Black Mountains dominates the western view, its rim towering above the mosaic of fields at its feet. Wooded slopes make a softer horizon to the east.

DOVE DALE

Derbyshire/Staffordshire border
Between Hartington and Thorpe

Correctly – or cartographically, anyway – Dove Dale is that wooded, limestone, highly picturesque part of the valley of the Dove that lies just to the north of Thorpe, sometimes called Little Switzerland. But almost every part of the little river's course is extraordinarily pleasant, whatever names its banks are given. And, nearly as important, much of it can be followed by footpath,

PEACEFUL RIVER *Footpaths follow the Dove as it flows under beech trees' overhanging branches, through the tranquil Staffordshire countryside of Dove Dale.*

all the way from its birthplace among the gritstone and shales of Axe Edge in Derbyshire down to Burton in Staffordshire, where it joins the Trent; from there, the combined waters flow down to the cold North Sea.

The gentle ghosts of Izaak Walton, author of *The Compleat Angler*, and his friend Charles Cotton linger about the head of Dove Dale, near tumulus-crowned Wolfscote Hill. Here, the stream's flow is slowed by a number of tiny weirs that create resting pools to encourage trout and grayling to linger in the vicinity. Downstream is Milldale and Viator Bridge, an old packhorse bridge whose narrowness was remarked

THE COMPLEAT ANGLER

Izaak Walton, author of The Compleat Angler. His anecdotes and gentle style ensured the success of his book and its place in English literature. He was born in Stafford in 1593 and lived in the area for most of his 90 years.

Walton's ghost is still said to haunt Dove Dale.

upon 300 years ago in Walton's book – confirmation that it is not passable by modern motor vehicles.

Below Milldale are the Dove Holes, caves carved deep into the limestone long ago before the Dove had worn its way down to its present level. Here, Dove Dale proper begins, a deep gorge heavily clad with ash and alders, out of whose dense cover limestone crags and pinnacles leap skywards. Surely in all England there can be few grander spectacles than the river at this point, guarded by Ilam Rock with its flat, grassy top on one side, and by the multiple spires of Pickering Tor on the other. Further south still is Reynard's Cave, and a natural arch formed by the collapse of part of the cave roof.

Everywhere there are pillars, spurs and outcrops of limestone – Jacob's Ladder, The Twelve Apostles, Tissington Spires, Lovers' Leap. The last is named after an unfortunate Irish dean and his female companion who, with their horses, managed to fall off it in 1761; only the lady survived.

The Twenty Stepping Stones link the Derbyshire and Staffordshire banks of the river, which makes one last great sweep round Dovedale Castle – a crag, not a fortification – and runs on to break through the southerly guardian hills of Bunster and Thorpe Cloud, leaving the limestone behind, to hurry on through the shales past Ashbourne to Burton.

DOVER'S HILL
Gloucestershire
1 mile northwest of Chipping Campden

On a clear day it is possible to see the Black Mountains of South Wales and The Long Mynd, almost 60 miles away, in Shropshire, from the top of Dover's Hill. The hill has a view indicator which gives details of the panorama from the 754ft summit. A plaque records that Captain Robert Dover's 'famous Olimpick Games' were held on the hill each Whitsun from 1612 to 1852. The games included wrestling, coursing and horse racing.

DRAYCOTE RESERVOIR
Warwickshire
5 miles southwest of Rugby

A country park surrounds Draycote Reservoir, 2 miles long and $\frac{3}{4}$ mile wide, at the foot of Hensborough Hill. From the hilltop there are fine views across the reservoir and the surrounding countryside. To the south is the gentle vale of the River Leam, from which water is pumped to the reservoir to supply the town of Rugby. Beside the water there are picnic places and a children's adventure playground. Below the hill are the 'ridge and furrow' undulations, the remains of the medieval system of strip farming when villages were allocated strips of land for cultivation.

DROITWICH
Hereford and Worcester
6 miles northeast of Worcester

Until recently, Droitwich was best known for the therapy treatment afforded by its brine water baths. The water was pumped from a lake over a bed of rock salt deposited 200ft below ground, and as it contained $2\frac{1}{2}$lb of salt in each gallon, 10 times more than sea water, it was extremely buoyant. Water is still pumped, with a reduced brine content, to an open-air pool in Droitwich Park.

Droitwich has the elegant atmosphere of Bath, and has some black-and-white timbered buildings, yet it is a lively market town. The Church of the Sacred Heart and St Catherine has walls and a ceiling covered with striking mosaics depicting the life of St Richard.

DUDLEY CASTLE AND ZOO
West Midlands
8 miles west of Birmingham

An unusual feature of Dudley's medieval castle, which stands on a splendid hill site, is the fact that it is surrounded by a zoo. Only the stone keep, gatehouse and parts of the curtain wall remain of the 13th-century castle, but there is also an impressive range of Tudor buildings, including the great hall, living quarters, kitchens, pantry and buttery, which are now being restored. The zoo is in 40 acres of attractively wooded grounds and contains a comprehensive collection of wildlife from all over the world.

In a wooded valley below Castle Hill are the ruins of a Norman priory. Wren's Nest Hill, 1 mile northwest of Dudley Castle, is a National Nature Reserve which also contains fossils of creatures over 300 million years old.

EARDISLAND

Hereford and Worcester
4¼ miles west of Leominster

The road into Eardisland from Leominster passes scattered black-and-white cottages and an old stone barn before reaching Staick House, just by the river. This is a superb timber-framed mansion, its beauty enhanced by topiary in the front garden, creeper-clad walls, leaded windows and a mossy roof. The oldest part is 14th century, and the most recent addition is the 17th-century dovecote-gabled east wing, which runs down to the road. Beyond the house oak beams, brick, roughcast and wisteria-webbed stonework mingle in a row of cottages on the river bank. These overlook the front gardens of an equally attractive row of houses and cottages on the other side of the Arrow, which date from the mid-16th century. The whole scene is best appreciated from the bridge across the river below Staick House, which also overlooks Millstream Cottage, formerly known as the Old School House.

EARDISLEY

Hereford and Worcester
4¼ miles south of Kington

Black-and-white half-timbered cottages line the single street of Eardisley, whose name is recorded in the Domesday Book as *Herdeslege* – Herde's clearing in the wood. At that time the village stood at the centre of a vast forest, the last surviving tree of which stands on Hurstway Common, half a mile east of the village centre. Called the Great Oak, it has a girth of 30ft.

EARL'S HILL

Shropshire
7 miles southwest of Shrewsbury

A narrow lane off the A488 leads to one of the most enchantingly varied fragments of wild countryside in Shropshire. Iron Age settlers built a ramparted fort on the craggy summit of Earl's Hill, 1049ft high; perhaps they, too, appreciated the beautiful lap of the Habberley valley to the south. Buzzards circle, swifts dart and dive; delicate blue harebells quiver in the grass and dwarf dandelions, wild thyme and gorse grow on the thin soil.

Earl's Hill is in the care of the Shropshire Trust for Nature Conservation, which has laid out a delightful nature trail that leads to the summit of the hill, from which there are spectacular views all around. Over its length, the trail runs through ash and oak woods, across upland meadows and along a stream in a deep valley. A walk through the reserve reveals places where ash saplings grow out of tumbled scree from crags above; where mosses and yellow stonecrop thrive; where the hummocks built by yellow ants provide tiny gardens of clover, speedwell and forget-me-not; and where cowslips grow in the long grass.

Pied flycatchers can be found down by the brook and, more commonly, dippers and grey wagtails. Woodpeckers, tits and warblers live in the woods. Butterflies are abundant: peacocks and commas emerge from winter hibernation in late March and in summer the pearl-bordered fritillary can also be seen.

BUTTERFLIES AT EARL'S HILL

Peacocks get their name from their 'eyes' that resemble peacock's tail feathers.

Peacocks feed on garden flowers such as buddleia.

The ragged edges to the comma's wings camouflage the butterfly among the dead leaves when it hibernates. The butterfly gets its name from the white 'comma' on the underside of its wings.

EASTNOR
Hereford and Worcester
1 mile east of Ledbury

There are two castles at Eastnor – one an ancient ruin, the other modern, a creation of the prosperous early 1800s. The older of the two, Bronsil Castle, was built by Richard Beauchamp, son and heir to John Beauchamp of Powycke, Lord Treasurer to Henry VI, in the 15th century, but was based on an older structure. It was burned in the Civil War and the only remains – not open to the public – are the moat and part of a gatehouse tower.

Eastnor Castle is a Norman-style mansion with tall, turreted towers. It was built about 1812 for the 1st Earl Somers to the design of Sir Robert Smirke, who also designed the British Museum. The castle, looking every inch a 'Norman' edifice – with turrets at each corner and a central keep – overlooks a lake and parkland. It remains in the family who built it and who still run the estate. It is open to the public on certain days in summer and contains collections of armour, tapestries and paintings. In the great days of steam locomotives, one of the Great Western Railway's Castle Class locomotives bore the name Eastnor Castle, and its nameplates are displayed in the entrance hall.

EDGE HILL
Warwickshire
7 miles northwest of Banbury

Magnificent beech trees line the road running along the top of the ridge, known as Edge Hill, at the foot of which the first major battle of the Civil War took place on October 23, 1642. The castellated Edge Hill Tower, now part of the local inn, The Castle, was built as a folly by Sanderson Miller, a local squire and architect in the 18th century, to commemorate the position of Charles I's royal standard at the start of the battle. There is a fine view from the top of the tower.

ELFORD
Staffordshire
4 miles north of Tamworth

Lying on a curve of the River Tame, Elford has a church which is well worth a visit. St Peter's Church was mostly rebuilt in the 19th century, but retains its late 15th-century Perpendicular tower and its fine collection of tombs, mostly in the Howard Chantry Chapel. The earliest is the 14th-century alabaster table-tomb of Thomas de Arderne, a knight who fought at Poitiers, and his wife. On the sides of the tomb are 22 figures with angels bearing coats of arms.

ELLESMERE
Shropshire
8 miles northeast of Oswestry

Old streets, mellow Georgian houses, half-timbered buildings and a parish church, St Mary's, which has a remarkable 15th-century wooden chancel roof, are at the heart of the small market town of Ellesmere which lies at the centre of Shropshire's 'Lake District'. The town gets its name from the haunt of the merehen, or lake bird, now called moorhen, though it has no connection with moors. There are nine lakes in all, which are also the home of herons, kingfishers, mallard, tufted ducks and great crested grebes. Cormorants, wigeons, teals and pomarine skuas may be seen in winter. The lake at Ellesmere – known as the Great Mere – covers 116 acres and is a popular spot for boating and fishing. On the lakeside are the Cremorne gardens. There are two local legends to explain how the town got its Great Mere.

Both say that there was once a well in a field near the town, from which all the inhabitants were permitted to draw water. In one legend, the farm to which the well belonged changed hands, and the new tenant

GREAT CRESTED GREBES AND TUFTED DUCKS

The great crested grebe is unmistakable with its conspicuous double crest and dark ruff. On the meres round Ellesmere, mother grebes can be seen carrying their chicks on their backs in spring.

Tufted ducks were strangers to Britain before 1849, now they are our commonest diving species. The males have a purple head with a drooping crest. The females also have a crest but are brown, with paler sides.

refused to let anyone draw water. Retribution was swift, for one morning when the tenant's wife went to fetch water, she found that the whole field had become a lake.

In the second story, the well was the only source of water for the townsfolk of Ellesmere, and a new landowner imposed a charge for every bucketful. The people prayed that God might redress their wrongs, and one night the water in the well rose until it flooded the land.

CONTRASTING BIRDS *Busy black coots and languid white swans feed together on the mere at Ellesmere.*

ELMLEY CASTLE

Hereford and Worcester
4 miles southwest of Evesham

There is no castle at Elmley today. The once-proud fortification, built in the 11th century fell into decay in the 16th century.

The village, at the foot of Bredon Hill, is one of the most beautiful in England. It has a wide main street, bordered by a tree-lined brook down one side, which presents a memorable picture of black-and-white cottages, thatched roofs, drystone walls and gardens.

At one end of the street stands a 15th-century stone cross, fairly well preserved.

EVESHAM

Hereford and Worcester

15 miles southwest of Stratford-upon-Avon

ABBEY SURVIVOR *The bell tower remained intact when Evesham's abbey was dismantled at the Dissolution.*

The market town of Evesham on the River Avon is the centre of the fruit-growing industry of the Vale of Evesham, which is noted for the mass of fruit blossom it displays in the spring. Despite great expansion the town keeps its elegance. Close to the ruined abbey by the river are fine Georgian houses and a few half-timbered buildings, the best of which is 15th-century Booth Hall, now restored and occupied by a branch of a national bank. At the centre of the town stands the 110ft high Bell Tower. Built in 1539, and part of the now-ruined Benedictine abbey, the tower is flanked by the 12th-century All Saints' Church and the 16th-century Church of St Lawrence. Abbot Reginald's Gateway, a 12th-century timber-framed building, leads to the two churchyards. The old town stocks are preserved on the green outside the town museum.

F

FARNBOROUGH
Warwickshire
6 miles north of Banbury

Stone cottages, a village store and the 17th-century Butcher's Arms Inn line Farnborough's winding main street. The parish church of St Botolph stands on high ground, which gives added height to the lofty spire built by Sir Gilbert Scott in 1875. The rest of the church is medieval, with some traces of Norman work.

At one end of the village street stands Farnborough Hall, a 17th-century mansion built of russet ironstone with dressings of grey sandstone. The house is owned by the National Trust, and the principal rooms have fine plasterwork to harmonise with the Italian paintings and sculptures. The house looks out across a picturesque lake to Edge Hill, scene, in 1642, of the first battle of the Civil War. The landscaped park has a terraced walk, a Classical temple, and an oval pavilion with an ornate plasterwork ceiling in the upper room. An obelisk of 1751 on the terrace marks the edge of the estate.

FECKENHAM
Hereford and Worcester
6 miles northwest of Alcester

Timber-framed cottages and elegant, red-brick Georgian houses face each other across Feckenham's quiet main street, which once formed part of a Roman road. The village is set around a small, tree-dotted green on which daffodils grow in the spring. A path from the green leads between the huge, weathered headstones in the graveyard and up to the Church of St John the Baptist. Parts of the church date from the mid-13th century and, inside, carved figures of angels playing musical instruments look down on the nave. On the west wall a benefaction board of 1665 records: 'King Charles the First of Blessed Memory Gave to ye ffree scoole of ffeckenham ye yearly Sume of £6 thirteen shillings and ffoure Pence Payable out of ye fforest land.' The old school is now a private house, but a trust still distributes the money – on books and uniforms for the boys and girls of the village school. The village was once important for the manufacture of needles and fish-hooks – industries now centred in Redditch, 4 miles north.

FOWNHOPE
Hereford and Worcester
6 miles southeast of Hereford

In the Domesday Book the village name is recorded as Hope – the Saxon word for a settlement under the side of a hill. 'Fown' was added later to make the distinction from Woolhope, possibly referring to a painted building. The village stands above the River Wye, beneath the tree-covered slopes of Cherry Hill and Capler Wood – both sites of pre-Roman camps. It has one of the largest churches in the county, early

Norman with a 14th-century broach spire, clad with wooden shingles. Inside are a fine 12th-century Norman stone carving, showing the Virgin holding the infant Jesus, and a 14th-century parish chest, 9ft long, carved from a single log of oak. Outside the churchyard, reminders of the days of harsh justice, are the old village stocks and whipping post.

Fownhope is famous locally for its annual Heart of Oak Club Walk, which takes place in the first week in June, when members carry flower-decorated sticks in procession to the 15th-century Green Man Inn where, it is said, the Roundhead Colonel John Birch stayed before taking Hereford from the Royalists in 1645.

FLOWER POWER *Apricot roses light up the russet ironstone of an old village house in Farnborough.*

The village's most famous son, born at Rudge End in 1795, was Thomas Winter, who became a professional prizefighter under the name Tom Spring – still a seasonal name but one more appropriate to his sport. A bare-knuckle fighter, he was champion of All England in 1823–4. He had one fight of 77 rounds (a round lasted until someone was knocked down) which lasted an epic 2 hours 29 minutes.

GARWAY

Hereford and Worcester
5 miles southeast of Pontrilas

The Church of St Michael and All Angels at Garway was one of the round churches of the Knights Templar, an order of knighthood founded about 1118 to guard pilgrims on their way to Jerusalem; it dates from the late 12th century. Part of the original round nave is visible, but the present nave is 13th century and the Norman chancel arch remains.

GLADESTRY

Powys
4 miles west of Kington

Set in a gap in one of Radnor Forest's sandstone ridges, this hamlet is typical of many in mid-Wales. Church, chapel, inn, court-house and cottages huddle together beside Gladestry Brook, overshadowed by heather and bilberry-clad sheepwalks. This is where lowland arable and livestock farming gives way to upland sheep-farming territory; the nearby hills reach more than 1600ft high.

VILLAGE VIEW *The sandstone outcrop of Grinshill Hill towers over the village and looks out across the Severn Valley.*

GNOSALL

Staffordshire
6 miles west of Stafford

Two pubs, the Navigation Inn and the Boat Inn, stand on opposite banks of the Shropshire Union Canal at the attractive waterfront area of Gnosall, bright with gaily coloured boats. This part of the village, known as Gnosall Heath, dates largely from the time the canal was opened in the early 19th century. Buildings from that period include the Coton Mill – originally a steam-powered flour mill, but now a private house.

GOODRICH CASTLE

Hereford and Worcester
4 miles southwest of Ross-on-Wye

Towers and walls of rich red sandstone, springing from a dry moat cut deep into solid rock, create the impression that Goodrich Castle grew from its rock foundations rather than being built upon them.

The castle, whose name originated as Godric's Castle, stands high above the meandering Wye on a beautifully wooded spur. The oldest part, the three-storey keep, was built about 1160 for Godric Mappestone. Its purpose was to guard a river crossing during the turbulent period when the Wye was a river of considerable military importance. No better position could have been chosen, for the view over the river and the surrounding countryside is superb – a military advantage in the 12th century and a scenic one now.

Corner towers braced by spurs and triangular buttresses strengthened the castle's outer wall, and complicated traps were devised to deter invaders. The long tunnel under the gate tower, for example, was blocked by a portcullis, and while intruders were held up there, hot lead or water could be poured on them from openings above.

GREAT WITLEY

Hereford and Worcester
5 miles southwest of Stourport

Where peacocks once strutted, jackdaws now swoop from the ruined shell of one of England's most sumptuous houses. Edward VII, when Prince of Wales, often used to stroll in the gardens of Witley Court; today only bumps in the grass reveal where the terraces stood, while a few bedraggled yews mark the lines of the formal walks.

Two magnificent fountains stand relatively unscathed by the fire, demolition and vandalism that have left the house a roofless and unstable ruin. One fountain has an immense statue of Perseus on a horse prancing 26ft above the ground. It used to throw a jet of water 90ft into the air, but has been dry since 1937, the year of the fire, when the long decline began.

In contrast, St Michael's Church, attached to the ruined house, is immaculately restored, with a baroque interior of unbridled opulence that would seem more at home in Italy than in the heart of the English countryside. Built by Lord Foley and consecrated in 1735, it was lavishly embellished 20 years later by the 2nd Lord Foley.

The glorious paintings on the ceiling, by the Italian artist Antonio Bellucci, once graced the Duke of Chandos's mansion at Canons near Edgware, Middlesex. When that house was broken up in 1747 the paintings were brought to Great Witley together with the painted glass windows and the ornate case of the organ which Handel used to play at Canons.

GRINSHILL
Shropshire
7 miles north of Shrewsbury

Large, attractive houses line the narrow lane running through the heart of Grinshill. It is a small, well-cared-for village, lying beneath a steep and thickly wooded hill. The most imposing house is the Jacobean Stone Grange. It was built in 1617 as a retreat for the teachers and pupils of nearby Shrewsbury School, who fled to it whenever plague struck the county town.

MYTHICAL HERO *One of the last reminders of Witley Court's former glory is an enormous fountain with Perseus on horseback rescuing Andromeda from a sea-monster.*

HAMPTON BISHOP

Hereford and Worcester
4 miles east of Hereford

The half-timbering, thatched roofs and lovingly tended gardens of Hampton Bishop lie strung out along the village street, and are perhaps best appreciated on foot. The handsome, frequently photographed church makes the best starting point. The tower and almost half the walls are original Norman, well integrated with 13th and 14th-century additions. The most striking feature, the black-and-white timber-framed belfry with its six bells, is perched atop the tower. Inside, behind the altar, is a red-sandstone canopied screen of the 15th century.

The small thatched cottage next to the church is typical of many in the village. Box Tree Cottage, some distance away, still has original 15th-century timber crucks supporting it. The Old Court Cottage's 16th-century timbers also still support a neat thatched roof.

HANBURY

Hereford and Worcester
5 miles south of Bromsgrove

A mile outside the little village of Hanbury lies an early 18th-century red-brick mansion. Hanbury Hall is in the style of Wren, although the architect is unknown, and the date 1701 is carved above the door. The entrance hall is relatively simple, the full impact being reserved for the staircase. Here the walls are lavishly painted with scenes from the life of Achilles, watched by gods and goddesses looking down from the high ceiling. From a viewpoint near the village church the countryside sweeps away to the southwest.

HARTLEBURY CASTLE

Hereford and Worcester
2 miles southeast of Stourport

For over 1000 years Hartlebury Castle has been the home of the Bishops of Worcester. Only the moat survives of the original castle, as the present red-sandstone mansion was built on its site in 1675. The mansion was completely restored in 1964. The state rooms include a great hall with portrait gallery and an 18th-century rococo saloon. The castle also contains the library of Bishop Richard Hurd, a noted 18th-century divine. In the north wing is the Hereford and Worcester County Museum, which has exhibits of local crafts and industries.

HATTON LOCKS

Warwickshire
1 mile to 3½ miles west of Warwick

From the bridge crossing the Grand Union Canal at Hatton Locks, 21 lock gates stretch away in the distance – 17 to the east and 4 to the west – known as

'The Golden Steps to Heaven'. Beside the bridge stands the British Waterway Board's maintenance depot, a Victorian building of red and plum-coloured brick with a three-legged crane at the dockside. There is a car park on the north side of the canal.

HAUGHMOND ABBEY

Shropshire
4½ miles northeast of Shrewsbury

One of the most impressive of all abbey ruins, the 12th-century Haughmond Abbey was partly demolished in 1539 at the Dissolution of the Monasteries. What remained was converted into a private house, which was burnt down during the Civil War. The entrance is through a 17th-century garden gate, and attached to what was the abbot's lodgings there is a 16th-century bay window.

HENLEY-IN-ARDEN

Warwickshire
9 miles northwest of Stratford-upon-Avon

In Tudor times Henley stood in the thickly wooded Forest of Arden. The trees were felled for fuel to smelt iron before the advent of coal, and only sparse clumps of trees remain. But some of the forest survives in the many oak-framed Tudor buildings along the town's main street. The 15th-century Guildhall is still used by the ancient manor court, which appoints constables and other local officers and there are two old inns, the White Swan and the 15th-century Blue Bell.

The parish church of St John the Baptist is 15th century, and has fine stone carvings. The River Alne flows gently by the undulating countryside where there are fine walks. Near the earthworks, which are the sole remains of Beaudesert Castle, is the 12th-century Church of St Nicholas.

HEREFORD

Hereford and Worcester
13 miles south of Leominster

Once the Saxon capital of West Mercia, Hereford is steeped in history. It is not simply a museum piece, however, but very much a busy commercial and social centre. The city is surrounded by orchards and rich pastures, grazed by herds of red-and-white Hereford cattle which provide some of the finest beef in the world. One of the old inns famous for its beef is The Green Dragon, an old posting inn with panelling dating back to 1600.

This cathedral city on the banks of the River Wye

ELM VAULTING *After Hereford Cathedral's west tower collapsed in 1786, wych elm and plaster were used to keep the weight of the new nave ceiling to a minimum. The ceiling was not painted until over 70 years later.*

was founded about AD 700. The oldest area of the city was bounded by a ditch which stretched south of the river to enclose Bishop's Meadow. The fortifications were intended to protect Saxon Hereford from the Welsh. In the 11th century the walls were built and were extended northwards 200 years later. A well-preserved section still stands near the 15th-century Wye Bridge. A tablet in nearby Gwynne Street records where Nell Gwynne was born.

The city skyline is dominated by ecclesiastical buildings, notably All Saints' with its crooked spire, and the Cathedral Church of St Mary the Virgin and St Ethelbert. There has been a cathedral at Hereford since the city was founded. Most of the present building dates from the 12th century, and the central tower and choir stalls from 200 years later. The immense sandstone building has a notable array of effigy tombs, some dating back to the founding of the church, and an inspiring nave ceiling. The cathedral contains a world map – the Mappa Mundi – drawn on vellum in about 1300, and a chained library of 1500 books – the world's largest.

The Coningsby Hospital, founded in 1614, incorporates a 12th-century dining-hall of the Knights of St John, and in the gardens at the rear are the remains of a Dominican monastery.

Hereford's major product, cider, is celebrated by a Museum of Cider in Grimmer Road. Other museums include a Waterworks Museum at Broomy Hill and the St John Coningsby Museum in Widemarsh Street. The Bulmers Steam Centre in Whitecross Road, home to famous steam locomotives including the *King George V*, is open at weekends during the summer.

High Town, the traffic-free city centre, has for its centrepiece The Old House, built in 1621 and moved to its present site this century. South and southeast of High Town a number of narrow streets and alleyways retain something of the character of bygone Hereford.

SAFE READING *Hereford Cathedral has the largest chained library in the world. Many of the books and manuscripts are beautifully bound and illuminated, the oldest date from the 9th century. Over 50 of the volumes were printed before 1500.*

Down the Wye to orchards and meadows in a golden valley

The majestic buzzard soars over a landscape where castles stand amid rolling farmlands and cider orchards. Wooded ridges separate the tributaries of the Wye into pastoral valleys dotted with ancient churches, country estates, and black-and-white villages typical of the Welsh Marches.

NORMAN GEM *The little Church of St Mary and St David at Kilpeck was built in 1135, and is an almost perfect example of Norman architecture.*

HILLTOP TOMB *Arthur's Stone, on Dorstone Hill, was a burial chamber around 3000 BC. Legend says that it was used in the worship of the god Thor, hence Thor's Stone which became corrupted to Dorstone.*

FARMHOUSE GARDEN *The garden of Abbey Dore Court, a Dore valley farmhouse, has many rare plants in its rockeries.*

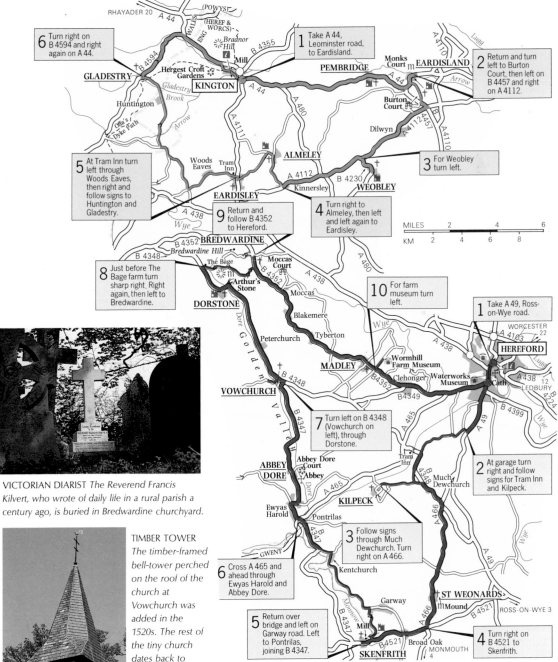

6 Turn right on B 4594 and right again on A 44.

1 Take A 44, Leominster road, to Eardisland.

2 Return and turn left to Burton Court, then left on B 4457 and right on A 4112.

3 For Weobley turn left.

5 At Tram Inn turn left through Woods Eaves, then right and follow signs to Huntington and Gladestry.

9 Return and follow B 4352 to Hereford.

4 Turn right to Almeley, then left and left again to Eardisley.

8 Just before The Bage farm turn sharp right. Right again, then left to Bredwardine.

10 For farm museum turn left.

1 Take A 49, Ross-on-Wye road.

7 Turn left on B 4348 (Vowchurch on left), through Dorstone.

2 At garage turn right and follow signs for Tram Inn and Kilpeck.

3 Follow signs through Much Dewchurch. Turn right on A 466.

6 Cross A 465 and ahead through Ewyas Harold and Abbey Dore.

5 Return over bridge and left on Garway road. Left to Pontrilas, joining B 4347.

4 Turn right on B 4521 to Skenfrith.

MILES 2 4 6
KM 2 4 6 8

VICTORIAN DIARIST *The Reverend Francis Kilvert, who wrote of daily life in a rural parish a century ago, is buried in Bredwardine churchyard.*

TIMBER TOWER *The timber-framed bell-tower perched on the roof of the church at Vowchurch was added in the 1520s. The rest of the tiny church dates back to Norman times.*

HEREFORDSHIRE BEACON

Hereford and Worcester
½ mile southwest of Little Malvern

On Herefordshire Beacon stands one of the finest earthworks in Britain, a 32 acre fortified settlement built 1115ft above sea level on this windy summit. The earliest structure dates from about the 3rd century BC. It is reached from the busy hub of the Malvern ridge walk, there is a car park opposite the Malvern Hills Hotel on the A449. British Camp, as the hill-fort is called, is well marked. Almost too well: so many walkers climb up to it that the Malvern Hill Conservators, who look after the hills, have been obliged to build tarmac paths. Yet the fortification itself, once

reached, is so immense, so indifferent to the tramp of human beings upon it, that it entirely retains its quality of endurance and mysterious pre-history.

It stretches away along the ridge to the south. Its broad level centre is the earliest part, surrounded by a bank and ditch – the ramparts were dry-stone walled. It is thought that in the 12th century a castle keep was built within this flat summit, and according to legend Owain Glyndwr, prince of Wales, made an unsuccessful attempt to defeat the English somewhere in the vicinity early in the 15th century.

From the centre of the fort the successive banks and ditches, built at later dates, widen like ripples in the great grassy hill. There are several entrances, and an ancient track climbing up from the west. One of a

line of such forts extending from the Dorset coast into northern Wales, British Camp is one of the largest and most impressive, covering 32 acres and with a lower rampart more than a mile long. Tradition says that the British chief Caractacus made his last, but unsuccessful, stand against the invading Roman army here.

The views from Herefordshire Beacon are magnificent. In the valley below a glint of water between the trees is the British Camp Reservoir, which supplies water to Great Malvern. In the grasslands surrounding the hill-fort grow wild mignonette and harebells, with heather on its southern slopes. Yet the past is most important here. Archaeologists suggest that 1500 to 2000 people may once have lived here, although it is strange that there is no natural water supply inside the

THE MALVERN HILLS *From the summit of Herefordshire Beacon, the Malvern Hills stretch northwards to their highest point, the 1395ft peak of Worcestershire Beacon (top right).*

fort's defensive ramparts. John Masefield, born $3\frac{1}{2}$ miles away in Ledbury, wrote after a childhood visit:

'People there had made the earth their father and protection; and the earth remembered that, and they, as parts of the memory of the earth, could still impress and terrify. Often they have terrified me.'

A footpath through the camp leads to Clutter's Cave, hacked from an outcrop of volcanic rock. It is 6ft high and 10ft deep, and may have been a hermit's cell or a shepherd's shelter.

HIDCOTE MANOR GARDEN

Gloucestershire
4 miles north of Chipping Campden

Glance through any modern plant catalogue and you come upon products of this garden. There are popular 'Hidcote' varieties of lavenders and hypericums, for example. But the name is known equally through a whole approach to modern gardening which has become a byword of 20th-century taste. Uniting formal planning with informal planting, it is known to gardeners everywhere as the Hidcote style.

The garden lies on the scarp of the Cotswolds some 4 miles from Chipping Campden. It covers, in reality, no more than 11 acres, but its fame – and complexity – are such that the physical scale means little. For this is a garden of many compartments, divided by bricked wall or clipped hedging, each enclosing its own design scheme. There are plots agleam with water, for instance, or heady with roses, or sculpted with evergreen topiaries, and almost everywhere at Hidcote borders brim with subtly blending or contrasting combinations of tree and flower and shrub. In all, the garden has been one of the most influential ever laid out. The garden's own creations, of course, hold special interest. There is the 'Hidcote' hypericum, for example, a now-popular evergreen shrub bearing bright yellow, saucer-shaped blooms. And there is the 'Hidcote' lavender, widely valued for its compact form and rich purple flowers. Additional delights include 'Hidcote' varieties of fuchsia, verbena, campanula and pentstemon, all prized and internationally known.

HIDCOTE GOLD

A bush rose with fern-like leaves and pendulant golden flowers was raised at Hidcote Manor in 1948 and named 'Hidcote Gold'. It is just one of many flowers named after the world-famous garden.

HIGH ERCALL

Shropshire
10 miles southeast of Wem

The sandstone and brick houses of High Ercall cluster around a T-junction near High Ercall Hall, the impressive remains of what was once a magnificent nobleman's mansion. It was built in 1608 for Sir Francis Newport, 1st Earl of Bradford.

In a garden behind the house stands an arcade of four arches mounted on round piers. There is nothing to show what they were for, but most likely they formed part of an inner courtyard or a loggia, which the hall was known to have.

St Michael's Church stands next to the hall, still mostly medieval, despite the Puritans' exaggerated claims in 1646 that it was 'demolished'. The tower dates from the 14th century. The base is badly worn, possibly by the weather, though parishioners say that it was caused in olden times by people sharpening their spears on it – and they may be right.

HIGHMEADOW WOODS

Hereford and Worcester
2 miles east of Monmouth

Oak and larch, beech and cedar, chestnut and spruce mingle gloriously in the vast woodland that sprawls over high ground across the river from Monmouth. Beneath the varied canopy, you can wind through the glades and up and down the slopes, following the waymarked trail northwards for almost 2 miles from the Staunton road to the Wye.

On the way, the path passes the enormous sandstone Suck Stone – 60ft long and 40ft wide – broken off from the hill above and thought to be the largest boulder in the country.

Where the path reaches the Wye, a suspension bridge for walkers spans the water, and on the other side you can take leisurely strolls either way along the towpath that was used in the days when the Wye was a busy commercial route. The path leading west runs below the Seven Sisters Rocks – tall spurs jutting from the trees – and mounts one of them to give a wonderful view down the river. Then it climbs to King Arthur's Cave, occupied by human and animal hunters in prehistory; bones of mammoth, bear, rhinoceros and bison have been found in it. Instead of crossing the footbridge you can follow the path eastwards above the river for $1\frac{1}{2}$ miles, to an unsurpassed view from the most impressive vantage point on the Wye's 130 mile course. Symonds Yat Rock stands 504ft above sea-level on a narrow neck of land almost cut off by a great ox-bow loop in the river. The patchwork of fields far below rolls away to the north.

HOAR CROSS

Staffordshire
7 miles west of Burton upon Trent

Neither village green nor main street forms the heart of Hoar Cross. Its houses and cottages are scattered along leafy lanes on the fringe of Needwood Forest, with an inn and a few houses at a crossroads, and Hoar Cross Hall and a church half a mile to the west.

The Church of the Holy Angels at Hoar Cross was built in memory of Hugo Meynell Ingram, of Hoar Cross

Hall, by his young widow. She chose for her architect one of the finest church builders of the day, George Frederick Bodley. The interior holds a wealth of decoration. The floor is paved with black-and-white marble. On the walls are 14 beautiful Stations of the Cross by two Antwerp woodcarvers, De Wint and Boeck. The vaulted chancel roof soars above the white marble tomb of Hugo Meynell Ingram.

Hoar Cross Hall was built for the Meynell Ingrams in 1862, in Jacobean style. The family moved out just after the Second World War, and now medieval banquets are staged there twice weekly in summer.

MOSAIC FLOOR *Blue and pink mosaics cover the floor of an Italianate arcade at the Church of St Catherine, Hoarwithy.*

HOARWITHY
Hereford and Worcester
7 miles northwest of Ross-on-Wye

A little corner of Italy stands in the Wye Valley water meadows of Hoarwithy. On a hilltop above the old stone buildings is the Church of St Catherine, which has a fine bell tower, arcades and mosaic floors that would fit in quite well amid the cypresses of Tuscany.

The church was the work of a wealthy Victorian parson, the Reverend William Poole. He arrived in 1854 to find his chapel 'an ugly brick building with no pretension to any style of architecture'. Over the years he changed all that, building a new church around the existing chapel. He brought in craftsmen from near and far, including Italy, and employed his own architect, J. P. Seddon. The result is a magnificent folly, a unique parish church with intricate tiled floors, a domed ceiling supported by columns of grey French and Cornish marble, a white marble altar inlaid with lapis lazuli, superb choir-stall woodcarvings showing 12 British saints and rich stained-glass windows.

BELL TOWER *The Tuscan-style church with a bell tower and arcades.*

St Catherine's is set off by the Englishness of the rest of the village. Tresseck, a black-and-white 16th-century building with a stone-gabled wing, a quarter of a mile to the west, is still a working farm. The cornmill, below the church, was working until the 1940s and is now a private house. It is distinguished by an old iron wheel set into the stonework.

On the southern approach to the village stands Bark House, a reminder that this was once a centre of an industry based on the oak trees which were plentiful in the area. Their bark was shipped by barge to Hereford where it was used for tanning. The riverbanks are lined with willow trees, and the village's name means white willow. Another reminder of old times is the tall, angular cottage – built as a toll house in 1865 – beside the iron bridge spanning the Wye. A horse-drawn ferry operated until 1856 when it was replaced by a bridge – the present one was built in 1876. The Upper Orchard Hotel dates from 1700.

HODNET

Shropshire
5 miles southwest of Market Drayton

Traditional Shropshire black-and-white buildings mark the core of the hill village of Hodnet. Most of the half-timbered houses cluster around St Luke's churchyard but, nearby, an eye-catching Tudor house stands in

picturesque isolation. There is also a modest 'folly' of Classical pillars.

From the ridge there is a clear view of Hodnet Hall and its 60 acres of wooded and pool-dotted grounds. The water gardens are linked to the house by formal terraces covered with lawns and massed rhododendrons and azaleas. In spring the banks are ablaze with daffodils and early flowering shrubs.

The hall, which was built in Elizabethan style in 1870, stands on the site of a castle which belonged to one of Shropshire's most renowned families, the Vernons. Today, Hodnet Hall is the home of the Heber Percys – among whose ancestors was Bishop Reginald Heber, a 19th-century rector of the parish and the composer of several famous hymns, including *From Greenland's Icy Mountains.*

The most interesting structure in Hodnet is the 14th-century sandstone Church of St Luke. Its tower, octagonal from top to bottom, is the only one of its kind in the county. The church contains a chained Nuremberg Bible, printed in 1479. Also on display are a breastplate, helmet and sword which belonged to a Vernon.

HOLME LACY

Hereford and Worcester
4 miles southeast of Hereford

An interesting feature of the Church of St Cuthbert at Holme Lacy is the 14th-century arcade dividing the nave and south aisle, which are almost of the same width. The late 17th-century font is carved, and the stalls have carved misericords.

There are many monuments to members of the Scudamore family from the 16th century, including one of 1571 with alabaster effigies.

HONINGTON

Warwickshire
11 miles southeast of Stratford-upon-Avon

On a gentle slope, rising from the River Stour where it meanders through a flat green valley, stands Honington Hall, one of the finest mansions to survive from the Restoration era.

Built in the 1680s of red brick, the hall – which is open to the public in the summer on Wednesday afternoons – has an imposing series of busts of Roman emperors set in niches over the ground-floor windows. Inside is a superb display of mid-18th-century plasterwork in the flamboyant rococo style. At the turn of the century, the Australian opera singer Dame Nellie Melba, a regular visitor to the hall, used to give private recitals in the majestic octagonal saloon.

Honington Hall was built by Sir Henry Parker, a Royalist alderman of the City of London, who profited from the Restoration of Charles II. He and his son Hugh are commemorated in an impressive monument in the stone Church of All Saints, just across the drive from the front of the hall. Although the tower dates from the 15th century, the rest of the church was built by Sir Henry in the 1680s. The spacious village street, with ample greensward on either side, is dominated by the gateway to the hall. From here, fine stone cottages are scattered up a slight slope and, below, a shady lane runs to the church. Magpie House, opposite, has fine diagonal timbers.

ILAM

Staffordshire
4 miles northwest of Ashbourne

The village church of Ilam, which is in the attractive Manifold Valley, contains a carved Norman font, and there are two Saxon crosses in the churchyard. The River Manifold, joined by the River Hamps, disappears underground near Beeston Tor in dry weather and reappears in the grounds of Ilam Hall; Dr Johnson experimented with a marked cork to prove that they were the same waters.

William Congreve, the Restoration playwright, wrote *The Old Bachelor* while convalescing in Ilam. Old Steeplehouse Farm, half a mile northwest, gives views of the Manifold Valley.

Bones and teeth of early animals, including cave lions and cave hyenas, have been found in caves, such as Elder Bush Cave, along the Manifold Valley.

ILMINGTON

Warwickshire
4 miles northwest of Shipston on Stour

Just beyond the northern edge of the Cotswolds the land rises again to form Ilmington Down, 854ft high and the highest point in Warwickshire. The village has all the Cotswold hallmarks – mellow stone-built cottages, lichen-covered stone roofs and mullioned windows.

The village has two greens: Lower Green overlooked by cottages, an inn and the village store; and Upper Green, below which are cottages and houses, the Norman church, St Mary's, and an orchard. Crab Mill, at the western end of Upper Green, dates from 1711, and the Manor House from the 16th century.

Just south of the village is the 17th and 18th-century Compton Scorpion Manor, home of Sir Adrian Beecham, son of the orchestral conductor Sir Thomas Beecham. Foxcote is an impressive early-Georgian house with nine bays.

In so English a village it is not surprising to find that some rural traditions are kept alive; sheep hurdles are still made there by a centuries-old method, and the Ilmington Morris Dancers perform regularly.

INKBERROW

Hereford and Worcester
5 miles west of Alcester

The village green at Inkberrow is bordered by a picturesque assortment of houses, some of black-and-white half-timbering and others, in pleasant contrast, in mellow red brick.

From the west side of the green, the three-storey Bull's Head Hotel looks across to one of the county's best-known inns, the timber-framed Old Bull, the model for the village pub at Ambridge in the BBC's long-running *Archers* serial. But it has an earlier and more distinguished literary association: Shakespeare stayed there in 1582 on the way from Stratford to Worcester to collect his marriage certificate.

Nearby is the Old Vicarage, a fine 18th-century brick building in the Tudor style and now divided into two dwellings.

Opposite stands Inkberrow's parish church of St Peter, dating from the 12th century but considerably rebuilt over the years. Its battlemented walls and tower are a familiar landmark. In safe keeping inside are some rare maps that were left in the vicarage by Charles I when he stayed there on May 10, 1645, not long before Naseby – the decisive battle of the Civil War, where he was defeated by Cromwell's forces.

IRONBRIDGE

Shropshire
7 miles northwest of Bridgnorth
See Coalbrookdale, page 39.

TIMELESS ILMINGTON *Stone-built cottages nestling behind verdant lawns and banks of summer flowers give Ilmington its timeless atmosphere of mellow tranquillity.*

K

KENILWORTH
Warwickshire
5 miles southwest of Coventry

There are better preserved castles in England than Kenilworth, but few can match it for grandeur and nobility.

The red-sandstone keep dates from Norman times, and additions were made in every century up to the

KING JOHN'S FORTRESS *The massive ruins of Kenilworth Castle recall the power and wealth of medieval kings and barons. King John made the castle virtually impregnable in the early 13th century when he built outer walls around the original 12th-century keep and then surrounded the whole fortress with a broad artificial lake. The main entrance to the island stronghold was over a causeway fortified by two gatehouses (see below right). On the strip of land between them, called the Tilt Yard, jousting contests were held.*

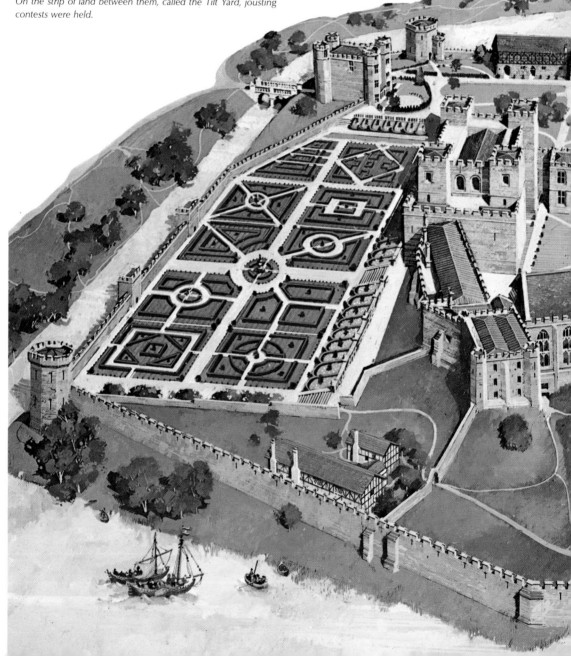

16th, including an outer court and towers built by King John, the banqueting hall of John of Gaunt and the gatehouse added by Robert Dudley, Earl of Leicester. Dudley was Elizabeth I's favourite, and she used to visit him at Kenilworth. The most famous occasion was in 1575, when the queen was entertained for 19 days, at enormous expense. Intrigued by the castle's history, it is hardly surprising that Sir Walter Scott was inspired to write a novel about it entitled, simply, 'Kenilworth'.

The best preserved building is the stables, built for the Earl of Leicester. The lower walls are of dressed stone and support the upper brick and timber-framed walls. Nearby is the Tiltyard, and it is probably here that the Great Tourney of Kenilworth took place in 1279, with more than 100 knights taking part. The outlines of the pleasure gardens laid out much later by the Earl of Leicester are still visible.

In its long and chequered history Kenilworth's most famous event was the siege of 1266 when the followers of the rebellious Simon de Montfort were encircled for eight months by the forces of Henry III. The king offered terms of surrender to the garrison, who cut off the hand of the royal envoy before sending him back. The Archbishop of Canterbury then excommunicated the garrison, whereupon the garrison's surgeon dressed in ecclesiastical clothes and excommunicated the archbishop, the king and all his followers. The defenders were eventually brought low by disease and forced to surrender.

The keep was partially destroyed after the Civil War and was never occupied after the Restoration.

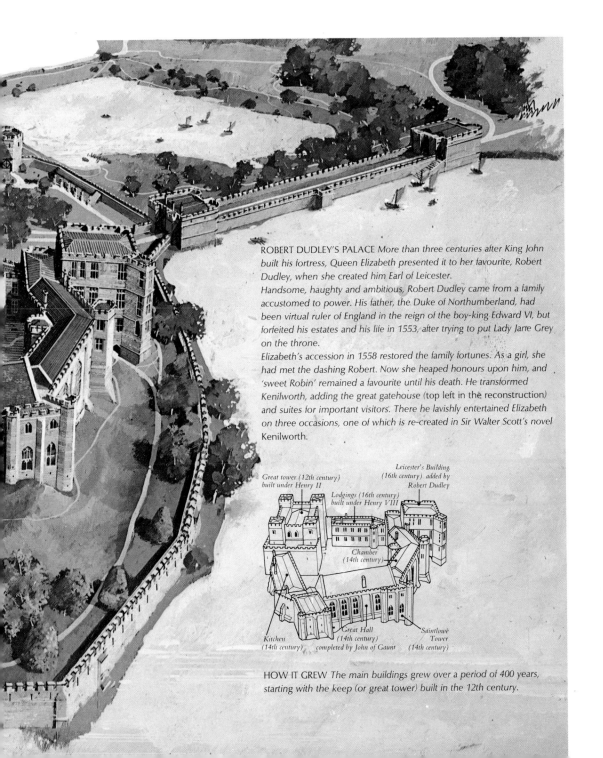

ROBERT DUDLEY'S PALACE *More than three centuries after King John built his fortress, Queen Elizabeth presented it to her favourite, Robert Dudley, when she created him Earl of Leicester.*
Handsome, haughty and ambitious, Robert Dudley came from a family accustomed to power. His father, the Duke of Northumberland, had been virtual ruler of England in the reign of the boy-king Edward VI, but forfeited his estates and his life in 1553, after trying to put Lady Jane Grey on the throne.
Elizabeth's accession in 1558 restored the family fortunes. As a girl, she had met the dashing Robert. Now she heaped honours upon him, and 'sweet Robin' remained a favourite until his death. He transformed Kenilworth, adding the great gatehouse (top left in the reconstruction) and suites for important visitors. There he lavishly entertained Elizabeth on three occasions, one of which is re-created in Sir Walter Scott's novel Kenilworth.

Great tower (12th century) built under Henry II
Leicester's Building (16th century) added by Robert Dudley
Lodgings (16th century) built under Henry VIII
Chamber (14th century)
Kitchen (14th century)
Great Hall (14th century) completed by John of Gaunt
Saintlowe Tower (14th century)

HOW IT GREW *The main buildings grew over a period of 400 years, starting with the keep (or great tower) built in the 12th century.*

KIFTSGATE COURT GARDENS

Gloucestershire
3 miles northeast of Chipping Campden

In 1920 there was nothing but a paved formal garden before the porticoed and pillared Georgian front of Kiftsgate Court. Now, much influenced by the style of the famous Hidcote Gardens near by, Kiftsgate has its pavilion of flowers. Small gardens open out like galleries or rooms, each with its own scheme of colour. The wide border is a profusion of silver, lavender and pink – with tissue-petalled paeonies, indigoferas and the purple-red of martagon lilies. Pass under a chestnut tree, then over a bridge, and there is the yellow border. The accents here are stronger, both in shape and hue. Golden euphorbias stand out sharply against shafts of delphinium blue, while tawny lilies and acers add deeper, warmer tones. The rose border is a clamour of colour broken only by the soft white of the irrepressible climber 'Kiftsgate'.

KILPECK

Hereford and Worcester
8 miles southwest of Hereford

At Kilpeck stands one of the most remarkable little churches in Britain – a strangely beautiful and almost perfect example of Norman architecture, with a superb array of rare carvings in red sandstone.

The name Kilpeck is a corruption of the Celtic *Kilpedic* (cell of St Pedic), and in the Domesday Book it was listed as 'Chipeete'. An early Celtic church there was replaced by an Anglo-Saxon one in the 6th or 7th century. The present Church of St Mary and St David was built on the same site in 1135, beside a Norman castle of which only the motte and a few fragments of masonry remain. The fact that the church has survived

DOORWAY DECORATION *Rich carvings on the south doorway of Kilpeck's Norman church include a Tree of Life.*

the ravages of more than eight centuries, in such a fine state of preservation, says much for the skill of the craftsmen who built it and for the care taken by generations of patrons and villagers.

The south doorway carvings include a Tree of Life, two soldiers with a slightly Egyptian appearance, a flying angel, birds and alarming-looking dragons. Right round the outside of the church is a frieze with more than 70 fascinating and fanciful carvings of heads – human, animal and monster.

Inside are a handsome chancel arch; a wooden gallery and a massive Norman font.

BORDERLAND SHEEP

Bred from Shropshire downland sheep and Welsh hill breeds, the hornless Clun Forest breed seen at Kington stock sales is well suited to the border hills.

Its dark muzzle and the black spots on its face and legs distinguish the Kerry Hill, a sheep descended from a Welsh mountain breed.

KINGTON
Hereford and Worcester
14 miles west of Leominster

High, rounded hills encircle the ancient market town of Kington, giving it a backdrop of great beauty whichever way you look. From their summits the hills survey glorious scenes. Kingswood Common, 2 miles south of the town, looks down to the Wye meandering gently to and fro across a wide, fertile valley, with wooded slopes beyond it. Smooth, small hills lie to the east, but in the south the Black Mountains loom dark and bold. On the other side of the town, Bradnor Hill rises sharply. A strenuous 2 mile walk from Kington Church climbs the hill to a magnificent 1282ft viewpoint which scans line upon line of hills as far as the majestic peaks of the Brecon Beacons. Just to the north are well-preserved sections of Offa's Dyke.

High Street and Bridge Street thread their way between the close-packed buildings of Kington, and narrow courtyards and alleyways are vestiges of the town's medieval gridiron street pattern. In the courtyard beside the Burton Hotel, the Old Gospel House has close associations with John Wesley, who is said to have written many of his sermons there. From the same courtyard a path winds to the River Arrow, emerging beside a fine Georgian mill-owner's house; the mill is still in partial use. Kington is the essence of a border town, in which big autumn sales of Clun Forest and Kerry sheep are held.

KINLET
Shropshire
9 miles south of Bridgnorth

An unspoilt village, Kinlet is an excellent centre for walking on the edges of the Wyre Forest. The partly Norman Church of St John the Baptist, set in parkland, has memorials recalling that two ancient families of Shropshire, the Blounts and the Childes, once lived at Kinlet. The monument to Sir George and Lady Blount is particularly noteworthy. Erected in 1584, it shows two figures kneeling under a canopy, while below them, visible through arches, is a corpse. One of their children, also depicted on the monument, is Dorothy, whose marriage so angered her father that after his death, it is said, he took to haunting her.

KINVER
Staffordshire
4 miles west of Stourbridge

Wool and, much later, iron screws and nails, created Kinver. The village lies between the great sandstone bluff of Kinver Edge and the double waterways of the River Stour and the Staffordshire and Worcestershire Canal. Part of the bluff bears the dramatic name of Hanging Hill, which rather disappointingly turns out to be the place where wool was hung up to dry. Most of the red-brick cottages in the High Street were built to house the early-19th-century nail workers.

St Peter's Church, perched on a 298ft spur above the village, dates mostly from the 14th century and incorporates the remains of an earlier, Norman church. On the north side of the chancel is a lovely 15th-century chapel, built by the Hamptons, lords of Stourton Castle.

Steep paths lead to the top of Kinver Edge, a dramatic hill that dominates the village. Its 198 acres of heath and woodland are National Trust property. From the summit can be seen four ranges of hills.

KNOCKIN
Shropshire
5 miles southeast of Oswestry

Mellow brick, sandstone and timber-framed 'magpie' buildings flank the broad street, which runs the length of the village of Knockin (pronounced 'Nukkin'). It was fortified by the Normans, and stones from the stronghold were used in the early 18th century to build two small bridges – and their adjoining sheep-dips – which span streams at the bottom of the street. All that remains of the castle is a grassy mound near the church.

KNOWLE
West Midlands
9 miles west of Coventry

The village has the distinction of having a church with three dedications – St John the Baptist, St Lawrence and St Anne. A chapel was founded here in 1396, the church was consecrated in 1402 and a college was founded in the church in 1416. Its west tower, buttressed and battlemented, soars above the 15th-century Guildhouse, a timber-framed building with close-set timbers and stone mullioned windows.

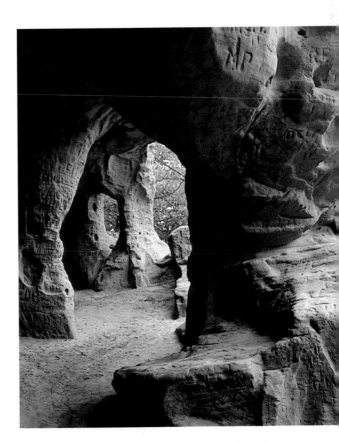

HOLY AUSTIN ROCK *In the Middle Ages, vagrants and hermits – probably including Holy Austin – found shelter in the caves weathered out from the soft sandstone in the face of Kinver Edge.*

L

LEDBURY

Hereford and Worcester
12 miles east of Hereford

In one of the most fruitful corners of the old county of Herefordshire is the beautiful and unspoiled little market town of Ledbury. For centuries Ledbury has flourished on the hops, fruit and red-and-white Hereford cattle that have been bred here since the 17th century, and its comfortable citizens have bequeathed it a wealth of black-and-white half-timbered houses. Those in the High Street include an old coaching inn, the 16th-century Feathers Hotel, and the 17th-century Market House. The Market House stands upon 16 stout timber pillars, and over the years it has served as a corn store, the town hall and a theatre for travelling players. An open market is still held in the sheltered space inside the pillars.

At the corner of Worcester Road and The Southend is Ledbury Park, a house which Prince Rupert of the Rhine used as headquarters when he occupied the town during the Civil War. In April 1645 some of his troops clashed with Roundheads under General Massey in the dining room of the gabled Talbot Hotel, in New Street. A running fight raged through the streets and churchyard, during which Rupert's horse was killed beneath him, and his Cavaliers finally drove the Roundheads from the town. There are small reminders of the fracas still to be found, including bullets embedded in the north door of the 12th to 14th-century parish church of St Michael and All Angels, which has more bullets on display inside. A soaring (126ft) steeple was added to the church's detached tower in the 18th century, and it looks down on the cobblestones and crooked, black-and-white cottages that border Church Lane. Horse-drawn carriages rattled past to the church until the 1740s, when iron posts were put up to stop the traffic.

On the west side of the High Street is St Katharine's Hospital, founded in 1232 for the relief of the poor. Of the medieval buildings, only one wing, containing the chapel and the great hall, remains. The chapel is in regular use, and the great hall with its timber roof was restored in 1971 for use as a parish hall. The separate Master's House nearby dates from the late 15th century, with 18th and 19th-century additions, and now houses the Tourist Office and a doctors' surgery. The row of almshouses next to St Katharine's was entirely rebuilt last century, and now contains 16 flats for elderly people.

LEEBOTWOOD

Shropshire
4 miles north of Church Stretton

Motorists purring along the trunk road that cuts Leebotwood in two are often oblivious to the existence of the village, so spread-out are its buildings, yet there is a rich store of history hereabouts.

The best starting point is the Church of St Mary, a plain and simple building dating from the 13th century. It has old box pews, and traces of a medieval painting can be seen on the north wall. The church stands on a hill overlooking the village, which lies in a wide valley.

The village began to assume its present shape in the mid-16th century, and some houses probably date from that period, although red-brick walls now disguise the timber-frame core. The Pound Inn, however, proudly displays its gleaming white walls to passing traffic on the main road, and even has white-painted chimneys poking up from a thatch that looks as though it had been flung over the building like a thick blanket. Although the inn bears the date 1650, the building actually dates from around 1480.

LEEK

Staffordshire
10 miles northeast of Stoke-on-Trent

In the 17th and 18th centuries, Leek was a centre of the silk thread industry. Albion Mill in Albion Street (off Compton Road), built in 1815, is the best preserved of the mills where the silk was twisted.

The mills gradually replaced silk twisting by hand in workers' cottages. Such cottages in King Street (all private dwellings) can be recognised by the long windows of the upper floor, where workrooms were connected so that a good length of continuous thread could be worked.

James Brindley, a Leek millwright, was the engineer who built Britain's first canal for the Duke of Bridgewater in the 1760s. The stone-built water mill in the town, now a Brindley Museum, was probably built by Brindley. The mill was used for grinding grain until the 1940s, and was restored in 1974.

LEDBURY'S POET DAUGHTER

The 19th-century poet Elizabeth Barrett Browning spent her childhood at a Moorish-style house, Hope End, 2 miles north of Ledbury. She described its secluded setting as '... dappled very close with shade, Summer-snow of apple-blossoms, running up from glade to glade.'

BATTLE SCENE *New Street, Ledbury, briefly became a battleground during the Civil War when Cavaliers and Roundheads clashed at the Talbot Hotel. The skirmish raged through the town.*

LEIGH BROOK
Hereford and Worcester
6 miles west of Worcester

The northern foothills of the Malverns that drop to the valley of the River Teme and its tributary, the Leigh Brook, are wild, wooded and remote. Although the towns of the Malverns are only a few miles away, they are concealed beyond the lofty summits.

Leigh Brook winds through a secluded valley of which 60 acres are managed as a nature reserve by the Worcestershire Nature Conservation Trust. The Knapp and Papermill Nature Reserve is reached by way of a cottage garden where a meandering lane crosses the brook. Dippers and kingfishers nest along the banks. Further on are woodlands and meadows where wild daffodils and early purple orchids grow.

Rising from the valley of the Leigh Brook to the 670ft peak called The Beck is Old Storridge Common, where ancient tracks – paved in places – lead up through birch woodland, ash trees, oaks and bracken. Here the low evening sun turns the dark slopes into a strangely foreign world: looking back on the climb, the rosebay willowherb is turned to purple fire, and there is neither roof nor chimney-pot visible anywhere.

Local legend says that St Augustine once conferred with the Celtic clergy from Wales on the sparsely wooded cone of The Beck. In Anglo-Saxon times, the spot was called Augustine's Oak.

LEIGHTON
Shropshire
6 miles north of Much Wenlock

Any village with the wooded Wrekin, the high escarpment of Wenlock Edge and the twisting River Severn as companions must be a contender for the title of Shropshire's loveliest village. There is not much of it, but the church, pub, hall and a few houses are just enough to make Leighton a discreet blend of rural community and unspoilt countryside.

Several black-and-white cottages line the road that runs through the village. Each has its own style, but all have gables and dormer windows decorated with a sawtooth design and a wooden spike at the apex.

The village church, St Mary's, contains many memorials to the Leighton family, including an effigy, probably dating from the 13th century, of a knight in chain mail.

LEINTWARDINE
Hereford and Worcester
7 miles west of Ludlow

Black-and-white cottages, and houses and shops of weathered brick and stone, line the streets of Leintwardine. The village, which stands on a hillside, is a network of narrow, crisscrossing lanes. On a grassy bank at the junction of High Street and Church Street is a wall with the filled-in doorway of the local lock-up.

The Church of St Mary Magdalene is evidence of the village's turbulent past, for its 14th-century tower is clearly defensive – 76ft to the top of its battlements, with 6ft thick walls. Among the church's monuments is one to General Sir Banastre Tarleton, a cavalry leader in the American War of Independence who was known by the rebels as 'Bloody' Tarleton.

LEOMINSTER
Hereford and Worcester
13 miles north of Hereford

This old wool town lies in a beautiful valley at the junction of the River Lugg and Pinsley Brook, among hopfields and orchards of cider apples. It has produced fine-textured wool, known as Lemster Ore, from its locally-bred Ryelands sheep since the 13th century. These same hornless, wide-backed animals helped to establish the great herds of Australia.

Just off Broad Street stands the 11th-century Priory Church of St Peter and St Paul, which has three naves. Here, too, is a ducking stool, used up to 1809 to still the tongues of nagging women.

BORDERLAND BUTTERFLIES

Male

In July and August, the dark green fritillary can be seen skimming above flowers and soaring to tree branches on Old Storridge Common, above the banks of the Leigh Brook. The green marks round the silver spots beneath its hind wings give it its name.

Male underside

Male

Female

Underside

Hedgerows or bushy hillsides are the holly blue butterfly's haunts – on holly in spring or ivy in autumn.

Underside

Male

Grey or 'grizzled' hairs on its brown-and-white wing markings give this butterfly its name. Its darting flight is so swift that it is difficult to follow.

LICHFIELD
Staffordshire
15 miles north of Birmingham

A changing but still charming cathedral city, Lichfield is dominated by the cathedral's three graceful sandstone spires, known as 'The Ladies of the Vale'. The spacious Close is still a haven of peace in which gracious 14th and 15th-century houses, together with the 17th-century Bishop's Palace, form the Vicar's Close, surrounding a stretch of vivid green lawn.

The first cathedral was consecrated in AD 700 by St Chad, but the present building was mainly completed

LADIES OF THE VALE *A local landmark, the tall sandstone spires of Lichfield Cathedral rise high above the treetops.*

COTTAGE CARVING *A decorated gable and dormer window at Leighton.*

between 1195 and 1325. The cathedral's west front is rich with sandstone statuary, and five statues on the northwestern tower and the bas-relief of Christ in Majesty above the central pillar are from the original cathedral. The 16th-century stained-glass windows in the Lady Chapel are among the best in England. They came from a dissolved Cistercian abbey in Herckenrode, in Belgium, early in the 19th century. In the cathedral library is one of the finest illuminated manuscripts in Europe. It includes the complete gospels of St Matthew and St Mark, and is called St Chad's Gospels, in memory of the missionary who became Bishop of Mercia in AD 669.

A marked town trail through the gridiron of streets passes most of the civic landmarks, including fine old timber buildings in Bore Street and Quonian's Lane. The house on the corner of Breadmarket Street where Samuel Johnson, essayist, critic and compiler of the famous *Dictionary*, was born in 1709 is now a Johnsonian Museum. In the cobbled square is a statue of Dr Johnson, and on the other side of the square is a monument to James Boswell, his biographer.

Dame Oliver's School and the grammar school, where Johnson was taught and in turn taught himself, both survive. The grammar school, now merged into a comprehensive school, also included among its pupils the essayist Joseph Addison (1672–1719) and the Shakespearian actor David Garrick (1717–79). At the Swan Inn nearby, Johnson used to meet his friends.

Another notable citizen of Lichfield was Elias Ashmole (1617–72), who founded the Ashmolean Museum, Oxford, in 1677. It is Britain's oldest public museum.

At Wall, 2 miles southwest, is the excavated bathhouse of a Roman posting station, Letocetum, on Watling Street. It is the most complete of its kind in Britain, and there is a museum.

LILLESHALL
Shropshire
3 miles south of Newport

On a rocky hill above Lilleshall village stands a 70ft high monument to the 1st Duke of Sutherland, a local landowner who died in 1833. According to the lengthy inscription on its base, he was 'the most just and generous of landlords' who 'went down to his grave with the blessings of his tenants on his head'. The monument was erected in 1833, and from its plinth there are superb views across the flat plains stretching westwards to The Wrekin.

Southeast of the village is Lilleshall Abbey, founded in 1148. Though now a ruin, the sandstone building is still impressive, particularly the arched doorway to the roofless nave and the tall Gothic window arch at the eastern end.

LLANYBLODWEL
Shropshire
5 miles southwest of Oswestry

One man, the Reverend John Parker, left his stamp on this village scattered along a secluded stretch of the River Tanat. Mr Parker was Llanyblodwel's vicar in the mid-19th century, and he rebuilt the Norman Church of St Michael to his own design, adding a curious, cigar-shaped tower which is connected to the body of

the church by an arch. An inscription on the arch reads: 'From thunder and lightning, earthquake and flood, good Lord deliver us.'

Despite the Welshness of its name – which means 'village of flowers' – Llanyblodwel is firmly in England, with the twisting national boundary just over 1 mile away. In the village centre stand a handsome old bridge and the Horseshoe, a 16th-century black-and-white inn, which until recently had been kept by the same family for more than 300 years. The old smithy is opposite, joined to a timbered barn.

LLANYMYNECH
Shropshire and Powys
10 miles north of Welshpool

Towering above a tangle of trees and bushes, the man-made limestone cliffs of Llanymynech Hill rise to 500ft above this 'frontier' village. The workings, where 60,000 tons of limestone were quarried each year in the middle of the 19th century, were abandoned before the First World War. Their cliffs now form part of the Llanymynech Rocks Nature Reserve, noted for carline thistle, clematis, wild thyme and other plants typical of limestone areas.

St Agatha's Church was built in 1845 and is a cheerfully eccentric little example of mock-Norman architecture. Its clock has faces big enough to be seen from Llanymynech Hill's quarry, where its designer, Richard Roberts, worked as a boy.

A footpath running south curves and climbs Llanymynech Hill on the eastern flank of the old limestone quarry. Crossed by the Offa's Dyke long-distance footpath, the hill is a magnificent vantage point with views embracing the mountains of Wales and the Shropshire plain, from which isolated sandstone hills rise like islands in a green ocean.

LONG COMPTON
Warwickshire
4 miles northwest of Chipping Norton

A saying in this village is that 'there are enough witches in Long Compton to draw a wagonload of hay up Long Compton Hill'. Local belief in witches existed at least until late in the 19th century, when a man accused of murdering a woman claimed she was a witch, and that there were 16 others in the district.

But there is no air of evil in Long Compton today – only stone and thatched cottages, antique shops and the remains of a medieval cross adapted as a drinking fountain. The only magic potions mixed are those for a studio making stained glass.

The Church of St Peter and St Paul dates from the 13th century, and has an unusual lych gate to the churchyard. The gateway is a two-storey thatched cottage with the ground-floor rooms removed. It now houses the village museum.

Just south of the village is a large stone, 8ft tall and 4ft wide, which stands apart from a Neolithic or Bronze Age circle known as the Rollright Stones. But local tradition gives a different version; it is said that the large stone was a king, and the smaller stones his courtiers, turned to stone by a witch to prevent him becoming King of all England. The stone is known as the King Stone, and the circle, the King's Men. A more distant group is called the Whispering Knights.

From Lichfield, through Cannock Chase to Needwood Forest

Between the heaths and woodlands of Cannock Chase and ancient Needwood Forest stand a romantic mansion, steeped in tradition, a romantic castle and a village that stages an ancient hunting dance, said to have originated from pagan rituals and dating from Saxon times.

COOL CORNER *When Abbots Bromley was a market town, its Butter Cross on the village green provided local people with a shady area in which to sell their butter and all their other dairy products.*

HEIRLOOM HERD *The ancestors of Blithfield Hall's Bagot goats were a gift from Richard II.*

FIRE INSURANCE *A fire mark on this house in the main street of Alrewas ensured prompt attention by the fire brigade.*

FOREST BIRD *Nuthatches are common in the woodland of Cannock Chase, recognisable by their black eye stripe, grey body and reddish flanks. The strong, pointed bill is used for cracking nuts.*

9 Turn right on A 513, then second left, to Shugborough; then return along A 513 and turn right to Great Haywood.

11 Turn right on A 518, then right to The Blythe.

12 Turn right to Newton, then left to Admaston and left again on B 5013.

STONE 10

8 For Brocton Nature Reserve turn left; then right to Milford.

STAFFORD 2

CHARTLEY CASTLE

Stowe-by-Chartley

SHUGBOROUGH

Milford Common

Farm

Hixon

Great Haywood

The Blythe

7 Turn right, on Brocton road, and beyond Anson's Bank car park turn right again.

Brocton

Newton

13 At end of causeway turn right, then fork left into Abbots Bromley.

Anson's Bank

Cannock Chase Country Park

10 Turn left to join A 51, then right on minor road for Stowe.

Admaston

B 5013

German & Commonwealth Cemetery

Penkridge Bank

Ladyhill Centre

Blithfield Res

ABBOTS BROMLEY

B 5234

CANNOCK CHASE

6 Turn right, on Rugeley road, then left on Penkridge Bank.

Marquis Drive Centre

Rugeley

14 Take B 5234. Fork right to Hoar Cross.

Hed.nesford

A 460

Hall

Hoar Cross

5 Turn right on A 460, then left and right to visitor centre.

A 5190

Castle Ring

4 Turn left, then right, to Hednesford.

Upper Longdon

Cannock Wood

15 Turn right, joining A 515 through Yoxall.

Gentleshaw

Yoxall

A 515

3 Turn left, then bear right to Gentleshaw; then turn right to Cannock Wood and Castle Ring.

Farewell

A 51

A 515

Fradley Junction

16 Turn left on A 513, then right onto Fradley road. (For Alrewas, straight ahead.)

2 Right, then left, on Upper Longdon road.

LICHFIELD Cath

A 513

ALREWAS

A 5

19 Turn left on A 515

17 For Fradley Junction turn right just before canal bridge.

1 Take A 51, Stone road, then turn left to Farewell.

A 38

18 Turn right and right again.

BIRMINGHAM 18

MILES 1 2 3 4 5

KM 2 4 6 8

HEATHLAND HUNTER *Foxes may be seen on Cannock Chase by the patient observer. Though alert and wary, with a keen sense of smell, they tend not to see stationary objects nearly so well.*

THE LONG MYND

Shropshire
3 miles west of Church Stretton

The great range of hills known as The Long Mynd, rising to 1700ft, is a world of its own. It encompasses 4530 acres of wild moorland, where red grouse whirr out of the heather, waterfalls cascade into half-hidden narrow valleys, springs rise icy clear through bog moss and pink bog pimpernel, bracken-covered hillsides and sunlit streams. During the last Ice Age, between 10,000 and 26,000 years ago, frost broke up the 800-million-year-old pre-Cambrian rocks of The Long Mynd to form a stony deposit blanketing the surface. This has given it its characteristic rounded outline, so unlike the jagged Stiperstones to the west.

The Burway, a single track climbing up a 1-in-5 gradient out of the snug little town of Church Stretton, which is tucked into The Long Mynd's eastern side, gives spectacular views of the surrounding diversity of the Shropshire hills. There are more intimate glimpses, too, of the deep valleys that cut through this high moorland. A track called The Port Way has run along the ridge for more than 3500 years, and the Burway joins its course there.

Much of The Long Mynd, which comes from the Welsh 'mynydd', meaning a bare mountain, belongs to the National Trust and parts are leased as grouse moors, with commoners having rights to graze their sheep and ponies. On fine summer weekends the sky above The Long Mynd is dotted with gliders from the Midland Gliding Club.

The best way to explore The Long Mynd is on foot, from one of the villages along its eastern flanks. The springs that rise on The Long Mynd have carved deep

DEEP SECRET *Cardingmill Valley is typical of the hidden valleys carved deep into The Long Mynd.*

valleys known as 'hollows', or 'batches', the most famous being Cardingmill Valley with the Light Spout waterfall at its head. Much less frequented and almost equally lovely is Ashes Hollow, reached from the black-and-white village of Little Stretton where a brook chuckles down between the houses. From here, too, can be found Callow Hollow, over an intervening hillside.

In the valleys there are many butterflies and birds, including the grey wagtail. On the high moor, where heather, gorse, sundew and bilberries grow wirily against the wind, ravens and buzzards fly; sometimes a white-rumped wheatear can be seen, and, more rarely, the ring ouzel, a mountain blackbird.

THE RARE RING OUZEL

Pale edges to flight feathers show in flight.

Males have a clear white crescent.

On the females the crescent is less marked.

In summer, ring ouzels can sometimes be seen flying above the high moors of The Long Mynd.

LOPPINGTON
Shropshire
4 miles west of Wem

They are not given much to change in Loppington. This is old farming country, and novelty is viewed with suspicion. You can see all around the stamp of conservatism, not least in St Michael's Church.

Roundheads garrisoned it during the Civil War, entrenched behind its battlemented tower. Local Royalists stormed it, and drove them out regardless of the damage done to their own church in the process. Records show that St Michael's was badly burnt and the roof ruined. However, the church was completely replaced in 1656.

In the renovated south porch an inscription notes that the churchwarden at the time was Nicholas Dickin, one of a notable family of local landowners, after whom the village pub, the Dickin Arms, is named. However, if the Royalists celebrated after their victory – and it was a rare one for the Royalists around here – it was most likely to have been in the

Blacksmith's Arms, which is much older. And they probably did it in much the same way as the regulars did until quite recently.

The pub was always what its name proclaims it as: the village blacksmith's. While horses were shod, beer was served. There was never a bar until 1984, when the building was renovated. Until then barrels were racked in the cellar and the ale hand-pumped upstairs on demand.

Subtle renovation and a thatched roof have kept its character. Even the villagers agree that the thatch is an improvement on the corrugated-iron roof, fitted in the 19th century, that replaced an earlier thatch.

An iron ring, 3in in diameter, is set in the middle of the road outside the Dickin Arms. It is the last bull ring in Shropshire. Until as recently as 1835, bulls were tethered there and baited as sport for the young bloods. A plaque in the pub wall tells of its use. They keep it not so much to celebrate an ancestral barbarity, but because to move it would mean change.

Loppington Hall, an 18th-century brick building with five bays and three storeys, contrasts rather harshly with the softness of the village, where the other houses are mostly brick and half-timbered, many with the cruck frame exposed.

One of the most attractive is The Nook, down the lane from the church, which for all its coy name is a working farmhouse. Its brick is mellowed by centuries of sunlight, yet the timbers are barely weathered. The churchyard has a well-worn look. In the interests of conservation the grass is kept uncut for most of the year, making it seem truly ancient rather than simply untidy. It fits in with the stone arches and Loppington's general air of changelessness.

LOWER ROCHFORD
Hereford and Worcester
2 miles east of Tenbury Wells

Behind a screen of trees the Teme winds through a valley where apple orchards are ablaze with blossom in spring. Fields neatly strung with hops are interspersed among the orchards, and several of the farms have oast houses with rows of wooden air vents like small ships under sail. The warm red brick of the farm buildings matches the glowing red soil through which the Teme cuts its swathe.

Set back from the road, between a farm and the river, St Michael's is an unspoilt little Norman church. An outstanding 12th-century doorway, with a Tree of Life carved within its arch, is set into the north wall, blocked up now but visible from outside.

The fine stained glass in the east window is an early work by William Morris.

NORMAN ARCH *Lower Rochford's church has a carved Tree of life in the arch of a blocked-up Norman doorway.*

In the early morning light, sheep graze in the dewy orchards beside the church.

LUDLOW
Shropshire
27 miles south of Shrewsbury

Two imposing buildings break the skyline above the beautiful border town of Ludlow: the sandstone and limestone castle and the spacious Church of St Laurence.

The castle was built between 1086 and 1094 by a Norman knight named Roger de Lacy. He chose the site shrewdly, so that the fortress had towering cliffs on two sides. From its lofty vantage point the castle helped to hold down the conquered Welsh and the rebellious men of the border.

The outer bailey is the size of a sports field, and may have been used as a refuge by the townspeople during times of strife. The massive keep was built up from the original gatehouse tower in the early 12th century, and the domestic buildings were added in the late 13th and early 14th centuries, mainly by the Mortimer family, who inherited the castle from the de Lacys. The Elizabethan buildings came when the castle became the seat of the Council of the Marches, set up to govern Wales and its wild borderlands.

In 1483 the 12-year-old Edward V was staying at Ludlow when he heard that his father Edward IV had died and that he was king. He left Ludlow with his young brother Richard, but on the way they were intercepted by their uncle, Richard, Duke of Gloucester who took them on to London. The boys were later murdered in the Tower and Gloucester became Richard III. Henry VIII's elder brother Arthur came here with Catherine of Aragon, his wife. After Arthur's death at Ludlow the course of English history was changed when Henry married Catherine. The terrace walk round the castle was laid out by Arthur for his bride. It was at Ludlow Castle that John Milton first saw the production of his masque 'Comus' in 1634. Today, a Shakespeare play is staged here every summer.

RAMPARTS AND ROOFTOPS *The tower of St Laurence's Church tops the battlements of Ludlow's ancient castle which in turn look down on the town they have guarded for centuries (overleaf).*

STEEP STREET
On Ludlow's most impressive thoroughfare, charming old houses cling to the slope of Broad Street as it plunges down to the River Teme.

BACK IN TIME
Ludlow's 18th-century Butter Cross now houses a museum.

TOP TIMBER *The Feathers Hotel is not just the finest timber-framed building in Ludlow, but maybe the whole country.*

Ludlow town grew up on the east side of the castle, and its magnificent jumble of medieval, Tudor, Stuart and Georgian houses is overlooked by the 135ft tower of St Laurence's Church. Built mostly in the 15th century, it is one of the largest parish churches in England. But its special glories are the beautifully carved misericords (backs of choir seats) in the chancel and its glorious east window. In the churchyard are the ashes of the poet A. E. Housman, author of 'A Shropshire Lad'.

Next to the church, in the Garden of Rest, is the Reader's House, so called because it was the home in the 18th century of the Reader, the Rector's chief assistant. West of the church are Hosier's Almshouses, originally endowed in 1486 by a rich local wool merchant, John Hosier. The present buildings, however, date from 1758.

Nearby is a classically designed 18th-century stone building, the Butter Cross, which lies at the heart of Ludlow's market place. The Butter Cross once housed a school but is now the town museum.

North of the Butter Cross, in the Bull Ring, is The Feathers Hotel, one of the finest timber-framed buildings in England. Enlarged in 1619, its front is a rich profusion of ornamental carvings – and its interior contains carved overmantels, embossed plaster ceilings and panelling. An ornate, first-floor balcony was added in the mid-19th century.

South of the Butter Cross is Ludlow's most impressive thoroughfare, Broad Street. The Angel Hotel, an old

coaching inn, has a back room called the Nelson Room. Lord Nelson was a hereditary burgess of Ludlow, and it was in this inn, in 1802, that his title was formally confirmed and he was given the freedom of the town.

At the foot of Broad Street – with its ranks of black-and-white, timber-framed shops and houses – is the Broad Gate. It was built in the 13th century, and is the only one of Ludlow's seven town gates to survive.

LYDBURY NORTH
Shropshire
3 miles southeast of Bishop's Castle

From a distance, the massive buttressed tower of St Michael's Church at Lydbury North looks as if it belongs to a castle, rather than a place of worship. There has been a church here since about AD 780, when a Saxon lord of the manor named Edwin Shakehead was cured of the palsy and dedicated his lands in gratitude. The present church is basically 12th century, but has been greatly altered since then. It is rich in medieval carving and the 17th-century candlesticks on the high altar are particularly fine.

The room above the south transept was used as a schoolroom from 1663 to 1847. The north transept, known as the Plowden Chapel, was built by a member of the local Plowden family after his return from the Crusades – one of the few still left in an Anglican church. The pews, partly restored in 1900, date from the early 17th century, as do the Creed and Ten Commandments painted above the rood screen.

NORMAN CASTLE *The round Chapel of St Mary Magdalene, built about 1100, is one of Ludlow Castle's notable features.*

STAINED-GLASS SPLENDOUR *For more than 500 years the glowing east window has lit Ludlow church.*

From Wenlock Edge to the grandeur of the Clee Hills

The wooded escarpment of Wenlock Edge runs northeast from Craven Arms. Behind and below it a network of narrow lanes zigzags across a landscape of streams and small valleys. In the heart of the area Ludlow is guarded by a fortress above the River Teme.

HOLY HILLSIDE *The yellow-stone All Saints Church at Richards Castle was built in the early 1890s against the side of a hill.*

ON GUARD *The church spire at Croft Castle rises in front of a corner tower of the fortress.*

HORNLESS *Bred in the 19th century from the original Hereford, Ryland sheep give lightweight fleece. Both sexes are hornless.*

FIRST NIGHT *John Milton's masque Comus was first given in Ludlow Castle on Michaelmas Night 1634.*

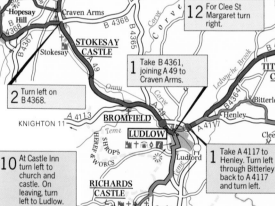

5 Turn right through Acton Scott; then continue and fork left to Hope Bowdler.

6 Turn right on B 4371.

7 Fork left, then turn left, to Cardington.

8 Turn right to Gretton, then right again.

9 Left on B 4371, then right, through Roman Bank to Beambridge.

10 Turn right on B 4368.

11 Turn sharp left through Peaton to Bouldon and fork right.

13 Turn right, round hill, to Cleobury North.

4 Turn sharp right on Long Lane, then left on A 49.

12 For Clee St Margaret turn right.

14 Turn right on B 4364.

3 Fork right over bridge, and right again in Hopesay.

1 Take B 4361, joining A 49 to Craven Arms.

2 For Titterstone Clee Hill turn left, signposted Dhustone.

2 Turn left on B 4368.

CHURCH IN THE TREES
The tree-ringed Church of St James at Cardington is overlooked by wooded, grassy hills.

10 At Castle Inn turn left to church and castle. On leaving, turn left to Ludlow.

1 Take A 4117 to Henley. Turn left through Bitterley back to A 4117 and turn left.

3 For viewpoint straight ahead; then return and take B 4214.

9 Turn left on B 4361.

4 For Burford turn right on A 456, then left. Return and follow A 456, then turn right on A 4112.

6 Turn sharp left on Eye Lane.

8 For Croft Castle straight ahead. Return and take B 4362, Ludlow road.

7 Right on B 4361, then fork left to Yarpole. At church fork left.

5 Turn left on A 49 to Leominster. Return and follow A 49.

MADLEY

Hereford and Worcester
6 miles west of Hereford

One of the finest and most spacious village churches in England – dedicated to the Nativity of the Virgin – looks out over the brick-built houses of Madley. It was built of local sandstone in the 13th and 14th centuries, and has remained virtually unaltered since 1320.

The church houses several treasures, including one of the largest medieval fonts in Britain. Some of the beautiful stained glass in the east windows is 13th century, and today artists come to Madley to view the stained glass and sometimes to paint the village itself.

Madley's historical claims go back to the 5th century, when it was the birthplace of St Dyfrig who is said to have crowned King Arthur.

MALVERN, GREAT AND LITTLE

Hereford and Worcester
7 and 11 miles southwest of Worcester

The pure spring water produced by the hard rocks of the Malvern Hills has been bottled and sold since the 18th century, when Great Malvern became a fashionable spa rivalling Bath and Cheltenham. Traces of those days can still be seen in the Georgian Mount Pleasant Hotel, the Regency ironwork of the Foley Arms, and the Victorian buildings lining the steep hillsides and tree-lined avenues leading to Great Malvern Station.

Great Malvern's greatest treasure, however, is the Priory Church of St Mary and St Michael, founded in 1085 but dating mainly from the 15th century. Its collection of 15th and early-16th-century stained-glass windows are second in England only to those of York Minster.

The north transept window, a gift from Henry VII, is particularly beautiful in glorious yellows. It contains portraits of the king and his elder son, Arthur, Prince of Wales. The church also has some good choir stalls and earlier work of the 12th and 13th centuries, with Norman nave arcades.

Opposite the priory, in Grange Road, is Priory Park which has a lake that was once the monks' fishpond. There is also an elegant Victorian bandstand where bands play on summer Sunday afternoons. Malvern Museum, housed in the Abbey Gateway, shows Malvern through the ages and is open daily in summer.

Little Malvern lies beneath Herefordshire Beacon on whose slopes the poet William Langland (1340–1400), is said to have dreamed his *Vision of Piers Plowman*. The village once had a 12th-century Benedictine monastery, and the court adjoining the Church of St Giles takes in part of its domestic buildings. All that remains of the original church is the central tower and east end, dating from the 15th century. The 15th-century stained glass in the east window depicts Edward IV and his family. Much of the 15th-century floor tiling remains and there are misericords. Little Malvern also has a priory.

MARKET DRAYTON

Shropshire
18 miles northeast of Shrewsbury

This was the birthplace in 1725 of Robert Clive – Clive of India. It is a town with a Wednesday market that has been held for 700 years. There are many good half-timbered houses dating from the mid-17th century.

In the 14th-century parish church are several Norman features, particularly a carved capital depicting William Rufus and his court. From the sturdy tower – said to have been climbed by the youthful Clive – there are fine views across the valley of the River Tern. The 16th-century grammar school where Clive was educated stands near the church, and has a desk carved with his initials.

Some 4 miles southeast of Market Drayton is Woodseaves Cutting, a man-made gorge which carries the Shropshire Union Canal to the west of Cheswardine. At the northern end of the cutting there is a wharf with a 19th-century warehouse.

MARTON

Warwickshire
5 miles north of Southam

The village of Marton stands on the Oxford to Coventry road. The River Leam skirts the village to the north, and the road bridge that crosses it still has masonry from the 15th century.

In Louise Close is the Museum of Country Bygones, open daily in summer. It began from the private collection of Mr George Tims, now the museum's curator. Everything in the museum comes from local farms and villages, and includes craftsmen's tools, dairying implements and agricultural machinery.

TEMPLE OF STEAM *Ornate columns and arches that carry the roof of Great Malvern's Victorian railway station would scarcely be out of place in a cathedral.*

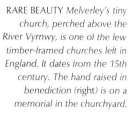

RARE BEAUTY *Melverley's tiny church, perched above the River Vyrnwy, is one of the few timber-framed churches left in England. It dates from the 15th century. The hand raised in benediction (right) is on a memorial in the churchyard.*

MELVERLEY
Shropshire
11 miles west of Shrewsbury

A remote and scattered hamlet, Melverley has one of Britain's most enchanting little churches. Perched above the River Vyrnwy and surrounded by ancient yews, the Church of St Peter has timber-framed walls of wattle and daub. The oak beams are joined with wooden pegs, and the black-and-white building, with its tiny tower roofed in grey slate, shelters beneath tiles green with lichen.

At Alberbury, about 2 miles southeast of Melverley

and close to Alberbury Castle, is the Church of St Michael. It has a massive tower of about 1220 on the north side, and the Loton Chapel, built in 1340. Its three-pipe manual organ is from Rowton Castle.

MERIDEN
West Midlands
6 miles west of Coventry

A 500-year-old stone cross on the village green is said to mark the exact centre of England. Meriden also claims to be the home of English archery, still practised by the country's oldest archery society, the Woodmen of Arden, established in 1785. Its membership is restricted to 81 archers. Their headquarters in the 18th-century Forest Hall stands by a field where the legendary outlaw Robin Hood is said to have competed in archery contests.

The village also has an obelisk on the green erected in memory of cyclists who died in both World Wars. On a Sunday each May cyclists come from all over the country for a memorial service. Nearby is a stone seat erected by the Cyclists Touring Club in memory of the cycling journalist W. M. Robinson – 'Wayfarer' – who died in 1956. Meriden became this cyclists' 'Mecca' because of its claim to be at the centre of England.

On a bluff overlooking the village, next to the half-timbered Moat House Farm of 1609, is the Church of St Lawrence, reputedly founded in the 11th century by Lady Godiva. About 1½ miles northwest is Packington Hall, ancestral home of the Earl of Aylesford, Lord Lieutenant of the county.

MIDSUMMER AND HOLLYBUSH HILLS
Hereford and Worcester
9 miles northwest of Tewkesbury

The southern summits of the Malverns are lower and more densely wooded than those to the north. Here on the twin peaks of Midsummer and Hollybush hills the men of the Iron Age built a great defensive settlement in about 400 BC. Owned by the National Trust, the hill-fort can be reached either along the Malvern ridge or up a long track from Hollybush Pass below, where the A438 curves over the hills from east to west. It is not easy to see the 'contour' fort from below, but the track turns into a sharp twist of footpath at the top of the ridge and emerges through woodland to the bare turfed summit.

Excavations were made at Midsummer Hill between 1965 and 1970, and revealed pottery and metalwork linking it with a similar massive hill-fort on Bredon Hill, northern outpost of the Cotswolds. Dry-stone-faced ramparts and 17 timber gateways enclosed some 19 acres, including both Midsummer and Hollybush summits. Within the walls is a natural spring and evidence of some 250 hut sites: it is believed that as many as 1500 people lived here before the Romans invaded in about AD 55. South of the fort on the adjoining hill are a Neolithic long barrow and several round barrows of the Bronze Age.

Dusk is a ghostly time here because of the pale green lights of the glow-worms that inhabit the grassy slopes. Midsummer Hill is one of the few places where this dwindling species of beetle can still be found.

MILFORD
Staffordshire
3½ miles southeast of Stafford

Some of the most delightful walks and drives in the county start at Milford, set in the beautiful valley of Staffordshire's modest little river, the Sow. The village is made up of attractive old cottages and newer, large homes, many of them half-timbered with sweeping lawns and well-tended gardens. At Upper Home Farm, on the western edge of the village a cart shed and a cow barn have been converted into new cottages, which won a Farm Building Award Scheme commendation in 1977. A stream in front of the buildings has been widened into a pool, which adds to the attractive scene. Opposite the Barley Mow Inn, the cottages and more elegant homes come to an end, and the road through the village opens on to the spacious Milford Common.

LIGHT OF LOVE

Midsummer Hill is one of the few places where the now rare glow-worm can be seen in England.

Winged male flies to glowing female.

The male is a slim brown beetle. The wingless female has a segmented body.

MINSTERLEY
Shropshire
9 miles southwest of Shrewsbury

The old centre of Minsterley lies on either side of a stream. The late 17th-century Church of Holy Trinity is a barnlike building in red brick, with stone surrounds to the doors and windows. Near the church are some half-timbered houses, including Minsterley Hall, home of the local Thynne family who also built the church.

MORDIFORD

Hereford and Worcester
4 miles southeast of Hereford

The wooded hills that spread east from Mordiford are laced with a tangled skein of narrow lanes, delightful and bewildering to the stranger. The lanes in turn are interwoven with many miles of footpaths and bridleways.

Mordiford stands on the River Lugg – a fine river for grayling – just above its junction with the Wye. Despite its plain name, the Lugg is a beautiful river, winding as sinuously as the Wye through rich farmland and orchards, and between lush water meadows

PINE-WOOD VISITORS

Siskins are often seen feeding with redpolls.

A winter visitor to Haugh Wood, outside Mordiford, is the siskin, a yellowy-green bird like the greenfinch, but smaller. It feeds on the seeds of pine and spruce.

dotted with pale willows. At Mordiford the river glides beneath the nine arches of the 600-year-old bridge. Each time the king rode over this bridge in medieval times the lords of Hereford had to give him a pair of silver spurs; that was their payment in return for the manor of Mordiford. From Backbury Hill, reached by a path leading northeast from the town, you can look down on the river, the town, and beyond to Hereford's sandstone cathedral and even the distant mountains of Wales.

Haugh Wood flanks the lane between Mordiford and Woolhope, and has a 3 mile waymarked Forestry Commission trail circling within it. It makes a tranquil interlude to wind among the dappled glades, with glimpses through the oaks from the high ground to the flat land outside the woods. A winter and early spring visitor is the vivid, little siskin.

MORE

Shropshire
2 miles northeast of Bishop's Castle

Attractive black-and-white houses cluster around St Peter's Church at More, which has a jaunty bell-cage above its squat tower. Inside the church, a 17th-century library is kept in two cupboards or 'presses', with the churchwardens' instructions for looking after the books hanging on the wall beside them. They cover almost 200 years of religious subjects from 1470 to 1669.

MORETON CORBET

Shropshire
5 miles southeast of Wem

A Norman castle enclosure with a tower stood at Moreton Corbet until Cromwell dismantled it; what stands there now and bears the name Moreton Corbet Castle is the stark ruin of a once-magnificent house built in 1579 by Sir Andrew Corbet. In the Civil War it was captured and burned in a night attack by Parliamentarian troops. It was never rebuilt.

The flat surrounding countryside accentuates the bold outlines of the house, its tall gables reaching to the sky where rooks take flight from empty windows.

MORVILLE

Shropshire
5 miles southeast of Much Wenlock

The steep, wooded slopes of Meadowley Bank provide a green velvet setting for Morville, a scattered limestone village on the main road between Much Wenlock and Bridgnorth. From the road the view is inviting, with a church and a hall facing each other across a wide lawn and the gilded domes of two rooftop cupolas rising above the trees.

Closer inspection reveals that the cupolas crown the stable pavilions of Morville Hall, an Elizabethan house extensively rebuilt in the 18th century. They stand facing each other across the broad sweep of grass in front of the hall, to which they are connected by curved walls. The hall itself is in unpretentious Georgian style, with lattice windows, a parapeted roof and porticoed doorway. The only ornamentation is on the faces of the two projecting wings, where four columns, each topped by a stone ball, rise to the level of the third storey.

Much of the stone is from the Benedictine priory buildings which once stood on the site, and there is evidence of the original Elizabethan staircases. Morville Hall is owned by the National Trust, but can be visited only by written application to the tenant.

The village church is the only one in Shropshire dedicated to St Gregory. After the dedication ceremony, performed in 1118 by the Bishop of Hereford, lightning killed two women and five horses in the village. Most of the church is Norman, and the south door has 12th-century ironwork. The nave has 17th-century woodcarvings of St Matthew with an angel, St Mark with a lion, St Luke with an ox and St John with an eagle; the Norman tub font is carved with large faces.

There is little more to Morville other than the church and the hall, but what there is completes the picture of rural charm. The village school is a rugged Victorian building watching over the weathered remains of a sandstone whipping post. Nearby is the Acton Arms, as smart as the pale beige paint that decorates its outside walls.

Aldenham Park, a few miles west of the church, was built at the end of the 17th century by Sir Edward Acton. His family lived there from the 14th century and includes a number of remarkable men. One was Sir John Acton, who went to seek his fortune in Italy before inheriting Aldenham. He ended as Prime Minister to King Ferdinand IV of Naples during the Napeoleonic Wars. There he reorganised the navy and army. At the time it was rumoured in Naples that he had arranged the murder of Prince Caramanico, who was one of his rivals.

MOSELEY OLD HALL

Staffordshire
4 miles northeast of Wolverhampton

The brickwork facing of Moseley Old Hall is a Victorian coating over a much older timber-framed building. On the evening of September 7, 1651, four days after the Battle of Worcester, Charles II arrived at the house as a fugitive, heavily disguised with his hair cropped and his face stained with walnut juice. When search parties called at the house, he hid in a secret chamber near his room. Charles escaped to Bristol by accompanying a party of supporters as a servant.

The bed and secret hiding place can be seen today, together with fine furniture, documents, portraits and other relics of the Whitgreaves, the family who sheltered Charles.

MUCH MARCLE

Hereford and Worcester
7 miles northeast of Ross-on-Wye

On February 17, 1575, Marcle Hill began to move – and kept on moving for three days. This strange movement of a mass of soil and rock, about 25 acres in extent, uprooted trees and hedges, killed cattle and sheep and even destroyed a small chapel in its path. The chapel bell was found during ploughing 265 years later. The cause of this convulsion, which moved the hill about 400yds, remains unexplained.

The village played a large part in the development of cider making as a major local industry. As far back as the 1600s the local farmers had sold their surplus cider. One of the first men to start an actual factory for cider making in the 19th century was a Marcle farmer named Henry Weston, whose firm still operates at Bounds Farm.

RUINED GRANDEUR *Silhouetted against the sky, the eyeless windows of Moreton Corbet Castle stare across the countryside, as they have since the house was burned by Parliamentarian soldiers during the Civil War.*

The Church of St Bartholomew, mainly 13th century, contains some of the finest carved effigies in the county. One, carved from a solid block of oak, dates from about 1350 and depicts a man – thought to be local landowner Walter de Helyon – lying cross-legged with hands clasped in prayer. Another commemorates the beautiful Lady Grandison, who died in 1347.

Near the church are several old black-and-white farm cottages, and the village has two historic houses – Hellen's and Homme House. Hellen's, an ancient manorial house of brick and stone begun in 1292, is mainly 16th century. It has a dovecote built in 1641. The house is occasionally open to the public. Homme House, which is not, dates in part from the early 16th century. It was the seat of the Kyrle family and is still owned by their descendants.

MUCH WENLOCK
Shropshire
13 miles southeast of Shrewsbury

Set in a dip to the northeast of Wenlock Edge, the tiny market town of Much Wenlock is a friendly patchwork of twisting streets, half-timbered houses, black-and-white cottages and limestone buildings.

The town, which was granted its first charter in 1468, grew beside a priory dedicated to its first abbess, St Milburga. Milburga came from a family of saints – her mother and two sisters were all saints and her father, Merewald, King of Mercia, founded the priory about AD 680 as a nunnery. Two centuries later the priory was disrupted by the Danes, and 200 years after that it was rebuilt by Lady Godiva's husband, Leofric. Finally, in 1540, it was closed by order of Henry VIII. Its extensive ruins, which are open to the public, lie at the end of the Bull Ring. Adjoining the priory is an L-shaped, early 16th-century building that was once the infirmary and the Prior's Lodge.

In the middle of the town is the mainly 16th-century Guildhall, its overhanging first floor held up by stout oak pillars. One of these pillars was the town whipping post, and still carries the iron staples to which the prisoners' wrists were tied. Beside the whipping post are the wheeled stocks in which wrongdoers were carted about the town. The last time this happened was in 1852. The Butter Market – for the sale of perishable produce – was held beneath the building.

The Guildhall has three gables, one of them over a passageway leading into the yard of Holy Trinity Church. The Norman church, with its stubby, battlemented tower, has a Jacobean pulpit whose carved panels include, somewhat oddly, some two-tailed mermen. On the other side of the street, opposite the Guildhall, is the local museum, and farther along in Sheinton Street are the half-timbered Old Gaolhouse, built in 1577, and the mainly 17th-century Manor House. The only exposed cruck-framed building in the town is St Owen's Well House, in Queen Street. It is next to a well dedicated to the 6th-century Welsh saint, who may have visited the area.

In the High Street is Raynalds' Mansion, built in about 1600, which takes its name from John and Mary Raynalds who lived there. The timbered building has three steep gables with carved balconies in each of its bays which John Raynalds added in 1683. Across the road, a medieval timber-framed building that was once the old Falcon Inn is now a bank.

A native of Much Wenlock, Dr William Penny Brookes, introduced physical education to British schools. In 1850 he also started his Olympian Games in the town. The annual event became so famous that in 1860, when games modelled on those of ancient Greece were held near Athens, the marathon winner's trophy was called the Wenlock Prize. Sadly, the doctor died in 1895, a year before the modern Olympic Games were started at Athens. An athletics meeting is

MEDIEVAL TOWN *Holy Trinity's weathered tower has overlooked Much Wenlock's rooftops since Norman times.*

RAYNALDS' MANSION *Carved balusters adorn the twin balconies of the timbered house.*

ROMANESQUE SCULPTURE *Two finely carved stone panels still remain on the walls of the ruined octagonal washhouse at Much Wenlock Priory. One (above) shows two men standing under arches. The other (right) depicts Christ – centre – sleeping in a boat on the lake.*

still held annually at Much Wenlock in his honour.

Benthall Hall, 4 miles northeast, is a 16th-century stone house with sparkling mullioned windows. South-west is Wenlock Edge, where the ghost of a robber is said to keep watch over his stolen gold in a cave. An outcrop is called Ippikin's Rock, after the robber.

Shipton Hall, an Elizabethan manor house, lies 6 miles southwest of Much Wenlock. Built of stone in 1587 to replace an earlier timber house, the interior combines Georgian furnishings with Tudor woodwork. There is a medieval dovecote.

MUNSLOW

Shropshire

8 miles southeast of Church Stretton

Munslow village, strung out along a sharp S-bend in the road running below Wenlock Edge, is pretty enough, with a terrace of black-and-white gabled cottages, stone houses and a high stone wall oozing aubrieta, stonecrop and toad-flax. The best of Munslow, however, lies off the road in the direction of the church, reached by a twisting lane that winds among steep little hills.

St Michael's Church sits in a wooded hollow and is surrounded by immaculate houses and barns, all built with Wenlock limestone. The elegant Georgian rectory, now a private house, has a fine front porch supported by two pairs of columns, with mature lawns leading down to a small pool. St Michael's has a Norman tower, topped by an 18th-century parapet, a splendid 14th-century wooden porch, and some 500-year-old stained-glass windows.

Aston Munslow, a mile to the southwest, has also developed away from the main road and is graced with several black-and-white buildings, including the Swan Inn, which has a dormer-like storey nodding forward over steps leading to the entrance.

But of all the charming buildings tucked away along a maze of back lanes, the most interesting is the White House. It is a fascinating architectural jumble of medieval, Elizabethan and Georgian styles.

The additions, seemingly made with little regard to blending with the previous styles, give the White

House a rather rambling appearance, but therein lies its charm: there can be few places where so many contrasting styles can be seen under one roof.

In Saxon times there was a manor here, known as Estune, but the earliest part of the present house dates from the 14th century. In the 16th century a gabled wing was added, and when this was partly destroyed by fire in the 18th century it was replaced by a Georgian addition. In every room the skill and craftsmanship of the original builders can be seen. All the original woodwork is still there, down to the locking pegs in the beams, and the medieval hall has a ceiling supported by a magnificent cruck frame.

Other features include an oval window, heraldic glass, linenfold panelling and secret staircases. The fine state of preservation is undoubtedly due to the fact

CORVE DALE Near Munslow, the River Corve winds past 16th and 17th-century manor farms on its journey to meet the River Teme at Ludlow. Harvest time transforms the fields into a multicoloured patchwork of browns, greens and yellows.

that the house has been lived in continuously.

There are other interesting buildings in the grounds, including a 17th-century coach house and a cider house complete with cider press, a granary, a 16th-century stable block and the ruins of a 13th-century dovecote. These outbuildings now form part of a Museum of Buildings and Country Life, established by the present owner, which is open to visitors on Wednesdays, Saturdays and Bank Holiday Mondays between April and October.

N

NAPTON ON THE HILL
Warwickshire
7 miles west of Daventry

The hill rises to almost 500ft above Warwickshire's flat countryside, and Napton has stood there since Saxon times. Thatched cottages, Georgian and Victorian houses and modern dwellings border the lanes around the village green, and towering above all, on the crown of the hill, is an early-19th-century tower-windmill. The old miller's cottage next door contains remnants of the original bread oven.

On the brow of the hill is the Church of St Lawrence, dating from the 12th century, which local legend says arrived there by mysterious means. It was originally planned to stand by the village green, but when the stones were placed ready for building they moved up the hill overnight. No one ever knew who

GLASS FLOWERS *Stained-glass panels of flowers are a feature of St Lawrence's Church at Napton.*

moved them, but rather than tempt fate, the church was built in the new position.

The Oxford Canal winds its way around the hill, attracting boating enthusiasts and anglers.

NESSCLIFFE
Shropshire
8 miles northwest of Shrewsbury

Nesscliffe Hill, where rhododendrons ramble amid the trees, is said to have been the hideout of 'Wild Humphrey' Kynaston, a 16th-century outlaw remembered as the Robin Hood of Shropshire. The cave named after him is reached by a flight of narrow steps, hollowed by countless feet and carved into a sheer cliff of red sandstone. From the top of the hill, where the remains of an Iron Age fort can be discovered amid the undergrowth, there are fine views over the Shropshire plain to Oswestry and the Berwyn mountains.

NEWPORT
Shropshire
2 miles north of Lilleshall

The Normans built Newport as a 'new town', designed around a winding main street with the Church of St Nicholas on an island at the centre. The red-sandstone church still stands at the town's northern end, and though massively restored in the 19th century retains its medieval character. Along the main street pleasant timber-framed shops and houses contrast with rows of Georgian and Victorian red brick.

Newport's most eye-catching building is the Town Hall, now used as business premises. Built in 1860, it is in Italian style with tall arched windows, stone facings and an ornate clock. The windows and stone facings are painted a dazzling white, while the rest of the brickwork is pale blue, giving the building a distinctly 'Wedgwood' look.

Cherrington, 5 miles west of Newport, possesses a beautiful half-timbered house built in 1635. It is said to be the house immortalised in the nursery rhyme 'The House that Jack Built', though no one seems to know who Jack was. The rhyme was first published in 1755 in *Nurse Truelove's New Year's Gift*.

PURPLE SUMMER SPLENDOUR

Flowers in May and June

Capsule with small, flat seeds.

The evergreen rhododendron was brought to Britain from Asia Minor more than 200 years ago and was widely planted for game cover in woods. Now about 200 species and varieties grow in parks and gardens, flowering in early summer. One species, however, ponticum, grows in the wild and spreads rapidly in shady, sheltered places.

Grows to 20ft high on sandy, peaty soil throughout Britain.

A river gorge where industrial history was forged

The steep-sided Severn valley, spanned by the world's first iron bridge, is rich in relics of the Industrial Revolution. Coalbrookdale had one of the world's largest iron foundries, and there is a Museum of Iron in a former warehouse. To the north, The Wrekin guards a plain.

COLOUR RANGE *The landscaped gardens at Hodnet Hall have a vivid and varied range of flowers, shrubs and forest trees. Primulas and irises grow beside the many lakes and pools set among trees.*

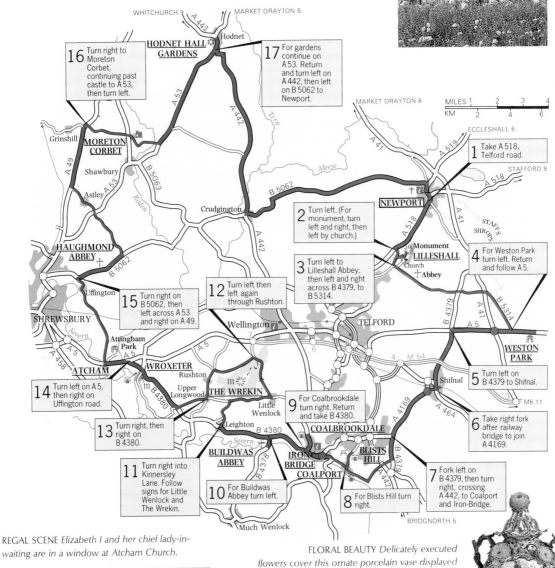

16 Turn right to Moreton Corbet, continuing past castle to A 53, then turn left.

17 For gardens continue on A 53. Return and turn left on A 442, then left on B 5062 to Newport.

1 Take A 518, Telford road.

2 Turn left. (For monument, turn left and right, then left by church.)

3 Turn left to Lilleshall Abbey; then left and right across B 4379, to B 5314.

4 For Weston Park turn left. Return and follow A 5.

5 Turn left on B 4379 to Shifnal.

6 Take right fork after railway bridge to join A 4169.

7 Fork left on B 4379, then turn right, crossing A 442, to Coalport and Iron-Bridge.

8 For Blists Hill turn right.

9 For Coalbrookdale turn right. Return and take B 4380.

10 For Buildwas Abbey turn left.

11 Turn right into Kinnersley Lane. Follow signs for Little Wenlock and The Wrekin.

12 Turn left then left again through Rushton.

13 Turn right, then right on B 4380.

14 Turn left on A 5, then right on Uffington road.

15 Turn right on B 5062, then left across A 53 and right on A 49.

REGAL SCENE *Elizabeth I and her chief lady-in-waiting are in a window at Atcham Church.*

FLORAL BEAUTY *Delicately executed flowers cover this ornate porcelain vase displayed at Coalport Museum, Ironbridge.*

MONASTIC DWELLING *The graceful ruins of Haughmond Abbey, founded for Augustinian monks in about 1135, stand in their own tranquil grounds.*

NORTH HILL

Hereford and Worcester
1 mile west of Great Malvern

North Hill is the most northerly of the Malverns, rising to 1307ft. Although not the highest, it is wilder and less trodden than its neighbour, Worcestershire Beacon. The path begins from a car park just below the brick Clock Tower in Great Malvern, passing a gaunt quarry face before curving on to the precipitous slopes of the east escarpment. There are other routes, but this gives magnificent views of Great Malvern – from here it is possible to see how closely it clings to the rock face. Through the shrub and woodland the pink and buff stone of Malvern Priory stands out clear against the Severn plain beyond.

The path winds past Ivy Scar Rock as it levels a little. Younger than the pre-Cambrian rocks which make up most of the Malvern Hills, this great lichen-covered rock face is dark and fine-grained. The succulent wall pennywort grows on its surface, and an ancient oak wrests its way out of a fissure.

After curling round the hill, the path drops into woodland and then climbs the broad track of Green Valley, once part of the old way across the hills from Great Malvern. At some points on the track, the ancient paving stones thrust their way through the turf. The old track was planted with an avenue of sycamores 40 years ago.

The summit of North Hill is grazed by sheep and is bare of the bracken, rowan trees and gorse found lower down. Only thin fescue grass and wild thyme grow here.

WHERE WILD THYME GROWS

Many, two-lipped flowers in dense flower-head.

Four-sided stem, hairy on two opposite sides.

Long-growing, sprawling stems of wild thyme form a dense carpet on grassland, rock ledges and sand dunes in Britain. Its tiny, rose-purple flowers attract honey bees.

EASTERN PROSPECT *Looking east from North Hill's bracken-clad slopes, the flat expanse of the Severn plain is spread out below.*

OFFA'S DYKE

Shropshire
From the River Severn to the River Dee

Offa, King of Saxon Mercia, ordered the dyke to be dug in the late 8th century, to define the boundary between his territory and Wales. It runs for nearly 170 miles from the River Severn to the Dee, with some gaps where there was originally thick forest. A footpath follows most of its course.

A particularly well-preserved 7 mile stretch of the dyke starts at Knighton, 16 miles west of Ludlow on the A4113. There is an information centre in the village.

CROWNED HEAD *A silver coin showing King Offa, who issued the first Anglo-Saxon coinage.*

OMBERSLEY

Hereford and Worcester
3 miles west of Droitwich

Even in a county celebrated for its black-and-white, timber-framed dwellings, the architecture of Ombersley is outstanding. The village street is bordered by a whole medley of buildings in this style; their gables, chimneys, differing rooflines, and seemingly haphazard frontages together form a scene typical of old Worcestershire.

Particularly notable is the King's Arms pub, partly 15th century and with a 17th-century plaster ceiling. The early-17th-century Dower House, in its leafy setting, is another fine timber-framed dwelling. Nearby are two medieval cottages – Cresswells, with a fine twisted chimney, and the Thatched Cottage.

The parish church of St Andrew, which still has its original box pews, was consecrated in 1829 and serves both the village and the estate of Ombersley Court, built in the early 18th century as the family home of Samuel, Lord Sandys. The mansion, with its impressive pillared portico and replastered front face, stands in landscaped grounds on the edge of the village.

On a grass verge at the centre of the village is a rare 'plague stone' recalling that the Black Death, which reached England in 1348, swept through this part of the country. The trough-like stone, originally placed outside the village, was as close as traders from outside would come. The villagers left money in the stone and traders left their goods nearby.

OSWESTRY

Shropshire
16 miles south of Wrexham

For centuries English and Welsh fought for possession of Oswestry until, in 1535, Henry VIII's Act of Union made the town officially part of England. However, Welsh is still widely spoken there.

The area – beneath the foothills of the Welsh mountains – was settled in the Bronze Age. At Old Oswestry, north of the town, are the remains of a vast Iron Age hill-fort, one of the most elaborate examples of its kind in the world. It was occupied from about 550 BC until AD 75, when the Romans overran it. Two banks and ditches originally protected the hill. Later a third bank was added, and finally an enormous double rampart, enclosing the whole. The entire area covered is about 56 acres. There is evidence of reoccupation during the Middle Ages.

The town's name is probably a corruption of Oswald's Tree, referring to Oswald, a Christian king killed here in 642 by Penda, the pagan king of Mercia. But there are two versions of the origin of Oswald's Tree. One story is that Oswald erected a wooden cross or 'tree' before his battle with Penda. The other has it that the dead king's body was hung from a tree.

Another legend tells how an angel flew off with part of Oswald's dismembered body and dropped it. On the spot where it fell a spring welled up; it is now known as King Oswald's Well and is said to have curative powers. The parish church is dedicated to St Oswald. Much rebuilt after damage by Parliamentarian troops in 1642, it still has some 13th-century stonework. It once stood outside the town walls.

In the 8th century, Wat's Dyke and, later, Offa's Dyke were built to mark the border of Anglo-Saxon Mercia with Welsh territory. Remains of both lie west of the town.

The Normans built a motte-and-bailey castle here soon after the Conquest to keep down the increasing Welsh raids.

In 1559 plague killed nearly one-third of the inhabitants of Oswestry. The Croeswylan Stone, or Cross of Weeping, in Morda Road, marks the spot to which the market was shifted during the affliction.

Three great fires between the 13th and 18th centuries and the ravages of the Civil War combined to destroy much of the town. Oswestry was Royalist, but was taken and held by the Parliamentarians who, after the war, destroyed the castle. Only fragments of it now remain on a grassy hilltop, which provides fine views from the centre of the town.

Many old buildings were demolished when Oswestry became a railway headquarters in 1860. One that escaped was 17th-century Llwyd Mansion, the town's best half-timbered building. On its side is a double-headed eagle crest, granted to the Lloyd family by the Holy Roman Emperor for distinguished service during the Crusades. Other timber-framed buildings include the Fox Inn and the Coach and Dogs, whose wattle-and-daub is revealed by a glass panel set into the wall. Oswestry School, in Upper Brook Street, was founded in 1407 and is believed to be the oldest secular school in the country. Beautifully restored in 1983, it now houses the Holbache Museum of Childhood, whose treasures include more than 300 dolls from as far afield as China and Japan, dating from 1720 to 1920. Oswestry is also a centre for fishing in the rivers of the

PREHISTORIC RAMPARTS *The banks and ditches of a huge Iron Age fort encircle the hilltop at Old Oswestry.*

nearby Welsh valleys, pony trekking in the hills and rambling along Offa's Dyke.

Wilfred Owen (1893–1918), the First World War poet, and Sir Walford Davies (1869–1941), Master of the King's Musick, were both born in the town.

Six miles north, just inside the Welsh border, is the beautifully preserved Chirk Castle, completed in 1310 and inhabited continuously since – at present by the descendants of Sir Thomas Myddelton, a 17th-century Lord Mayor of London.

TIMBER TOWN *A hotchpotch of black-and-white, timber-framed houses line the main street in Ombersley.*

HOUSE AND GARDEN *Packwood House has stood replete in Tudor glory since the middle of the 16th century. It is noted for its magnificent gardens. The walled Carolean garden has a gazebo at each corner, but the pride of Packwood is the yew garden (right) with its immaculately clipped trees.*

PACKWOOD HOUSE

Warwickshire
1 mile east of Hockley Heath

Packwood House is a fine example of Tudor building, a timber-framed beauty dating from between 1556 and 1560, with 17th-century additions. Its 50 acres of gardens include the Carolean Garden, which has a gazebo at each corner. One of these has a furnace and flue used to heat water pipes in an adjacent wall against which peach trees were successfully grown.

The most remarkable feature, however, is the yew garden where clipped yew trees are said to be set out to represent the Sermon on the Mount. One large tree is known as 'The Master', and on each side are the Evangelists and Apostles. Rows of smaller trees stand for the listening multitude. The garden was laid out by John Fetherston, owner of Packwood in the mid-17th century. The rooms of the house contain fine tapestries and English furniture.

PEBWORTH

Hereford and Worcester
6 miles northeast of Evesham

Time has hardly touched Pebworth's Friday Street, and if Shakespeare strolled down it today, as he used to when he lived at nearby Stratford-upon-Avon, he would have little difficulty recognising it. The half-timbered cottages standing there now are the same ones he knew, many of them still trimly thatched and set in colourful country gardens. And if anyone asked him he might be able to explain how the village got its nickname – Piping Pebworth. Is it true, as people say, that after getting drunk at Bidford-on-Avon, just over the border into Warwickshire, he slept the night under a crab-apple tree; and next morning, waking up with a hangover and vowing never to drink in Bidford again, he composed the uncharacteristic jingle which keeps the nickname alive, as well as those of several other nearby villages?

Piping Pebworth, Dancing Marston, Haunted Hillborough, Hungry Grafton, Dodging Exhall, Papist Wixford, Beggarly Broom and Drunken Bidford

The village is built in a figure-of-eight on a hill, and the mixture of red brick and Cotswold stone shows how close it lies to Warwickshire and Gloucestershire. The 15th-century Church of St Peter crowns the hill.

PEMBRIDGE

Hereford and Worcester
6 miles east of Kington

Half-timbered cottages and inns, jumbled round a medieval market place, make Pembridge an oasis of old English grace.

The open market hall, with its stone-tiled roof supported by eight oak pillars, dates from the early 1500s and once had a second storey. It shares the triangular market place with the rambling New Inn — also known locally as 'the inn without a name'. Founded in 1311, it was enlarged with matching gabled wings in the 17th century. Two ghosts are said to haunt the inn: one of a girl who appears only to women, the other of a red-coated soldier armed with a sword. Another old inn, the Greyhound, is a short walk east past the post office. It has stood, its overhanging upper storey supported by carved timber brackets, since early in the 16th century.

Old stone steps lead from the market place up to a knoll and the Church of St Mary. It is thought to have been built between 1320 and 1360, replacing an earlier Norman church. Its most remarkable feature is the detached, pagoda-like bell-house. Mighty timbers, bracing one another in crisscross fashion inside stone walls, relate to a Scandinavian building method adopted in East Anglia but surprising on the Welsh Marches. The walls are slitted with embrasures through which bowmen could fire, indicating that the belfry also served as a stronghold during border skirmishes. In the church itself, the west door is bullet-scarred from a Civil War attack.

Opposite Ye Olde Steppes, where Bridge Street starts north towards the River Arrow, are Duppa's Almshouses. Four remain from the six built in the 1660s. Another row of six almshouses, Trafford's, is at the eastern end of the village and dates from 1686. Glan Arrow Cottages, near the river, were built in the 1500s, and the row of three houses now known as Bridge House, beside the riverbank footpath, has a 14th-century hall.

PERSHORE

Hereford and Worcester
8 miles southeast of Worcester

This market town, rich in well-kept Georgian buildings, is set among woodlands and fruit farms where the delicious Pershore plums are grown. The town is reached from the east by crossing a 14th-century six-arched bridge over the River Avon. Parts of Pershore Abbey, originally Norman, survived the Reformation to serve as the parish church. The magnificent lantern tower was built about 1330. Nearby is St Andrew's Church, which contains 13th to 15th-century work.

PITCHFORD

Shropshire
6 miles south of Shrewsbury

Pitchford is a typical Shropshire farming village, where red-brick houses complement the red sandstone of solidly built Pitchford Farm. Lying on a quiet back lane, the village has no shops or pubs, but it does have one of the most notable Elizabethan houses in England, Pitchford Hall.

The hall was built between 1473 and 1549 for the Ottleys, members of a wealthy Shrewsbury family who acquired the estate in 1473, then lived there for 300 years. The hall represents the peak of the timber-frame building period, and is a riot of black and white. From their stone foundations to the stone-tiled roof, the walls are a maze of beams forming diamond and chevron patterns. The mansion stands in a setting of trees and water.

One of the best views of the hall is from the lodge at the northern end of the village, when all the superb details come into perspective, particularly the elegant star-shaped chimneys and pretty roof gables. A close view can be gained from the drive that leads from a second lodge, half a mile north of the village, to the Church of St Michael and All Angels which stands on a slight rise next to the house. Near the church a giant lime tree supports a timber-framed 'tree house' of 1714 in its massive branches.

St Michael's is considerably older than the hall, dating partly from the 12th century but mostly from the 13th. It is a small, unpretentious building of red sandstone with buttressed walls and a steeply sloping roof topped by a weatherboarded belfry. In the north wall, Norman herringbone stonework can be seen below a blocked window. Inside the church is an oak effigy – measuring 7ft – of the Knight Templar Sir John de Pitchford (1237–85).

PONTRILAS
Hereford and Worcester
11 miles southwest of Hereford

This hamlet at the southern end of Golden Valley is notable for two interesting houses: Pontrilas Court, which is a 17th-century gabled stone house, and Kentchurch Court, 2 miles southeast, which dates from the 11th century. A fortified manor house with a 14th-century great gateway and tower, Kentchurch Court was remodelled by John Nash in 1795 and has fine 17th-century wood-carving, attributed to Grinling Gibbons. Owain Glendwr (Owen Glendower), the Welsh hero who fought against the English, spent the last years of his life there in the early 15th century.

DAZZLING DISPLAY *The black-and-white front of Pitchford Hall dazzles the eye with its diamond and chevron patterns.*

R

RAGGEDSTONE HILL AND GOLDEN VALLEY
Hereford and Worcester
1 mile south of Hollybush

According to legend, this dark double peak of the Malverns – bleak, bare and jagged from almost any viewpoint – has a menacing shadow. In medieval times a young monk from Little Malvern Priory is said to have fallen in love, and as a penance for breaking his vow of chastity was ordered to crawl each day on his hands and knees the $2\frac{1}{2}$ miles from the priory gate to pray on the summit of Raggedstone Hill. One day, exhausted and bitter, he reached the peak but instead of praying he called down a curse on all those on whom the shadow of Raggedstone might fall. Cardinal Wolsey, the powerful chancellor of Henry VIII, once lived at nearby Birtsmorton Court, and one afternoon fell asleep in the garden: the shadow of Raggedstone passed over him and his downfall began from that moment.

On the marshy eastern levels below Raggedstone Hill is Golden Valley – not to be confused with the valley of the same name between Dorstone and Pontrilas – from where the hill looks sinister enough, but remote. Golden Valley is another stretch of the wild Malvern sheep-grazed commonland, covered with yellow gorse, thorn and oaks, turf and bracken.

RAGLEY HALL
Warwickshire
2 miles southwest of Alcester

From its stately perch on a hill of rolling parkland, Ragley Hall surveys the Arrow Valley and the Cotswold hills beyond. The grey-stone house, with sweeping stone stairs leading up to the grand classical columns of the entrance, was designed in the Palladian style by Robert Hooke in 1680 for the Seymour family, who have lived there ever since.

A portico and the interiors designed by the architect James Wyatt (1746–1813) were added in 1780. James Gibbs (1682–1754), best known as the architect of St Martin in the Fields, London, designed the decorated great hall, which has moulded plasterwork. There are collections of paintings, china, furniture and books. The house is set in a 500 acre park with extensive gardens and a lake.

RAVENSHILL WOODLAND RESERVE
Hereford and Worcester
7 miles west of Worcester

An enchanting survival of the woodland that once stretched from Malvern Chase to the Wyre Forest, Ravenshill Woodland Reserve is managed by the Worcestershire Nature Conservation Trust. Some 30

kinds of native tree, including oak, ash, wild cherry, yew and spindle flourish there. Parts of the 50 acre reserve have been commercially planted with hardwoods, conifers and poplars, and hazel trees are being coppiced in places. Coppicing is an ancient system of woodland management, which involves lopping the main stem of a tree back to a stump. Fresh shoots spring from the stump and provide a crop of poles, which are cut every 7 to 20 years, depending on the species of tree.

More than 170 different plants have been recorded in the reserve, including the locally rare herb paris, the bird's-nest orchid, and the creamy-pink spikes of the broad-leaved helleborine. In spring there are bluebells

and wild daffodils, primroses and wild violets.

The paths in the reserve are clearly marked, and from the highest point there are fine views of the Malverns, Worcester Cathedral, and the Severn plain.

RIBBESFORD
Hereford and Worcester
1 mile south of Bewdley

Beside the road the Severn runs broad, deep and slow compared with its boisterous tributary the Teme. An avenue of horse chestnuts leads to the hamlet of Ribbesford, which consists of no more than a farm, a

LOFTY GRANDEUR *The flamboyant Great Hall at Ragley, built in 1750, rises to the full height of the house.*

cluster of dwellings, a big house aloof across the fields, and St Leonard's Church.

The church dates from about 1100, and over its Norman doorway is a carving of a hunter shooting with a bow and arrow at a strange creature.

Inside, the church is sombre from Victorian refurbishment. However, there is a fine stained-glass west window in delicate colours designed by Edward Burne-Jones, and medieval painted glass showing St George and the dragon survives in another window.

RICHARDS CASTLE

Shropshire/Hereford and Worcester

3 miles south of Ludlow

Richards Castle straddles the Shropshire/Hereford and Worcester border, and has two notable churches, one in each county. The late Victorian Church of All Saints was designed in 1891–2 by R. Norman Shaw, the architect who designed New Scotland Yard. It stands on a hill, and a notable feature is the massive tower at the southwest. Shaw drew inspiration from Gothic periods for the style of the windows and other features.

On the Hereford and Worcester side of the village is the Church of St Bartholomew, which has a Norman nave, but also much later work. The detached bell-tower was added about 1300. Some medieval stained glass remains, and there are 17th-century box pews.

RIPPLE

Hereford and Worcester

5 miles north of Tewkesbury

A local story tells how in 1437 a farmer's attempt to spite the rector ended in ignominious failure and exposure. Apparently, the rector or lord of the manor once had the right to take the best cow of a herd when the owner died. This farmer, however, was determined that the rector of Ripple – with whom he was on bad terms – should in no way benefit by his death. So, falling dangerously ill and sure that death was close, he sold his entire herd, rather than let the rector take even one of his cows.

But instead of dying, he recovered. The rector heard about his plan and dragged him before a court. There, the unfortunate farmer was sentenced to walk, carrying a candle, three times round the churchyard on a cold winter's night, dressed only in a nightshirt.

The largely 12th-century Church of St Mary has scarcely changed since it was built. Inside is a marvellous series of carvings on the backs of the choir seats (misericords) which have survived intact from the 14th and 15th centuries. Outside, the churchyard looks onto the handsome 18th-century red-brick Rectory. Nearby lies the tomb of Robert Reeve, known as the Ripple giant and said to have been 7ft 4in tall. He died aged 56, in 1626, from over-straining himself while mowing a meadow for a bet, according to a local story.

The centre of the village is the tiny green, with its ancient stone cross, overlooked by whitewashed cottages. Manor Cottage, built in the 18th century, was once an almshouse, and close by the former Nag's Head Inn, now Ripple Cottage, is a reminder of days when the road through Ripple was an important coaching route.

JANUARY – *collecting dead boughs.*

FEBRUARY – *hedging and ditching.*

MARCH – *ploughing.*

MAY – *crops blessed.*

JUNE – *hawking scene.*

JULY – *Lammas (Loaf-mass) Eve.*

RURAL ROUND *The 14th-century misericords – the carved undersides of tip-up choir seats – in St Mary's Church, Ripple, tell the month-by-month story of the rural year.*

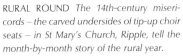

AUGUST – *reaping.*

SEPTEMBER – *malting corn for brewing.*

OCTOBER – *pigs foraging for acorns.*

NOVEMBER – *pig killing.*

DECEMBER – *spinning by the fire.*

APRIL – *bird scaring.*

THE ROACHES

Staffordshire
4 miles northeast of Leek

The Pennines have kept a special triumph to mark the very end of their long march down Britain – the fantastic, battlemented ridge called The Roaches. Like nearby Ramshaw Rocks and the oddly named Hen Cloud, The Roaches are on the millstone grit. Though they never rise to more than 1700ft, their weird, weathered shapes and their foreign appearance in the landscape make them enormously impressive.

The best side from which to attack The Roaches is the southwest. From Upper Hulme a minor road takes you up the first part of the climb, then just past Hen Cloud there is a path on the right that slopes northwards up the escarpment. Halfway up there is surprising wooded pasture and easier slopes. But the final 200ft or so to the top is something of a scramble.

The views, however, are well worth the breathlessness. Away to the northeast the land dips and rises to the heights of Axe Edge, and to the southwest, shimmering in the haze, is the eccentric shape of Tittesworth Reservoir. Almost due west is The Cloud, the hill that stands over Congleton, and beyond that the rolling Cheshire Plain.

DOUBLE IMAGE *The graceful spire of the parish church at Ross-on-Wye (right) is reflected in the river.*

CLOISTERED CALM *An air of peace reigns among the arches and pillars of the Market House in Ross-on-Wye. The ground floor of the red-sandstone building is open.*

ROSS-ON-WYE

Hereford and Worcester
11 miles northeast of Monmouth

The heart of Ross-on-Wye is the 17th-century Market House, built of red sandstone, which presides over the crowded Market Square. The ground floor of Market House is open; the upper floor, supported by weathered pillars and arches, is now the library. Here are displayed two mementoes of the town's allegiance to Charles II. A bust of the monarch is shown on a white stone medallion on the east wall, and the southeast corner of the building has the curious monogram 'FC', intertwined with a heart. The device is generally taken to mean 'Faithful to Charles in Heart', and was put there by the town's greatest benefactor, a wealthy barrister named John Kyrle (1637–1724).

He restored the tapering spire of the medieval Church of St Mary and gave it a magnificent tenor bell. He also sponsored the causeway to the nearby Wilton Bridge and donated the town's main public garden, The Prospect, with its unbroken views of the surrounding woods and mountains.

No one knows where John Kyrle is buried, but there is a tombstone to him inside the church. His former

home is opposite the Market House, but the half-timbered Elizabethan building is now divided into two shops. At the back of one of them, a chemist's, is an old garden laid out to Kyrle's original design, with a maze of box hedges about 12in high. Visitors are allowed to see the garden on request.

Flanking the other side of Market House is a splendid black-and-white building with heads carved on its beams. In coaching days this was the Saracen's Head inn, and today it is an estate agent's office.

ROYAL LEAMINGTON SPA
Warwickshire
8 miles south of Coventry

Leamington became 'Royal' in 1838, when Queen Victoria visited the spa, and during the 19th century the town reached the peak of its fame as invalids flocked to take advantage of the town's mineral springs. Many stayed at the Regent Hotel, the largest hotel in England when it was opened in 1819.

The saline spring waters were first recorded in 1586, but they owed their rise in popularity to a local doctor, Dr Jephson, who did much to publicise the waters. He

is commemorated by the Jephson Gardens on the banks of the Leam which runs through the town.

The gardens and river are overlooked by elegant Regency and Victorian terraces, and those leading off the main shopping street, The Parade, are fine examples of late Georgian architecture. Newbold Terrace has houses probably built by John Nash, who designed London's Regent's Park terraces. The Royal Pump Rooms were built in 1814 over one of Leamington's seven springs.

RUYTON-XI-TOWNS
Shropshire
9 miles northwest of Shrewsbury

Next to the black-and-white Smithy House at the west end of the strangely-named village of Ruyton-XI-Towns is a monument commemorating the time in 1308 when Ruyton joined with ten other communities to form a small, rural borough.

Ruyton straggles along a main street more than 1 mile long, which runs atop a steep sandstone bluff above the River Perry. It has the reputation of being one of the longest high streets in the country.

S

ST WEONARDS

Hereford and Worcester
7 miles north of Monmouth

The church tower of St Weonards is a landmark for many miles around, and about it church farm, village mound and mellow sandstone houses cluster tightly together. Largely of 14th-century origin, the church has fragments of 15th-century Flemish glass, possibly made by Flemish glassmakers who settled near the village at that time.

The village mound, or rump, is the reputed burial place – in a golden coffin – of St Weonard. It is in fact a prehistoric structure, emphasising the long history of settlement in the area.

MAGNOLIA AND JAPANESE MAPLE

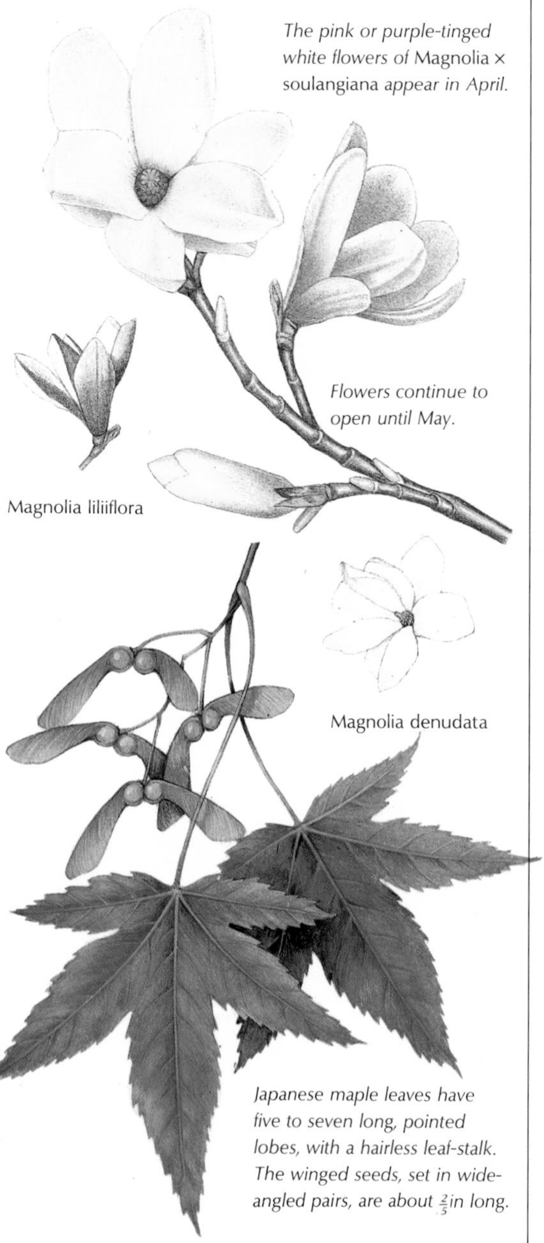

The pink or purple-tinged white flowers of Magnolia × soulangiana *appear in April.*

Flowers continue to open until May.

Magnolia liliiflora

Magnolia denudata

Japanese maple leaves have five to seven long, pointed lobes, with a hairless leaf-stalk. The winged seeds, set in wide-angled pairs, are about $\frac{2}{5}$ in long.

SEZINCOTE

Gloucestershire
1¼ miles west of Moreton-in-Marsh

Sezincote is a Mogul palace – complete with minarets, onion domes and peacock-tail arches – which rises like a mirage among the leafy oak woods of Gloucestershire. The house was completed in 1805 for Charles Cockerell, who had served in the East India Company. With growing British interest in the subcontinent, 'Indianesque' building styles became fashionable at home. But Sezincote survives as something unique in Europe: a complete building executed in the Mogul style of the 16th century.

The park and garden were landscaped with advice from Humphry Repton. Besides providing the parkland with landscaped woods and a sweeping lake (made to resemble a river), he also helped to select some of the Indianesque ornaments.

The ornaments are to be seen in the old garden, which lies to the north of the house. Known as the Thornery, this area consists of a luxuriously planted pool chain. At the head is a temple dedicated to the Hindu sun-god Surya; below, the stream passes under an Indian Bridge topped by Brahmin Bulls. Lower still is the Snake Pool, taking its name from a three-headed metal serpent which entwines the trunk of a dead yew. The snake is ingeniously devised to spout water.

Magnolias and flowering cherries contribute their spring colours to the Thornery. Irises and lilies enliven the summer scene, to be succeeded by massed blooms of hydrangeas. In autumn, fiery miscellanies of Japanese maples keep the colours alive in the garden.

Large-leaved aquatics, together with weeping beeches, pears and willows, all provide sculptural effects, and there are many aged specimens among the trees, including a grove of cedars.

SHALLOWFORD

Staffordshire
5 miles northwest of Stafford

The tiny village of Shallowford has an assured place in the annals of English literature, for it was here that Izaak Walton lived and wrote his famous book *The Compleat Angler, the Contemplative Man's Recreation.*

Walton was born in Stafford in 1593, and went to London as a draper's apprentice. There he became a friend of the poet John Donne, and later wrote his biography.

After the Civil War broke out, Walton spent much of his time in Staffordshire, and eventually bought

VALE OF FARMS *Rolling wooded slopes overlook the fertile meadows of the Teme valley east of Shelsley Walsh.*

Halfhead Farm at Shallowford. He was 60 when he wrote his great book, and was to live another 30 years. He did much of his fishing with a friend in the River Dove on the border of Derbyshire.

When Walton died he directed that the income from the farm should be used each year to apprentice two poor boys of Stafford to a trade, to provide a dowry so a servant girl could marry, and to provide coal 'for some poor people ... in the last week in January or in every first week in February ... the hardest and most pincing times'.

The farm cottage is now furnished as a typical late-17th-century house, such as Walton would have known, and is sometimes open to the public.

SHELSLEY WALSH

Hereford and Worcester
7 miles northeast of Bromyard

A jewel of a little church, plain on the outside but with a fine interior, snuggles at the foot of a steep wooded hill. Only a farm and handsome, 16th-century manor house keep it company to make up the hamlet of Shelsley Walsh.

The splendour of the Church of St Andrew's breathtaking interior lies in its woodwork. The 15th-century oak screen, intricately carved with vine motifs and fruit, doubles back into the nave of the church to form a little private chapel. Above the screen a huge beam spans the nave; this, too, is carved with vine leaves, and surmounted by a bold wooden cross. A century older than the screen are the timbers of the roof, with sturdy rough-hewn beams and planks simply painted with stars.

SHIFNAL

Shropshire
7 miles south of Newport

Shifnal, a market town which has fine half-timbered and Georgian houses, was described by Dickens in *The Old Curiosity Shop*. St Andrew's Church, originally Norman, was one of the few buildings to escape a great fire in 1591 which destroyed most of the town. The church, built of local sandstone, has 16th and 17th-century monuments, and two chancels, one original and the other built in the 14th century. The hammerbeam roof is handsome and there are several fine stained-glass windows of the mid-1800s.

SHOBDON

Hereford and Worcester
12 miles southwest of Ludlow

Once there was a 12th-century priory here, which was pulled down by Viscount Batement, Treasurer of the Household of George II and a friend of Horace Walpole – the author and antiquary whose own house, Strawberry Hill, did much to popularise the 18th-century Gothic style. In its place he erected a chancel arch, with three pointed arches, and two doorways, to act as a romantic 'eye-catcher' in the park of Shobdon Court. He then rebuilt the present Church of St John the Evangelist in fanciful Gothic style, with everything painted blue and white.

SHREWSBURY

Shropshire
12 miles west of Telford

Shropshire's county town is beautifully situated within a loop of the Severn. Everywhere are superb black-and-white buildings, including Abbot's House (1450); the tall gabled Ireland's Mansion (1575); and the early 16th-century Rowley's House, which has a museum of Roman remains.

Its narrow streets branch off from two main thoroughfares, as in Roman towns. Shrewsbury may have been founded by Britons who abandoned the Roman city of Viroconium, the remains of which can be seen at Wroxeter, 5 miles southeast.

A castle commanding the approach to Shrewsbury was built soon after the Norman Conquest, but the present structure dates chiefly from about 1300.

Parts of the old town walls, including a 13th-century tower, also survive. Nine bridges connect the town to the opposite bank of the Severn.

St Mary's Church dates back to the 12th century and has a lofty stone spire, fine medieval carving and stained-glass windows. The circular St Chad's designed in 1792 by George Steuart, stands in a prominent position overlooking the Severn. It is one of the country's few round churches and has a tower which looks like a minaret topped by a dome.

The town's library is now housed in the original early 17th-century buildings of Shrewsbury's public school. The naturalist Charles Darwin, was born in Shrewsbury in 1809, and attended the school. A statue of him stands in front of the library.

The Lion is an ancient coaching inn with a splendid ballroom. Among its famous 19th-century visitors were the singer Jenny Lind, the violinist Paganini, and Charles Dickens. Parts of the inn still reveal its 15th-century timber-framed origins. Joined on to one end of the building is the Henry Tudor House. Here Henry, Earl of Richmond, stayed after landing in South Wales on his way to the Battle of Bosworth Field and, eventually, to his coronation as Henry VII.

JESSE WINDOW *The great east window of St Mary's Church, Shrewsbury is filled with 14th-century stained glass. The three panels shown above trace the genealogy of Christ back to Jesse, father of David.*

Peaceful villages among the verdant Shropshire hills

Rolling hill country south of Shrewsbury is dominated by the windswept plateau of The Long Mynd and the stark crags of the Stiperstones. The River Clun flows past quiet villages and Cound Brook curves down from Condover and on to the three Strettons in their own valley.

GABLED GATE *The timbered lych gate at St George's Church in Clun was built in 1723.*

A MIDSUMMER LIFE *The common blue butterfly is found throughout much of Britain in midsummer.*

Male

Female

DEVIL'S CHAIR *The jagged outcrop called the Devil's Chair is one of the formations that give Stiperstones its sinister reputation.*

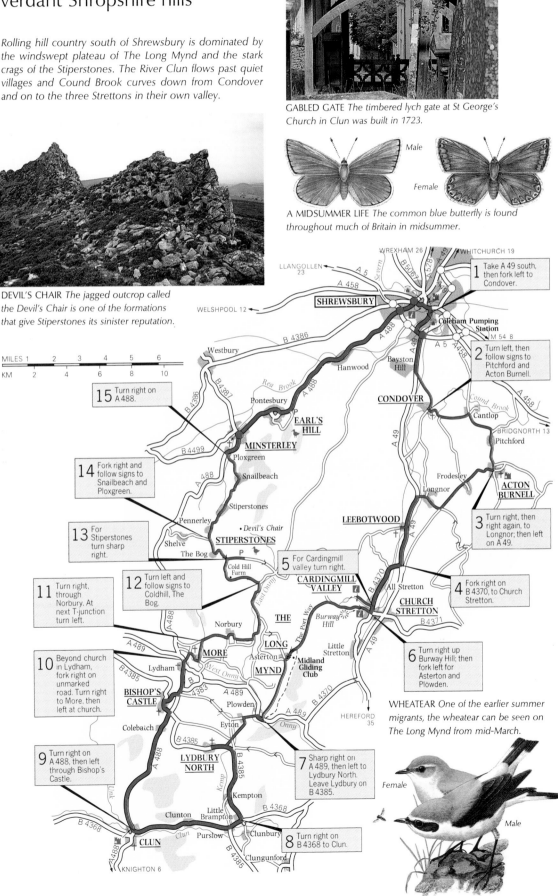

WHEATEAR *One of the earlier summer migrants, the wheatear can be seen on The Long Mynd from mid-March.*

Female

Male

MILES 1   2   3   4   5   6
KM   2   4   6   8   10

1 Take A 49 south, then fork left to Condover.

2 Turn left, then follow signs to Pitchford and Acton Burnell.

3 Turn right, then right again, to Longnor; then left on A 49.

4 Fork right on B 4370, to Church Stretton.

5 For Cardingmill valley turn right.

6 Turn right up Burway Hill; then fork left for Asterton and Plowden.

7 Sharp right on A 489, then left to Lydbury North. Leave Lydbury on B 4385.

8 Turn right on B 4368 to Clun.

9 Turn right on A 488, then left through Bishop's Castle.

10 Beyond church in Lydham, fork right on unmarked road. Turn right to More, then left at church.

11 Turn right, through Norbury. At next T-junction turn left.

12 Turn left and follow signs to Coldhill, The Bog.

13 For Stiperstones turn sharp right.

14 Fork right and follow signs to Snailbeach and Ploxgreen.

15 Turn right on A 488.

SHUGBOROUGH
Staffordshire
5 miles east of Stafford

An imposing Ionic portico dominates the east front of the mainly 18th-century mansion of Shugborough, set in a bend of the River Sow where it joins the Trent. The west front of the house is almost as impressive, with a three-storey bay window set between two cast-iron verandahs.

The interior of the mansion reflects the scholarly tastes of the Anson family, Earls of Lichfield, who have been at Shugborough since 1624. The Red Drawing Room, designed by Samuel Wyatt in 1794, has a coved ceiling decorated with magnificent plasterwork. Owned by the National Trust, Shugborough is open daily except Monday from mid-March to mid-October.

The park surrounding the house is open all year and contains an unusual collection of monuments. Some,

BOLD FRONT *Shugborough's colonnade dates from the 1760s, when the house was redesigned in Classical style.*

like the Tower of Winds, are copies of Classical Greek buildings. But there is also an elegant little Chinese House designed by an officer of a ship commanded by Admiral Anson, whose defeat of the French in 1747 is commemorated by a triumphal arch. Two marked tours of the monuments start from the car park.

The Staffordshire County Museum is housed in the domestic buildings of the house, and includes the restored brewhouse, coach-house and laundry, and a reconstructed tailor's shop and village general store. It is open from Tuesday to Sunday, but closes on Saturdays in winter.

Adjoining the estate is the Shugborough Park Farm, open at the same times as the museum. Its livestock are mainly Staffordshire breeds of cattle, sheep and pigs, and a small museum displays farm equipment.

SOLIHULL

West Midlands
7½ miles southeast of Birmingham

At the time of the Domesday survey, 900 years ago, the area which is now Solihull was one of the most sparsely populated parts of the country. The village began to take shape after the founding of St Alphege's Church in 1220, and by 1242 the village was granted a charter for a weekly market. Today Birmingham's sprawl has reached it, but Solihull is still a town in its own right.

The buildings are a pleasant mixture of old and new with many examples of timber-framed Tudor houses and shops. Particularly attractive are the George Inn, the 15th-century Old Berry Hall, which still has part of its moat, and Solihull Hall. Solihull School was founded in 1560.

SOUTHAM

Warwickshire
7 miles southeast of Royal Leamington Spa

Red-brick, bowfronted shops and the whitewashed Black Dog inn face Southam's Market Hill. The town grew up on the old cattle droving road from Wales to London; less peaceful visitors were the Royalist and Parliamentarian troops during the Civil War, and Charles I stayed there overnight on his way to the first major battle of the war at Edge Hill in 1642.

The main street, with a bridge over the River Itchen, makes a broad sweep past the parish church of St James with its handsome, 16th-century timber roof, 14th-century tower and 15th-century octagonal spire.

An inn, originally called The Horse and Jockey, has been renamed The Old Mint, a reminder that in medieval times Southam 'tokens' were minted in the district. These were a form of local currency in small denominations – used because local people found normal coins too high in value for everyday use. Some Southam farthings are collectors' pieces or are in museums.

SPETCHLEY PARK

Hereford and Worcester
3 miles east of Worcester

There is so much to discover at Spetchley Park, for the plantsman and landscape enthusiast alike. The Georgian mansion is flanked by wide lawns, reaching down to a lake. A succession of gardens lies to the east, each different in content and mood. Olive trees and pomegranates share the shelter of the former melon yard with tender flowering shrubs. The exterior walls of the large kitchen garden provide a framework for crowded borders, and the air vibrates with scent and colour. Roses, paeonies, camellias, viburnum and berberis jostle for space with numerous other species. Four yew-framed plots make up the unusual Fountain Garden – a wonderland of trees and shrubs within 36 beds, divided by paths. A deer park lies beyond the ha-ha to the south of the house where herds of red and fallow deer graze among fine old oaks.

In the little village of Warndon, 3 miles north, the Norman Church of St Nicholas has a timbered tower and a 15th-century font. The church has many fascinating features – in its vestry are some sculpted cherubs and a pelican, said to be from Worcester Cathedral.

SKENFRITH

Herefordshire/Gwent border
9 miles west of Ross-on-Wye

The distinctive sight and sound of a large water wheel emphasises the timelessness of this compact border village, just in Wales. The mill stream is fed from a weir on the River Monnow, and the mill still grinds corn in the time-honoured way. The Monnow also forms part of the moat of Skenfrith Castle, whose remains, owned by the National Trust, lie at the heart of the village. The filled-in, grassed-over moat which faces Skenfrith's single row of houses has now become the village green.

St Bridget's Church was built in the early 13th century. The dark, cool interior is a jumble of old graveslabs, medieval pews, a minstrels' box and the Morgan tomb, carved with effigies in Tudor costume. The Monnow washes the edge of the churchyard, entering and leaving the village in a steep, wooded valley.

STAFFORD

Staffordshire
14 miles south of Stoke-on-Trent

A charming county town on the River Sow, Stafford was listed as a borough in the Domesday Book in 1086, and has history dating back to before the Norman Conquest.

The town retains its medieval street pattern, built around the ancient market square. Many of the original half-timbered buildings have now disappeared, but some fine examples remain. The most outstanding is the 16th to 17th-century, many-gabled High House, which sheltered Charles I and Prince Rupert for three nights in 1642. In the same street, Greengate, is the Tudor Swan Hotel. George Borrow (1803–81) the travel writer, worked at the inn as an ostler and described it in *Romany Rye*.

The 12th to 15th-century parish church of St Mary lost much of its medieval stone and wood when it was restored in the 1840s. But it retains its 13th-century nave and tower, and a fine Norman font. Izaak Walton (1593–1683), author of *The Compleat Angler*, who was born in Eastgate Street, was baptised at this font. There is also a bust to him in the north aisle.

The Royal Brine Baths, opened in 1892, used brine extracted from salt deposits discovered in Stafford in the 19th century. The Baths have now been converted for freshwater swimming.

The William Salt Library, in Eastgate Street, is a fine 18th-century house containing a large collection of pictures, maps, manuscripts and other items illustrating the history of the borough and county.

Stafford Castle, 1½ miles southwest of the town, was rebuilt in the 19th century on the site of a 14th-century castle, but is now in ruins.

One mile to the east of Stafford is Baswich, whose little Church of the Holy Trinity was rebuilt during the 18th century, although the medieval tower was kept.

ARNOLD BENNETT

The novelist Arnold Bennett immortalised Stoke-on-Trent in his novels of the 'Five Towns'. He was born in Hope Street, Hanley in 1867, but left Stoke when he was 21 and never lived there again. Nevertheless he used the

'Five Towns' in his best-known novels, including Clayhanger, The Old Wives Tale and The Card, changing the names to Knype (Stoke), Bursley (Burslem), Hanbridge (Hanley), Longshaw (Longton) and Turnhill (Tunstall). Bennett spent most of his life in London, where he died in 1931. He was a prolific writer of newspaper articles and short stories as well as his novels.

AIRS AND GRACES *Arnold Bennett, as depicted by the cartoonist David Low.*

THE STIPERSTONES

Shropshire
11 miles southwest of Shrewsbury

When all around is sunshine, the chances are that there will be a dark cloud smudging the bleak and ragged ridge of the Stiperstones, at 1762ft the second highest hills in Shropshire. Even the most unimaginative feel a sense of desolation and unease when in the shadow of the Stiperstones, or on their grim, rock-strewn summit. One of the curious rock formations is called the Devil's Chair, and it is said that when cloud hides the Stiperstones, the Devil has taken his seat. According to legend, witches and demons have met here for centuries.

The Stiperstones lie 5 miles northwest of the great moorland back of The Long Mynd. The rocks were formed about 500 million years ago, when shales and sandstones were laid down under a shallow sea. Later folding of the rock brought the Stiperstones quartzite, hard white sandstone, to outcrop at a steep angle. During and after the Ice Age, frost shattered the quartzite into the jagged tors and tumbled screes that cover the summit today. Because of their geological interest and vegetation – a transition between the southern heaths and the northern moors – the Stiperstones were bought by the Nature Conservancy Council in 1981 to become a 1015 acre National Nature Reserve.

The Romans found lead on these hills and started a tradition of thriving independent mines which continued through medieval times until in 1835 at the height of the industry, 3500 tons a year were being produced. The centre of the area was the village of Shelve, west of the Stiperstones, the mines running eastwards to The Bog and north to Snailbeach. At Snailbeach, waste tips of white calcite, like some strange lunar landscape, still remain. The miners were part-time farmers and a tradition of smallholdings grew up in the area, the fields marked out by dry-stone walls. But by the beginning of this century the lead industry had collapsed.

There are several paths up to the Stiperstones, and the views, should the day be clear, are magnificent, looking west into Wales and southeast to The Long Mynd. The easiest path leads off the single track road that leads northwest from the village of Bridges, on the eastern side up to The Bog.

STOKE-ON-TRENT

Staffordshire
135 miles northwest of London

The names of Wedgwood, Minton, Copeland and Spode are known all over the world as incomparable examples of fine pottery and porcelain. All these wares are manufactured in this corner of north Staffordshire, and excavations prove that pottery has been made here since long before the Roman occupation.

The five towns of Tunstall, Burslem, Hanley, Longton and Stoke, made famous in Arnold Bennett's novels, amalgamated in 1910 with a sixth town, Fenton, to form the one town of Stoke-on-Trent, now a city of 36 square miles.

It was in 1759 that Josiah Wedgwood, born in Burslem in 1730, set up his own business. The beauty of his pottery, after the brilliant Classical sculptor and designer John Flaxman had stamped his own creative genius on it, established a fashion for Wedgwood all over the civilised world. The industry grew to an importance which has never diminished. The Regency church in Stoke-on-Trent has a memorial to Wedgwood, and the Wedgwood Memorial Institute in Burslem commemorates the site of his first factory.

Arnold Bennett's family lived from 1880 at 205 Waterloo Road, Cobridge, and Hanley was the home of Reginald Mitchell, designer of the Spitfire fighter plane, for most of his life.

At Smallthorne, about 4 miles north of Stoke, near Burslem, is Ford Green Hall, a fine Elizabethan timber-framed house and probably the oldest dwelling to survive in the Potteries.

A VICTORIAN POTTERY THAT STILL LIVES

The Gladstone Pottery at Longton was built in the 1850s and closed in the mid-1960s. It is now a working museum of the potter's craft, and is the only potbank in Britain where visitors can see demonstrations of various stages in pottery-making as it was in Victorian times. There are also galleries which illustrate how British and foreign pottery developed, tracing the progress of sanitation and the growing use of ceramics for decorating tiles, washbasins and chimney pots.

BOY POWER *The potter's wheel was turned by a boy, to revolve the turntable, while a woman handed clay to a man throwing pots.*

TOP POTS *Ornate chimney pots were a Victorian decoration.*

H AND C *A late 19th-century washstand with floral design.*

TILE STYLES *Birds, flowers and famous men were favourite subjects.*

STOKESAY

Shropshire

6½ miles northwest of Ludlow

The few houses and farm buildings that make up Stokesay lie in the shadow of a perfectly preserved piece of medieval England – Stokesay Castle, one of the oldest surviving fortified manor houses in the country, which has remained almost unchanged over seven centuries. The settlement, originally known as Stoke (meaning 'dairy farm'), became the property of the de Say family following the Norman Conquest, and Stokesay, as it eventually became known, was their home until about 1240.

Although the lower two storeys in the north tower survive from this early period, Stokesay as it now stands was largely the work of Lawrence of Ludlow, a wealthy wool merchant who probably bought the castle in 1281 and set about turning it into a grand country residence. He demolished much of the older building and put up a cavernous Great Hall, comfort-able living quarters, south tower and a protective wall. The manor house, one of the first of its kind, was built between 1285 and 1305 and was the home of Lawrence's descendants for the next 300 years. Its superb condition today is due largely to the care given it by successive owners, and to the fact that it has changed hands only five times in 700 years. During the Civil War, it escaped virtually undamaged after being surrendered to Cromwellian troops in 1645.

The result of Lawrence's handiwork is an extremely attractive building which, nevertheless, gives the impression that its creator was not sure what he wanted it to be. The south tower is fortress-like with its buttressed walls and battlements. The north tower, however, is domestic and has a timber-framed projecting upper storey and a steeply sloping roof. Between the two towers the great hall has tall Gothic windows and pointed gables, facing the courtyard on one side and open country on the other.

The Great Hall also has an attached solar, an addition which appeared in many 13th-century

houses, and was the place where the family withdrew after meals. Stokesay's solar measures 29ft by 19ft, and its fittings date from the 17th century. Presumably because the sun could not always be relied upon to provide warmth, the room has a stone medieval fireplace with an elaborately carved Flemish overmantel.

Also worth seeing are the massive roof of the Great Hall, with timbers made from whole trees, and a timber staircase set into the wall – the oldest of its kind in the country.

Stokesay's parish church, dedicated to St John the Baptist, was partially destroyed by Cromwell's men. It was rebuilt in the mid-17th century and is, therefore, that rarity, a Commonwealth church. Inside there are elegant canopied pews where the gentry sat and plain box pews for humbler folk.

HIGH LIFE *Stokesay Castle began as a Norman stronghold, and was later transformed into a manor house.*

STONE
Staffordshire
7 miles north of Stafford

A pleasant, mellow old town, Stone has ruins of an ancient priory and some solid 18th and 19th-century houses in its long High Street. Admiral Jervis, who became Earl St Vincent after his naval victory at Cape St Vincent in 1797, is buried in the parish churchyard. Peter de Wint, one of England's greatest watercolourists, was born at Stone in 1784.

STONELEIGH
Warwickshire
2½ miles east of Kenilworth

The tiny River Sow flows through Stoneleigh on its way to join the Avon, and the early-19th-century Sow Bridge forms an elegant approach from the east to this attractive village. There are many timber-framed houses and cruck-framed cottages with brick infilling, a black-and-white gabled farmhouse and a smithy.

Stoneleigh Abbey, the ancestral home of the Leigh family, is a magnificent blend of the remains of the old abbey, founded in 1154, and a Georgian mansion.

In the abbey grounds is the National Agriculture Centre, where research is carried out into farming techniques, and these techniques are demonstrated to the public on certain open days during the year. The abbey and grounds are open daily except Tuesdays and Saturdays. The Royal Show is held in the grounds in July.

STOURPORT-ON-SEVERN
Hereford and Worcester
3 miles south of Kidderminster

The town of Stourport is sometimes known as the Venice of the Midlands, because it stands at the junction of the rivers Severn and Stour and the Staffordshire and Worcestershire Canal. It owes its existence to the building of the canal in the 18th century. Before that it was a quiet village, but afterwards it became the busiest inland port in the Midlands after Birmingham.

STOW HILL
Shropshire
2 miles northeast of Knighton

The great curved upland of Stow Hill guards the valley of the Teme. It is 1391ft high and an ancient 'green lane', a track that may have been used as long ago as the Bronze Age, spans the length of it.

Along the track, the views grow broader at every step: south into Hereford and Worcester to the Welsh borders, west into Wales, east to the Clee Hills, north to The Long Mynd. A lane drops down northeastwards between stands of conifers on high grasslands. There are dew-ponds here, with buzzards and ravens circling in the sky above. Over the southern edge of the hill, steep rocky slopes fall away to the Teme winding below. At the end of the trackway is the River Redlake, meandering cheerfully over pebbles through a charming valley and under a small wooden bridge. A footpath leads to the imposing summit of Caer Caradoc.

STRATFORD-UPON-AVON

Warwickshire

20 miles northwest of Banbury

England's greatest dramatist and poet William Shakespeare dominates Stratford-upon-Avon, and has made it one of Britain's biggest tourist centres. Even so, the town has managed to retain its identity as a small, delightfully mellow, old market community in the rural heart of England. With its memorable buildings, broad streets, meadow-flanked river and canal bright with boats, it would be a rewarding place to visit even without its links with Shakespeare. Many package-tour pilgrims snatch only a fleeting impression of the town's character as they are hustled between Shakespeare's Birthplace, his grave, the riverside theatre and Anne Hathaway's Cottage. It is the visitor with time to linger and explore who sees Stratford at its best.

William Shakespeare was born in Henley Street on or about April 23, 1564. His father, John Shakespeare – or Shakspere, according to the parish records – was a glover and wool dealer who later became the town's bailiff, or mayor. His mother, Mary Arden, was the daughter of a yeoman farmer from the nearby village of Wilmcote. Her home, complete with cider-mill, dovecote and other outbuildings housing old farm implements, dates from the early 16th century and has been owned by the Shakespeare Birthplace Trust since 1930. Mary married John Shakespeare in 1557. Documents show that her husband had been living in Henley Street for at least five years before the wedding.

Their house in Henley Street was sold in 1847 to what later became the Shakespeare Birthplace Trust. The price was £3,000. Only 41 years earlier the building had changed hands for £210. Posters advertising the sale described the house as 'the most honoured monument of the greatest genius that ever lived'.

More than 500,000 people visit Shakespeare's Birthplace every year. Its rooms are furnished with items typical of middle-class homes in the time of Shakespeare. An unusual feature of the kitchen is a 17th-century 'baby-minder', fitted to keep small children away from the huge fireplace with its roasting spits and cast-iron pots. Upstairs, the room in which the playwright is believed to have been born has a window engraved with the signatures of notable visitors, including the novelist Sir Walter Scott and the Victorian actor Sir Henry Irving.

The part of the building which John Shakespeare used for his business, and which later became an inn, is now a museum containing documents, rare books, portraits, and the desk young William is said to have worked at as a schoolboy. The garden is planted with many of the trees, flowers and herbs mentioned in Shakespeare's works.

Shakespeare was almost certainly educated at Stratford Grammar School, which was at least 250 years old when it was re-founded by Edward VI in 1553. It still stands in Church Street and may be visited by organised parties during the Easter and summer holidays, after a written application has been granted. Beneath the school, under the room where Shakespeare would have attended lessons, is the old Guild-hall, used in those days by groups of travelling actors. Shakespeare may well have seen his first play there.

In 1582 Shakespeare married Anne Hathaway, a farmer's daughter. The cottage that was her home is in Shottery, 2 miles from the centre of Stratford. It is still linked to the town by footpaths that the young suitor may have walked when he walked out with Anne. In fact it is a thatched house of 12 rooms. The section of the house furthest from the road was badly damaged by fire in late 1969, but it has now been fully restored. In the parlour is the uncomfortable narrow bench, or settle, where Shakespeare is thought to have courted his future bride. The cottage remained in the Hathaway family until 1892. Much of the furniture belonged to them, and details of the cottage go back to the will of Anne's father, who died in 1581. In spring and summer the typically English cottage gardens are ablaze with flowers, including some fine roses.

Little is known about Shakespeare's early life, although he is said to have got into trouble for poaching deer from Charlecote Park, 4 miles east of the town. That may have been one reason for his leaving Stratford and becoming an actor at the Globe Theatre in London.

In 1597, at the height of his fame, the dramatist

COLLEGIATE CHURCH *The beautifully proportioned Holy Trinity Church is tucked away in a quiet corner of Stratford. Here William Shakespeare was baptised in 1564, and was buried in 1616. His wife, daughter and her husband, John Hall, lie beside his simple grave.*

IMMORTAL BARD *A bust of Shakespeare is above his grave.*

UPPER FORM *Shakespeare probably attended the Grammar School on the first floor of the old Guildhall.*

bought a house in his native town – New Place, on the corner of Chapel Street and Chapel Lane. It had been built by Hugh Clopton, a Stratford merchant who became Lord Mayor of London in 1492. Clopton's greatest gift to his home town was the many-arched stone bridge that still carries traffic over the Avon.

Shakespeare took up permanent residence at New Place in 1611 and died there five years later, on his 52nd birthday. He left the house to his elder daughter, Susanna, but it eventually passed back to the Clopton family, was completely rebuilt in 1702 and then demolished in 1759.

However, the foundations have been uncovered and now form part of the garden beside Nash's House,

another of Stratford's impressive timber-framed buildings. This takes its name from Thomas Nash, husband of Elizabeth Hall, Shakespeare's grand-daughter. The house is now a museum which tells Stratford's story since prehistoric times and paints a picture of the England that Shakespeare knew.

HOME AND GARDEN *Susanna Shakespeare lived with her husband Dr John Hall at Hall's Croft (overleaf).*

Behind Nash's House are the Knott Garden, with herbs and flowers laid out in intricate patterns, and the Great Garden, with lawns that are shaded by a mulberry tree said to have been grown from a cutting of one planted by Shakespeare.

The playwright was buried in the Collegiate Church of the Holy Trinity, an old riverside church dating in part from the 13th century and approached down an avenue of limes. The north door has a sanctuary knocker: any fugitive who reached it could claim sanctuary for 37 days. In the chancel, a bust of Shakespeare, quill in hand, is set in the wall above his gravestone. Above the bust is a carving of the Shakespeare coat of arms with its motto *Non Sanz Droict* (Not Without Right). The gravestone bears the words:

'Good frend for Jesus sake forbeare
To digg the dust encloased heare
Bleste be ye man yt spares thes stones
And curst be he yt moves my bones.'

The now-broken font in which Shakespeare was baptised can be seen, as can the parish register recording his baptism and burial. There are also monuments to Shakespeare's wife Anne and his elder daughter and her husband who are all buried in the church. Like Stratford in general, Holy Trinity has much to offer in addition to its memories of the dramatist.

There are fine examples of 15th-century woodcarving, superb stained-glass windows and several ornate tombs, the most outstanding of which is that of Joyce Clopton and her husband, the Earl of Totnes, who was James I's Master of Ordnance. Carved guns, cannon-balls and barrels of powder indicate his office.

Before Shakespeare died, his elder daughter Susanna and her husband, John Hall, lived in Hall's Croft, one of the town's most memorable medieval houses, owned by the Shakespeare Birthplace Trust. It is seen at its best from the spacious walled garden. John Hall was an eminent local doctor, and the house contains fascinating insights into 16th and early-17th-century medicine. The Halls' daughter Elizabeth, Lady Barnard, brought the playwright's direct line to an end when she died in 1670.

Although it had long been famous as Shakespeare's birthplace, Stratford did not stage a festival in honour of its famous son until 1769. It was organised by David Garrick, the actor-manager commemorated by the name of an old public house in High Street.

SON AND LOVER *In 1564 Shakespeare was born in this half-timbered house (above). Its garden has been set with plants and flowers mentioned in his works. As a young man he often walked 2 miles to Anne Hathaway's Cottage in Shottery, (right), and in 1582, at the tender age of 18, he married her.*

The first Shakespeare Memorial Theatre, opened in 1879, was destroyed by fire in 1926; its replacement was completed six years later. It is now known as the Royal Shakespeare Theatre, renowned for the quality of its productions. The adjoining Theatre Picture Gallery and Museum houses costumes worn by leading actors and actresses, relics of Henry Irving, David Garrick, Dame Ellen Terry, Sarah Siddons and other celebrated theatrical figures.

The lofty Gower Memorial near the theatre was unveiled in 1888. Beneath a seated figure of Shakespeare are life-size statues of Hamlet, Lady Macbeth, Falstaff and Henry V, symbolising, respectively, philosophy, tragedy, comedy and history.

The Guild of the Holy Cross, an influential religious brotherhood known to have existed before 1269, gave Stratford its grammar school, Guildhall and other buildings. The Guild Chapel, founded in the 13th century, stands beside the school. The nave tower and porch were rebuilt about 1496 by Hugh Clopton. Many leading citizens of the past are depicted in the chapel's stained-glass windows.

Inside, the wall at the western end of the nave bears the remains of a 'doom' – a mural depicting Judgment Day. Fortunate souls are shown ascending to Heaven, while sinners are being tormented by devils and cast into the flames of eternal damnation. The chapel, for which a £50,000 restoration appeal was launched in 1976, is used by the grammar school for daily services during term time. On the other side of the school is another legacy of the Guild of the Holy Cross – a row of almshouses built to house old or sick members of the guild.

Some of Stratford's architectural treasures, such as the Shrieve's House in Sheep Street and Mason's Court in Rother Street, are still used as private dwellings, and cannot be visited. Others are now used as shops, offices, hotels and inns. Judith Quiney's House, where Shakespeare's younger daughter lived after marrying Thomas Quiney, is the town's information centre. The Falcon Hotel, where the Shakespeare Club was formed in 1824, has panelling from New Place, its former neighbour across the road.

The Shakespeare Centre, flanking the garden of the dramatist's birthplace, was built as the headquarters of the Shakespeare Birthplace Trust and as a study centre. It was opened in 1964, to commemorate the 400th anniversary of Shakespeare's birth.

THE STRETTON HILLS

Shropshire
East of Church Stretton

Across the narrow Stretton Valley, to the east of The Long Mynd, is the miniature mountain range of the Stretton Hills. The valley itself follows an enormous fault, a break in the earth's crust, and separates the rounded whaleback of the pre-Cambrian Long Mynd from the even older and craggier summits of Caer Caradoc, The Lawley and Ragleth Hill.

The Stretton Hills are also among the most beautiful, and within about 10 miles encompass shady trackways, pebbled streams, bracken covered slopes and high, invigorating summits. Caer Caradoc is the highest peak at more than 1500ft. It can be reached either from the crossroads in the hamlet of Comley at its northern foot – a steep and breathless clamber up through bracken, past a blue dew-pond and over grassy turf and wiry bilberry – or by way of a lane and track that leads from the village of Cardington. These

THE SONG OF THE LARK

The skylark is usually found in the countryside, flying over open fields and downs and uttering its loud and persistent song. It often rises several hundred feet vertically, warbling for several minutes at a time.

The skylark has a sustained flight song, which it delivers while rising, hovering and descending.

Skylarks are a speckled brown with a crest.

ancient tracks and paths link Cardington with Church Stretton, winding through cushiony farmland and wild moorland under the crags of Caer Caradoc.

Harebells quiver in the grass on Caer Caradoc, and in early summer the bilberry – sometimes known as the whortleberry – flowers pink over the hills. In spring and autumn its tough, small leaves have a rose tint; the tasty blue-black berries can be picked in July and August. Heather and bracken grow on the hills, too, and larks abound, so that on the final scramble up the crags the thin turf seems alive with them.

STRETTON-ON-DUNSMORE

Warwickshire
6 miles west of Rugby

In the heart of the village – which stands on Dunsmore Heath and straddles the Roman Fosse Way – is a triangular green divided by a stream and crossed by low brick bridges. Around it are timber-framed and red-brick dwellings and farm buildings. A post office, some shops and two inns complete the rural scene, which is dominated by the lofty Victorian tower of All Saints' Church.

SUTTON COLDFIELD

West Midlands
7 miles northeast of Birmingham

A medieval market town, Sutton Coldfield is now a dormitory for Birmingham, 7 miles away. Its main attraction is the magnificent 2400 acre park to the west of the town, one of the best natural parks in Britain. Much of it is unchanged since it was given to the town in 1528. There are woods, valleys, open moors covered in gorse and heather, large lakes for boating, bathing and fishing, bird sanctuaries, and a championship golf course.

SWYNNERTON

Staffordshire
3 miles northwest of Stone

An attractive village on high ground, Swynnerton is surrounded by richly wooded country. There are a few well-thatched cottages, and the ancient blacksmith's forge, now a garage, looks out on to the main street, as does The Fitzherbert Arms, which dates from Jacobean times.

SYMONDS YAT

Hereford and Worcester
6 miles southwest of Ross-on-Wye

It takes a $4\frac{1}{2}$ mile car trip to get from one half of the resort to the other, although the two halves are only 100yds apart. This is because Symonds Yat is cut in two by the River Wye, with no bridge between. Spread out along the craggy slopes of a spectacular wooded limestone gorge, the village is a centre for walking and river cruising amid some of the best scenery of the Wye Valley.

Yat Rock, nearby, stands 473ft above sea level at the neck of a 4 mile loop in the river, giving panoramic views. The great loop of water circles Huntsham Hill and then curves back to within a quarter mile of its original course. To the north is the Queen Stone, strangely indented and probably a prehistoric ceremonial monument.

Regular boating trips are run up and down the river as they have been for centuries (Nelson was a visitor), and the Wye can be crossed in the village by small rope-guided ferries running between two pubs – one on each bank.

DOWN IN THE VALLEY *Symonds Yat Rock stands high above the Wye, overlooking a mosaic of wooded fields.*

T

TELFORD
Shropshire
14 miles east of Shrewsbury

Telford was named in honour of the Scottish-born civil engineer Thomas Telford (1757–1834), who was County Surveyor of Shropshire. He designed many of the county's bridges, tunnels and other buildings. He was also responsible for much of the work on the Holyhead Road (A5). This follows the line of the Roman Watling Street, through Oakengates and Wellington, both now part of Telford.

At the southwest corner of the town, the River Severn rushes through a limestone gorge. On its banks, in 1709, Abraham Darby the Elder (about 1677–1717) discovered how to smelt iron using coke instead of charcoal, a technical achievement which helped to launch the Industrial Revolution.

The role which the villages of Coalbrookdale and Ironbridge played in early industrial development is traced on sites in the gorge. One of these sites, at Blists Hill, has trams and steam engines, and preserves a section of the Coalport Canal.

The towns and villages which make up Telford still have many buildings which pre-date the Industrial Revolution, particularly in the Ironbridge Gorge. At Madeley, 16th-century Madeley Court was the home of Abraham Darby the Elder. The church was designed by Telford.

TENBURY WELLS
Hereford and Worcester
8½ miles northeast of Leominster

'The town in the orchard', announces a sign welcoming visitors to Tenbury Wells – an appropriate title, as the approach roads are lined with fruit farms, hop and nursery gardens. Henry III granted Tenbury a charter for a weekly market in 1249, and growers still flock in from outlying farms to sell their produce every Tuesday.

Some farmers arrive early to secure a good pitch at the market house in the centre of the town. This curious, oval-shaped brick building, with arched windows and an overhanging roof, was built in 1811 as a corn and butter market.

Several ancient inns testify to Tenbury's importance as a coaching town on the road between London and Wales. The Royal Oak, which probably dates from the 16th century, is a magnificent black-and-white building, its timbers forming an intricate web of squares, circles and diamond shapes. The Pembroke Inn is another timber-framed house with its first floor overhanging the pavement; its walls have settled over the centuries into delightfully crooked angles.

Oddest of all Tenbury's buildings – and the one that gave the town its title of 'Wells' – is the Spa building, a dilapidated folly at the rear of the Crow Hotel. Mineral waters were discovered there in 1839, and Tenbury enjoyed a short-lived boom as a health resort.

The baths were housed in a curiously decorated conservatory, with a metal-clad tower that looks like a space rocket with four nose cones, one above the other. Relics of the spa and other curiosities are housed in Tenbury Museum in Cross Street, which is open at weekends.

St Mary's Church has monuments to the Cornewall family, including a unique painted memorial in the

form of a triptych. Its doors open to reveal three life-size Elizabethan portraits. They are of Richard Cornewall, 9th Baron of Burford, his wife and eldest son, Edmund, who succeeded him. The 12th-century tower has Norman windows, though most of the rest of the church dates from the 18th century.

The River Teme skirts the north of the town and marks the Shropshire border. Across the medieval bridge and 1 mile west of the town is the hamlet of Burford, also flanked by the fast-flowing Teme.

FARM FARE *The oval-shaped market house in the middle of Tenbury Wells originally sold butter and corn.*

TOLL-KEEPER'S HOUSE

Thomas Telford built his Holyhead road in the late 1820s along the line of the Roman Watling Street. The toll-house, which collected a tariff from all traffic using the new road, has been reconstructed at the Blists Hill Museum of Buildings.

BY THE FIRESIDE *The wood-fired range in the kitchen (left) of the toll-house was used for cooking, boiling water and warming boots. The parlour (above) had its own kettle and supply of wood – tea was taken close to the cosy comfort of the fireplace by the toll-keeper on many a cold winter's night.*

MAN OF IRON *The Scottish-born engineer Thomas Telford (1757–1834) began his career as a mason and became a self-taught architect. He was made County Surveyor of Shropshire in 1787, and won fame for building the Ellesmere Canal. In 1828 he became president of the Institute of Civil Engineers.*

THREE SHIRE HEADS

Staffordshire/Derbyshire/Cheshire borders
4 miles southwest of Buxton

The triangle of high moorland between Leek and Macclesfield in the west and Buxton to the east is the birthplace of five rivers and the meeting place of three counties – Staffordshire, Derbyshire and Cheshire. The actual meeting place, called Three Shire Heads, is in the upper valley of the River Dane.

The wide rolling moorland is slashed across by tributaries of the Dane which have eroded through the sandstone and shales to produce attractively named edges such as Cut-thorn Hill and Turn Edge.

TITTERSTONE CLEE HILL

Shropshire
5 miles west of Cleobury Mortimer

This solitary escarpment dominates the landscape east of Ludlow. From its windswept, desolate upper slopes there are vast panoramas westwards towards the Welsh hills, and southwards across the rich farmlands of Herefordshire.

Titterstone Clee Hill was mined for coal during the Middle Ages, and the black basalt – 'dhustone', or black stone – which forms its upper part is still quarried today for road-building. On either side of the road to the summit is a moon landscape of worked-

A VIEW FROM THE HILL *Seen from the top of Titterstone Clee Hill, the fertile fields of Herefordshire are spread out like a brightly coloured patchwork counterpane.*

out pits and quarry workings. Beyond Clee Hill village a short detour down the Doddington road leads to a public viewpoint. Cars can be parked on the south of the road, from where there are wide-ranging views south towards the Malvern Hills.

LOFTY LANDMARK *Titterstone Clee Hill, seen from the south-west, towers over the landscape east of Ludlow.*

TONG

Shropshire
17 miles northeast of Much Wenlock

There can be few villages in England that have had their place of worship compared with Westminster Abbey. Perhaps the American consul to Birmingham in 1868, Elihu Burritt, was overstating it a bit when he called Tong church a 'little Westminster', but certainly it has a wealth of beautiful and impressive monuments to noble families.

Pride of place goes to the Vernons, whose tombs include that of Sir Richard, a 15th-century Speaker of the House of Commons, and his wife Benedicta. Close by lies Sir William, a Knight Constable of England, and his wife Margaret.

The Church of St Mary and St Bartholomew is a Collegiate church, though the college buildings for 'a warden and four priests, two clerks and thirteen poor people' have long since gone. Built of red sandstone, it has a central tower rising to a pinnacled spire.

Another link with the Vernons is the Great Bell of Tong, given to the church in 1518 by Henry Vernon. Recast twice in the centuries since, it now weighs 2 tons. A notice in the porch lists the special occasions on which it is rung – including royal births, royal visits to Tong, and visits by the head of the Vernon family.

LADY'S CHURCH *Lady Isabella de Pembrugge founded Tong's Church of St Mary and St Bartholomew, in 1410, so that Masses could be said for her three husbands.*

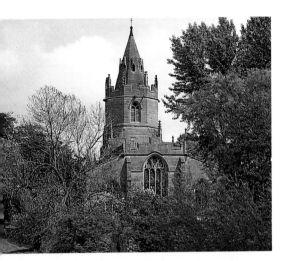

Set in undulating countryside, Tong village is small and attractive with three red-brick Georgian houses, a large Victorian one, only a couple of new houses and several black-and-white cottages tucked away in quiet corners. It was here that Charles Dickens (1812–70) set the closing chapters of *The Old Curiosity Shop*. Beyond the main road an ornamental lake is all that remains of the landscaped park of Tong Castle, re-modelled by Capability Brown in 1765. The castle was demolished in 1954 and the M54 motorway goes through the middle of the ruins.

Relics of two wars, some 300 years apart, can be found near Tong. At RAF Cosford, 2 miles south, are aircraft and other exhibits of the Second World War. Boscobel House, 3 miles east of Tong, is famous as the hiding place of Charles II after the Battle of Worcester in 1651. John Giffard, a staunch Catholic, built the house around 1600 as a hunting lodge, and a 'place for concealment' – conscious of the growing anti-Catholic feeling in the country.

But it was a huge oak tree in the grounds that was to provide a more significant refuge. Charles II – dressed as a peasant – hid in it after his defeat. For two days the Roundheads scoured the locality, before the search moved on and the king was able to make his escape to France.

The descendant of the original oak tree, grown from one of its acorns, still marks the spot – the inspiration for the 'Royal Oak' inn signs throughout the country.

NOT SO MERRY MONARCH

Charles II hiding in an oak tree is depicted in a contemporary woodcut.

RESTING PLACE *The tombs and effigies in Tong's church have been compared to those in Westminster Abbey.*

TRENTHAM GARDENS
Staffordshire
3 miles south of Stoke-on-Trent

Trentham Gardens and Park are Staffordshire's largest pleasure grounds. There are 500 acres of gardens and parklands with boating, fishing and swimming facilities. The gardens were mostly laid out by the architect Sir Joseph Paxton.

TUTBURY GLASS

Glass-making is centuries old in Tutbury, where glass-blowers can be seen at work.

Engraving the base of a wine goblet.

Checking an engraved wineglass for flaws.

Putting a handle on a tankard.

TUTBURY
Staffordshire
5 miles northwest of Burton upon Trent

Georgian and Regency houses rub shoulders in Tutbury's broad and spacious High Street. The odd building out is the black-and-white, half-timbered Ye Olde Dog and Partridge Hotel. Built in the 15th century, it has served as the town house of the Curzon family and as a coaching inn. The Red Rover, a fast night coach between London and Liverpool, used to call here in the 18th century.

The centre of Tutbury is a conservation area, creating an 'old' town at its heart and a 'new' town on its outskirts. From the old quarter, Castle Street leads up to the ruins of Tutbury Castle, set on an isolated, outlying rock. The castle dates from the 11th century, when it belonged to Henry de Ferrers, one of William the Conquerer's barons who fought at the Battle of Hastings. The present castle dates from various periods in the Middle Ages. The red-sandstone gatehouse was built in 1362 by John of Gaunt, Duke of Lancaster. The south tower, with its winding staircase leading to an ante-chamber and presence chamber, dates from 1442 to 1450. The 15th-century north tower has 67 steps leading to the top, from which there are panoramic views stretching from Needwood Forest – in which guests at the castle went hawking and hunting – to the Low Peak of Derbyshire.

Mary, Queen of Scots was twice imprisoned in the castle during 1568 and 1569, and the remains of her state apartments are in the courtyard. The high north tower contains fragments of rooms used by her secretary, personal physician and chief cook. The dungeons were used as storehouses and later as a prison for those who broke the game laws in Needwood Forest.

Near the castle is the Priory Church of St Mary, one

CASTLE RUINS *The north tower and gatehouse are all that remain of Tutbury Castle.*

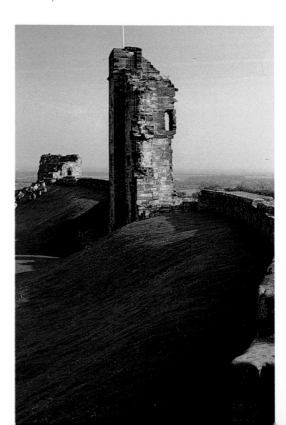

ARTISTRY IN STONE *Lavish doorway decorations and a finely carved head of Christ display the art of Norman stonemasons, who built the Priory Church of St Mary, in Tutbury.*

of the finest Norman churches in the Midlands. Built in the 11th to 12th centuries, the church is under the patronage of the Queen, as Duke of Lancaster. Its chief glory is the magnificent west front, which has a Norman door 14ft high and 9½ft wide with seven receding arches. The lectern was carved from a log of black bog oak believed to be some 6000 years old.

UPPER ARLEY

Hereford and Worcester
3 miles north of Bewdley

The village of Arley clings to the steep eastern bank of the River Severn. It is sometimes known as Upper Arley, to distinguish it from the village of the same name in Warwickshire. Arley is right off the beaten track and its hilly main street, which dips down to the very edge of the river, is a cul-de-sac.

At one end of the village is the parish church of St Peter, a fine 14th-century building with fragments of Norman ornament in the south wall of the nave, which indicate the existence of an earlier church. Its buttressed tower commands a fine view overlooking the river.

Bordering the village street as it climbs away from the river is an attractive mixture of buildings: old red-brick and white-rendered cottages, a few modern bungalows, a large vicarage and the Georgian splendour of The Grange. The whole appearance is reminiscent of a small seaside fishing village, and attracts anglers from a wide area.

Arley's ferry boat has been replaced by a single-span pedestrian bridge. This leads to the old Harbour Inn and the impeccably restored railway station, now part of the privately run steam-operated Severn Valley Railway.

COARSE FISHERMAN'S DELIGHT

Perch are fished for in many rivers, such as the Severn, and are recognisable by their dark, vertical stripes and arched, spiny dorsal fin. They are carnivorous, living on small fish including smaller perch. Perch may grow to 20in long, and large specimens of 3–5lb are occasionally caught by anglers.

SENTIMENTAL JOURNEY *Across the River Severn from Upper Arley a steam-hauled train of the Severn Valley Railway evokes the nostalgia of bygone days.*

UPTON HOUSE

Warwickshire
6 miles northwest of Banbury

A William-and-Mary mansion, Upton House is owned by the National Trust. The terraced gardens surrounding the house are laid out on gentle slopes against a background of woods. There is a large collection of paintings, which includes works by the English artist George Stubbs and the Flemish master Peter Breughel, as well as Brussels tapestries, Sèvres porcelain and 18th-century furniture.

UPTON UPON SEVERN
Hereford and Worcester
6 miles northwest of Tewkesbury

A modern bridge arches gracefully across the Severn at Upton, but the town's chief landmark is the massive Bell Tower which stands close by. The tower dates from the 14th century and is Upton's oldest building.

The tower was once part of the Church of St Peter and St Paul, which was badly damaged during the Battle of Upton Bridge in 1651. It was rebuilt in 1754, and in 1770 the church spire was replaced by the lantern and cupola which are distinctive features of the tower and have given it the local nickname The Pepperpot. It now houses the Pepperpot Heritage Centre which has displays showing the development of the town and the Battle of Upton Bridge.

UTTOXETER
Staffordshire
15 miles southeast of Stoke-on-Trent

The handsome half-timbered buildings that overlook Uttoxeter market belong to the 19th century. But a market has been held there since 1251. Bright awnings of stalls that crowd the narrow streets still enliven the town centre on Wednesdays and Saturdays.

A regular stallholder in Uttoxeter market 250 years ago was a Lichfield bookseller named Michael Johnson. When Johnson lay on his deathbed his son, Samuel, refused to go to the market in his father's place. The memory of this ignoble act so haunted Dr Samuel Johnson that as an elderly man he stood bareheaded in the rain in the market place for a day. Today a plaque commemorates this act of penitence.

VOWCHURCH
Hereford and Worcester
6 miles northwest of Pontrilas

The village of Vowchurch with its stone bridge across the River Dore lies in the centre of the Golden Valley. The 14th-century parish church has a fine Jacobean screen and an unusual roof, supported by oak posts within the building instead of by the walls. There is also a curious wooden bell-turret, built in the 1520s. Just across the river at Turnastone is another attractive church with a Norman doorway.

A narrow road leads westwards from Turnastone, past half-timbered farmhouses, into the hills with their marvellous views of the Golden Valley.

WARMINGTON
Warwickshire
5 miles northwest of Banbury

Buildings of rich, honey-coloured Hornton stone distinguish this enchanting village. It nestles beneath the steep, northern slopes of Edge Hill and looks out over an undulating patchwork of fields towards the valley of the River Cherwell. It was along this valley that Charles I's army marched in October 1642 to Edge Hill and the first major battle of the Civil War.

The army advanced westwards through Cropredy and Mollington before reaching Warmington and climbing the hill beyond St Michael's Church. People in the Manor House, and many other buildings still surviving, watched the Royalist troops pass by on their way to the bloody, but indecisive, fray.

Much earlier, during the reign of Henry I, Benedictines from Preaux in Normandy were granted the manor of Warmington by the Earl of Warwick, and established a priory there. Like its counterparts in the neighbouring Cotswolds, the village thrived when the wool trade was at its peak during the Middle Ages. The oldest houses and cottages date from that period.

The village's centre is a spacious green surrounded by some of Warmington's most memorable buildings. It rises gently toward tree-clad slopes on which stands the ancient Church of St Michael. The foot of the green is dominated by the 18th-century rectory.

At the top of the green, behind a pond attractive with ducks and water lilies, is the Manor House, built about 1600. Grove Farm House, in the southeast corner of the green, dates from the late 17th century.

The centuries-old houses of Court Close, below the church, at the opposite end of the village stand a short distance above the Plough, a cosy, early-17th-century inn. Nearby, a short lane climbs steeply to the main road and is overlooked by the mullioned façade of Ivy Dene, an attractive old house flanked by a curved archway.

Steps lead from Church Hill to the churchyard. A stone marks the last resting place of Alexander Gourden, a Scots 'captaine' who was buried two days after the Battle of Edge Hill together with Richard Sauner, one of Charles's officers, and seven other soldiers.

WARWICK
Warwickshire
20 miles northwest of Banbury

Above the tree-fringed River Avon rise the majestic walls and turrets of Warwick Castle. Seen from across the river the castle forms a bluff sentinel guarding the town beyond, where narrow streets cluster together behind a wooded ridge. It is a view thought by the novelist Sir Walter Scott to be unsurpassed in England. Warwick is a medieval walled town which barely survived a disastrous fire in 1694. But out of the ashes arose fine Queen Anne houses and a church tower, to blend with the gabled and timber-framed buildings that escaped the flames. Outside the walls, modern Warwick has spread with dignity, combining town and country in the heart of England's shires.

Warwick Castle was built in the 14th century on the site of a Norman castle which William the Conqueror gave to Henry de Newburgh, and with it the title of Earl of Warwick. For nearly 600 years the castle remained the seat of the Earls of Warwick.

Warwick Castle has two faces – the grim forbidding walls and towers with their dungeons and trappings of war, and the grandeur of its state apartments. The dungeon below Caesar's Tower has a grisly display of torture instruments, and inscriptions carved on the wall show that Royalist soldiers were held there during the Civil War. A collection of arms and armour in the Armoury includes a helmet said to have belonged to Oliver Cromwell, and the sword of Guy of Warwick. Sir Guy was a Saxon knight who, according to legend, vanquished attacking Danes by slaying their giant, Colbrand.

The state apartments, all overlooking the river, are dominated by the Great Hall – a room of baronial splendour. It is 62ft long, 45ft wide and 40ft high. The floor, of red and white Venetian marble, was laid in 1830. The room is notable for its furnishings, paintings and suits of armour.

The focal point of the state dining room is Van Dyck's portrait of Charles I, clad in armour and mounted on a white horse. Above a white-marble fireplace is a Rubens picture of two lions, which are said to have killed their keeper while the artist was at work.

The smallest room is the Blue Boudoir, with wall coverings of blue damask. A silver and enamel clock opposite the fireplace belonged to France's Queen Marie Antoinette, who was guillotined in 1793 during the French Revolution.

Outside the castle walls, the most interesting building to survive the fire of 1694 is the Lord Leycester Hospital. The group of buildings date from the 12th to 16th centuries and have been used as a guildhall, council chamber and grammar school. In 1571 Robert Dudley, Earl of Leicester, founded the hospital, or almshouses, for those wounded in the service of the queen and her successors.

St Mary's Church is believed to date back to pre-Norman times. It was made a collegiate church by Roger, Earl of Warwick, in 1123, which gave it similar

ARTISTIC LICENCE *This equestrian portrait of King Charles I, which hangs in Warwick Castle, is one of seven attributed to Sir Anthony Van Dyck – who probably painted only the face and hands.*

status to a cathedral. The fire of 1694 destroyed the nave and tower, but much of the medieval building survived, including Earl Roger's crypt.

The Beauchamp Chapel was built to house the tomb of Richard Beauchamp, who died in 1439.

The tomb is one of the finest of the medieval period in Britain. Purbeck marble was used for the base, and Beauchamp's effigy lies with hands raised towards the figure of Our Lady in the vaulted roof. A cage of hoops and bars around the effigy was designed to support a velvet pall. Close by is the tomb of Ambrose Dudley, who was made Earl of Warwick by Elizabeth I when the Beauchamp line died out.

Warwickshire's County Museum is housed in the Market Hall built in 1670. It was built in arches to provide under-cover space for stalls, but in the 19th century the archways were railed off and the area was used for the stocks. These were on wheels, and the culprit was made to pull them into the railed space before being locked in them. The stocks were used as a punishment for drunkenness as late as 1872.

A branch of the County Museum, displaying folk life and costume, is in the 17th-century St John's House. On the first floor is the museum of the Royal Warwickshire Regiment.

Some of the best examples of Warwick's rebirth in the 18th century can be seen in Northgate Street. Buildings in the Classical style line one side, including the Shire Hall.

The hall contains two octagonal courtrooms, a shape continued in the grim building next door – the County Gaol. The dungeon, dating from 1680, is 21ft in diameter with a stone-vaulted roof through which a single grating allowed light and air to enter.

On the south side of the town the 18th-century Castle Bridge spanning the Avon provides one of the best viewpoints of the castle.

WELFORD-ON-AVON
Warwickshire
4 miles southwest of Stratford-upon-Avon

A loop in the meandering River Avon embraces Welford on all sides save the south. From the north a narrow stone bridge crosses the river to meet the long main street, off which lies the village green with its chestnut tree and tall red, white and blue maypole. A footpath follows the Avon through the willow-hung water meadows southwest of the village.

Thatched, timber-framed houses and cottages abound in Welford. They stand in colourful gardens on both sides of the main street, down the lane leading to the church. The entrance to the churchyard is through a lych gate, a replica of one that had stood there since the late 14th century until time and weather made it unsafe.

VILLAGE IDEAL *Timber framing and thatch give Welford-on-Avon a picture-postcard charm.*

WEM

Shropshire
11 miles north of Shrewsbury

Wem was largely destroyed by fire in 1677, and the oldest surviving building, other than the parish church, is Dial Cottage in the High Street. Another survivor is the delightful black-and-white Old Hall.

Set among the shops in the High Street are some half-timbered houses which give the street a somewhat medieval look. This is also true of the parish church of St Peter and St Paul, which has a 14th-century doorway and lofty tower with battlements, buttresses and pinnacles.

In Noble Street is Hazlitt House, the boyhood home of the essayist and critic William Hazlitt (1778–1830).

WEM'S BLOODY CLAIM TO FAME

In 1684 Judge Jeffreys bought Wem for £9000. The next year he entered history when he presided at the 'Bloody Assize', sentencing thousands to death, transportation and flogging after the Monmouth Rebellion.

WENLOCK EDGE

Shropshire
From Craven Arms in the southwest to Much Wenlock in the northeast

Wenlock Edge runs ruler-straight for 16 miles across Shropshire from northeast to southwest: its steep limestone edge faces west; the eastern side has a gentler slope. It is hard to believe that some 420 million years ago it was a coral reef in a tropical sea.

Although distinct from a distance, Wenlock Edge is strangely elusive when approached. The only main road to cross it is the A458 at the northeast end, but a good secondary road runs along the northern half. From remote black-and-white half-timbered villages along its eastern slope, many tracks and paths across open farmland and through deep woods climb up to its unexpectedly level plateau. At Rushbury the Romans had an outpost, commemorated in the hill lane called Roman Bank.

In the northern half of the Edge lie many quarries, for the limestone was once used for building. Ippikin's Rock is opposite Lilleshall Quarry, now disused, beside the B4371 northeast of Easthope.

Major's Leap on the precipitous Edge near Stretton Westwood, on the B4371, owes its name to a Royalist officer called Major Thomas Smallman, who rode his horse over the cliff to evade Parliamentarian pursuers. His horse was killed, but his fall was broken by a tree and he escaped safely to Shrewsbury. His family

home, the 16th-century Wilderhope Manor, now belonging to the National Trust, is further south.

Wolverton Wood, west of the point where the minor road from Harton crosses the Edge, contains a secluded nature reserve with a shadowy entrance in the woods that lie in folds down the escarpment. Edge Wood Nature Reserve, managed by the owner in conjunction with the Shropshire Trust for Nature Conservation, is a deep, enchanting, rustling wood, with a mile-long nature trail where visitors can see ancient oaks, great holly trees, hazel coppices, a marshland area, and a wood consisting almost entirely of birches.

At another point on the trail, there is an old quarry and lime-kiln. This is one of the places where farmers dug limestone and burned it to produce lime, which they used as a dressing for their fields around the Edge. Near the kilns there are lime-loving plants such as common spotted orchids and spindle trees – bright with rose-red seed pods in autumn.

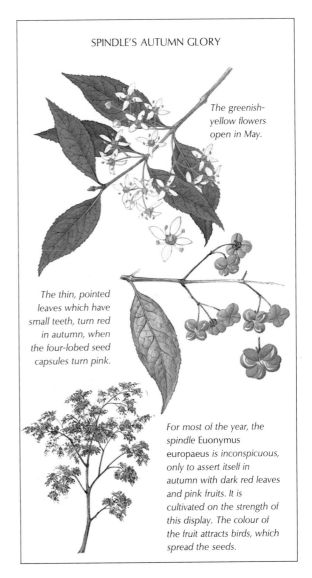

SPINDLE'S AUTUMN GLORY

The greenish-yellow flowers open in May.

The thin, pointed leaves which have small teeth, turn red in autumn, when the four-lobed seed capsules turn pink.

For most of the year, the spindle Euonymus europaeus is inconspicuous, only to assert itself in autumn with dark red leaves and pink fruits. It is cultivated on the strength of this display. The colour of the fruit attracts birds, which spread the seeds.

OLD ENGLAND *Over the rolling Shropshire countryside the traditional English landscape of field, wood and hedgerow spreads out below Wenlock Edge in a pattern which has become rare in many parts of the country (overleaf).*

WEOBLEY
Hereford and Worcester
10 miles northwest of Hereford

Timber-framed cottages and inns fan out from Weobley's wide central street. The island in the middle of the street, now a rose garden, was the site of a market in the heyday of this village, which until 1832 was a 'rotten' borough returning two members to Parliament. Weobley's name – pronounced 'Webley' – is derived from Wibba's ley, or meadow, and appears in the Domesday Book as Wibelai. The village is best seen from the remains of a massive motte and bailey on the south side, from which an avenue of oaks leads to the grassed-over site of several old houses burned down in the 1960s.

The road north from the 14th-century Red Lion loops around the fine Church of St Peter and St Paul. Its commanding spire and traceried eight-sided font date from the 14th century, but other features remain from the Norman era. Among many interesting ornaments and monuments is a marble statue of Colonel John Birch, an officer in Cromwell's army who quarrelled with his leader and claimed after the Restoration that he had been imprisoned no fewer than 21 times. He was later MP for Weobley.

BRED FOR BEEF

Hereford cattle, which are now reared throughout the world, were developed in the 18th century by a Weobley man, Benjamin Tomkins. He took a local all-purpose breed, and turned it into the prime beef breed we know today.

The cow, like the bull, is usually docile. It is kept for bearing and suckling beef calves, not for its milk yield, which is low.

Hereford bulls are distinguished by their white faces and red bodies.

Friesian cows are often mated with Hereford bulls to produce early maturing beef animals.

ROMANTIC RUIN *Its crumbling stonework gives an air of romantic desolation to Chartley Castle, near Weston Park.*

WESTON PARK
Staffordshire
6 miles east of Telford

The industrious Capability Brown laid out the gardens and parkland surrounding this 17th-century mansion, built by Lady Wilbraham and the home of the Earls of Bradford for almost 300 years. The house is one of the best examples of Restoration period architecture and contains a collection of pictures by English, Flemish and Italian painters.

In the spacious grounds are three lakes and there are walks through woodland. There is also a butterfly farm, a miniature railway, an aquarium and a museum of country bygones. The house and park are open from Wednesday to Saturday or by appointment.

About 3 miles northeast from Weston Park, and a short climb uphill from the road, are the ruins of Chartley Castle. In contrast to castles that are fenced off and carefully tended, Chartley still wears an air of romantic neglect.

WESTON UNDER PENYARD

Hereford and Worcester
2 miles east of Ross-on-Wye

Houses of old red sandstone blend harmoniously with
more recent buildings among a fine display of pretty
gardens in the hillside village of Weston under
Penyard. Men have lived on the site at least since
Roman times. The Romans called it Ariconium. They
founded it as a garrison town and later used it as a
smelting centre for iron ore from the Forest of Dean.

Only a few fragments remain of the medieval
Penyard Castle, 1 mile southwest of the village. But
some of its original stone is thought to be incorpor-
ated in the Rectory and in Bollitree Castle, a 17th-
century house just north of the village. Behind the
house is a startling range of outbuildings with high
walls, battlements and turrets – said to have been
added by an 18th-century owner to please his bride,
who wanted to live in a castle.

The Church of St Lawrence looks down from its
position above the main village. It has a fine arcade of
four Norman arches and a 14th-century bell tower
which gives superb views across the countryside. In
medieval times it was used as a watch tower.

WHITCHURCH

Shropshire
18 miles north of Shrewsbury

The town of Whitchurch is just inside Shropshire's
border with Wales, and its Highgate pub claims to be
the last in England. The Roman town of Mediolanum
once stood on the site.

St Alkmund's Church, with its distinctive, airy
Queen Anne style of architecture, dominates the
town. The original church collapsed one night in 1711,
and the new one was paid for partly from taxes levied
on visitors to the town's inns. St Alkmund's is large,
with an impressive west tower, pinnacled and balustraded. The interior has tall columns and a gallery;
there is a 17th-century font decorated with a Tudor
rose and the Prince of Wales's feathers, and monuments from the earlier church, including one to John
Talbot, 1st Earl of Shrewsbury (*d.* 1453).

Downhill from the church, the High Street is lined
with a remarkable variety of buildings. They include an
unusual structure clad in cast iron – once the Alex-
andra Temperance Hotel and later the works of J. B.
Joyce, clockmaker. Many of the town streets have old
names: Bargates, Bluegates, Watergate, Highgate,

Newtown (built on the site of the old castle), Pepper Alley and Bull Ring – the town centre where the last bull was baited in 1802. Whitchurch is the birthplace of Sir Edward German (1862–1936), composer of *Tom Jones* and *Merrie England*.

WHITTINGTON

Shropshire
16½ miles northwest of Shrewsbury

Swans, ducks and gulls patrol the moat of the ruined castle, rebuilt by the warlike Fulke Fitzwarine, that guarded Whittington for more than 400 years. It was built in 1221 to control a route across what was then a wilderness of bogs and sluggish streams. A well-preserved gatehouse is flanked by two towers.

Opposite the castle stands a church of mellow brick built between 1747 and 1805. Its 19th-century rectors included William Walsham How, composer of *For All the Saints* and other popular hymns.

Dick Whittington is said to have left the village to seek his fortune in London in 1371.

WILMCOTE

Warwickshire
3 miles northwest of Stratford-upon-Avon

Shakespeare's mother, Mary Arden, was brought up on a farm in the little village of Wilmcote. The farmhouse is there still, its venerable timber-framed walls bent with age and seeming to follow the rolling contours of the ground on which they stand. Inside, the stone and polished oak floors undulate too, and there is a delightful irregularity in the beams and rafters overhead.

The house is furnished in 17th-century style, with polished oak furniture, including a linen cupboard, a dough chest and even a wooden rat trap. The farm buildings contain a fine collection of country bygones, among them a huge cider press and a gypsy wagon.

A marked contrast to Mary Arden's house is the Victorian gothic church of St Andrew, which was built in 1841. It was an important place of worship for the Oxford Movement, whose members sought closer links between the Church of England and the Roman Catholic Church.

WOOLHOPE

Hereford and Worcester
10 miles west of Ledbury

A dome of limestone rising to 500ft above the face of green borderland country has literally put Woolhope on the map. Woolhope Dome, laid down more than 400 million years ago, has a complex geology of alternate shale and limestone outcrops which create an unusual mixture of ridge and vale scenery. All main roads go around rather than over the dome, but a minor road from Hereford follows a steep and narrow route through woodland and across an open common to reach the village perched on a southeastern slope. Here, in 1851, was founded the Woolhope Naturalists' Field Club, devoted to studying the natural history and archaeology of this fascinating area. Today the club is a national body and is known to naturalists all round the world.

Woolhope is sometimes called 'the walled village', because of its preference for stone walls rather than garden hedges. It has two attractive pubs: the black-and-white Butcher's Arms and the Crown Inn, its whitewashed walls and grey roof standing out among handsome red-brick houses. On the outskirts of the village is Wessington Court, a 19th-century Gothic mansion set high on a hill overlooking green fields and pastures. Its brick-and-stone lodge-gatehouse stands beside the road behind tall spiked railings and massive stone gateposts.

A fine timber-framed black-and-white house called Terrace Hall stands in Wessington, a mile down the road. It is the home of the Polish sculptor Walenty Pytel, and one of his creations, a 6ft tall metal flamingo, stands in the forecourt. Near it stands a Victorian lamp post, a piece of metalwork by an earlier, unknown artist.

Woolhope's Church of St George is a red-sandstone building with some 13th-century work, but with a modern stained-glass window which reveals the origin of the village's name. It depicts Lady Godiva and her sister Wulviva who gave the manor of Wulviva's Hope (hope meaning 'valley') to Hereford Cathedral in the 11th century. By 1234 the village had become known as Wulvivehope, which later became abbreviated to Woolhope.

The churchyard has a lych gate, a rickety but noble timber structure erected in Tudor times and known by its Herefordshire name, The Skallenge. From the steps just below it there are views across farmlands and fields to Holling Hill.

Woolhope exists mainly as a farming community, and at Lower Buckenhill, a mile south, a working farm with a farmhouse pure Tudor in style proudly displays its date, 1592, on the black-and-white front wall. Ancient grazing rights still exist on the common, Broadmore, which is clothed on its northern slopes by Haugh Wood, a mixed forest of broadleaf and conifer trees. It is part Forestry Commission and part National Trust property, and has a small herd of fallow deer.

At Brockhampton-by-Ross, 3 miles southwest of Woolhope, the stone and concrete Church of All Saints, built by W. R. Lethaby in 1901–2, has a central tower. The extremely steep arches of the nave spring low from the walls, without brackets. The tapestry was designed by Sir Edward Burne-Jones and made by Morris & Co., and there is some 20th-century stained glass by Christopher Whall. The altar has a fine alabaster statue of the Madonna.

ANCESTRAL HOME *Shakespeare's mother and her forebears lived in this comfortable 16th-century yeoman's house at Wilmcote. The barn (top) contains a museum of country bygones.*

WORCESTER

Hereford and Worcester
24 miles southwest of Birmingham

Sauce and fine china have carried Worcester's name around the world; and glove-making, a local craft since the 13th century, is still carried on alongside such modern industries as engineering and printing. The city centre has many splendid medieval buildings, crowned by the cathedral beside the River Severn. There are also carefully preserved reminders of Worcester's 19th-century industrial history.

The city is set amid rich farmland of meadows, apple and cherry orchards and hopfields. Agriculture has always played an important part in its economics.

In medieval times, the eastern boundary of Worcester was marked by defences which ran parallel to City Walls Road. These have been excavated, and Worcester's oldest buildings lie between them and the river front. The oldest church is St Helen's in Fish Street, established in AD 680, rebuilt many times, most recently in 1880, and now used to store ecclesiastical and secular records.

Dominating the city is the cathedral, founded as a Saxon monastery by St Oswald in 983. It stands on high ground, on the eastern bank of the Severn, with its out-buildings extending to the edge of the river and the city stretching away behind it. The earliest part of the present building, the Norman crypt, was constructed by St Wulstan, the only Saxon bishop to keep his office after the invasion of 1066. It was built for the safe keeping and worship of saints' relics. On each anniversary of St Wulstan's death on January 19, 1095, services are held in it. The circular chapter house, one of the first of its kind, was built about 1120, and 50 years later the west end of the nave was reconstructed. The choir stalls were also added in the 13th century.

The great tower was added in the 14th century, when much of the rest of the cathedral was rebuilt. Prince Arthur's Chantry, an elaborately carved chapel, was built in 1504 by Henry VII in memory of his son Arthur, who had died at Ludlow. It is remarkable for its fine tracery, heraldry and sculptures. Worcester Cathedral is the burial place of King John, who died in 1216.

The cathedral library, over the south aisle of the nave, contains a large collection of early manuscripts, including fragments of an 8th-century Gospel and deeds of land from the same period.

A monastery grew up around the cathedral, and was dissolved in 1540, but some of the buildings remain. Among them are the refectory, which is part of the King's School, the cloisters, a circular chapter house and the 14th-century Edgar Tower. The massive gateway of the tower, which formerly led to the priory, is still in use. South of the cathedral, across College Green, is the site of Worcester Castle, built in the 11th century and never more than a fortified enclosure.

The Methodist Church of St Andrew has a very different setting, standing over a shopping arcade high above Pump Street. It was opened in 1968 and is reached either by a lift, or by a winding staircase beside a large, colourful stained-glass window in modern abstract style. All that remains of the 15th-century St Andrew's Church is a tower and spire 250ft high

BOSS *Carved keystones at rib intersections in vaulting were known as bosses, and were often painted. They were carved with flowers, leaves or angels' heads, or depicted religious events. A boss in the south transept at Worcester probably shows St Wulstan's canonisation. Bosses were also used at beam intersections in timber roofs.*

RIVERSIDE MAJESTY *The massive bulk of Worcester Cathedral looks down on the quiet waters of the River Severn as it has done for 800 years or more.*

1 WEST DOOR *The main door, used for processions.*

2 NAVE *In monastic days, the nave had many chapels where monks and priests said daily Masses for various saints. Altars, which could be used for only one Mass a day, were placed against the west sides of pillars.*

3 TRIFORIUM *Arcaded walk above the nave arches and below the clerestory.*

4 TOWER *Most cathedrals have a central tower over the crossing, formed by the transepts, that separates the nave from the chancel.*

5 LADY CHAPEL *A chapel dedicated to the Blessed Virgin Mary, sited at the extreme east end of the cathedral. Veneration of the Virgin became popular in the 13th–14th centuries.*

6 PRESBYTERY *The sanctuary round the High Altar, where only officiating priests were allowed.*

7 CHOIR *The area reserved for the priests and choir, and monks in medieval days.*

8 PARLOUR *A room where the monks could converse. The chamber above was a treasury, where valuable vessels were kept.*

9 CHAPTER HOUSE *Where the chapter held meetings.*

10 REFECTORY *The monks' dining hall, or Frater.*

11 CLOISTERS *Covered walks between the cathedral and the abbey, often used by the monks as a study.*

12 GARTH *The area that the cloisters surrounded.*

13 FLYING BUTTRESS *An arched prop to counteract the thrust of vaulting.*

ROYAL RESTING PLACE *The marble likeness of King John was placed on his tomb in Worcester Cathedral two years after his death in 1216. It is the oldest royal effigy in England (overleaf).*

above riverside gardens. Its local name is the Glover's Needle.

The Commandery, just outside the old city walls in Sidbury, was founded in 1085 as a hospital by St Wulstan. It was rebuilt in the 15th century, and has a great hall with mural paintings. Charles II used it as his headquarters during the Battle of Worcester in 1651. The Royalist forces were defeated, and their commander, the Duke of Hamilton, died of his wounds in The Commandery.

Friar Street and its continuation, New Street, contain several 15th and 16th-century houses. Among them is Nash House, a four-storey, half-timbered Elizabethan building. Another, Greyfriars, was put up about 1480 as a hostelry for travellers, and is one of the few buildings of the friars to survive in the city after the Dissolution of the Monasteries. It contains some early fireplaces, panelling and furniture of the period. Also in Friar Street is the Tudor House, a 500-year-old timber-framed building which has been turned into a folk museum, depicting life in the city from Elizabethan times. It includes a Stuart room and a kitchen with a cast-iron cooking range. King Charles's House, a half-timbered building in New Street, was built in 1577. It was partly destroyed by fire in the 18th century, but the remainder has been restored and is used as a restaurant. The king hid in the house after his defeat in the battle outside the city walls, and fled through the back door as Parliamentarian troops entered at the front.

Charles II and his father, Charles I, are commemorated by statues on the façade of the Guildhall in High Street, designed in 1721 by Thomas White, a pupil of Sir Christopher Wren. Oliver Cromwell's head is depicted, too, nailed by the ears above the doorway, in illustration of the city's unswerving loyalty to the Stuarts. The whole frontage is one of the finest examples of early Georgian architecture in the country. Inside the building is a beautifully decorated Queen Anne assembly room and a collection of armour, including some left on the field after the Battle of Worcester. Civil War relics are also on display at the City Museum in Foregate Street, next to the 19th-century Shire Hall. One section of the museum is devoted to the Worcestershire Regiment raised in 1694, and the country's Yeoman Cavalry, formed exactly 100 years later. Apart from the usual uniforms and weapons, the exhibits include three Victoria Crosses and captured German and Japanese relics of the Second World War.

Worcester's porcelain industry was started in 1751 by Dr John Wall and a group of local businessmen. Their factory soon produced its own successful lines of Chinese blue-printed ware and, later, richly ornamented ware. The present factory of the Worcester Royal Porcelain Company in Severn Street is open to visitors by appointment.

The Lea & Perrins sauce factory in Midland Road was founded in 1825 by two local men, and they first created the recipe for their celebrated Worcestershire sauce five years later.

The city is the home of Britain's oldest surviving newspaper, Berrow's Worcester Journal, founded in 1690. Every third year the cathedral is the setting for Europe's oldest music festival, the Three Choirs Festival, which it has shared with Gloucester and Hereford since 1719.

The composer Sir Edward Elgar (1857–1934) was born at Broadheath, 4 miles northwest of Worcester, in a house which is now a museum, containing proofs of his musical scores and personal mementoes.

Worcester has one of the oldest racecourses in the country. In summer, county cricket is played on the attractive ground across the river from the cathedral. Boat excursions, through the green and wooded local countryside, start from Worcester Bridge.

ELGAR – ENGLAND'S TRIUMPHANT COMPOSER

Edward Elgar (1857–1934), the son of a Worcester music shop proprietor, was born at Broadheath on the city outskirts in a house which is now a museum dedicated to his life and work. One of the greatest British musicians, his compositions include the highly original 'Enigma Variations' and the famous march, 'Pomp and Circumstance', a favourite amongst the military bands.

The score of Elgar's second symphony which he wrote in 1910–11.

Pictures of the friends portrayed by Elgar in his 'Enigma Variations'.

Golf, chemistry and racing all fascinated the great composer.

Down through the lush Severn valley to the lofty Malvern Hills

The Severn valley broadens as it rolls south. To the west the Malvern Hills rise abruptly, and beyond them lie broad hop fields and cider-apple orchards. In the north, the cathedral city of Worcester is famed for fine porcelain and spicy sauce. At the former port of Upton upon Severn, to the south, 18th-century warehouses still stand by the river.

SOLE SURVIVOR *Of the old church in Upton upon Severn, only the tower is left standing.*

RESTORED *Pieces of stained glass, restored in Ledbury church during this century.*

PETAL POWER *The yellow-green flower-spikes of wild mignonette can sometimes be found growing on the open grassland of the Herefordshire Beacon. A short plant with divided leaves, it grows to only about 2ft and is in flower from June to September.*

TUNNEL VISION *A herd of cows ambles contentedly to grass through a tunnel by the River Teme's towpath near Worcester.*

FANCY FRONT *Regency ironwork adorns Great Malvern's Foley Arms.*

SMALL ORDER *Little Malvern Priory is well named, as its Benedictine monks never numbered more than a dozen.*

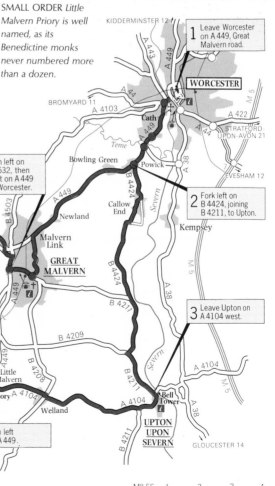

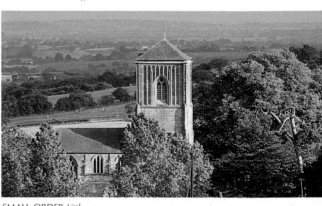

1 Leave Worcester on A 449, Great Malvern road.

2 Fork left on B 4424, joining B 4211, to Upton.

3 Leave Upton on A 4104 west.

4 Turn left on A 449.

5 For Eastnor turn left on A 438. Return and continue to Ledbury.

6 Turn right on A 438. At railway bridge, ahead on B 4214.

7 Turn right on B 4220, through Bosbury.

8 Turn right on A 4103.

9 Turn right on B 4219 to Great Malvern, then right on A 449.

10 Turn left on A 4532, then right on A 449 to Worcester.

KIDDERMINSTER 12 / BROMYARD 11 / STRATFORD-UPON-AVON 21 / EVESHAM 12 / GLOUCESTER 14 / TEWKESBURY 9

WORCESTER / Cath / Bowling Green / Powick / Callow End / Kempsey / Newland / Malvern Link / GREAT MALVERN / West Malvern / Storridge / BOSBURY / HEREFORDSHIRE BEACON / Little Malvern / Priory / British Camp / Clutter's Cave / LEDBURY / EASTNOR / Bronsil Castle / Welland / UPTON UPON SEVERN / Bell Tower

Teme / Severn / Cradley Brook / Malvern Hills

MILES 1 2 3 4
KM 2 4 6

WORCESTERSHIRE BEACON

Hereford and Worcester
1 mile southwest of Great Malvern

A clear day is desirable for climbing the 1395ft to the summit of the Worcestershire Beacon, the highest point of the Malvern Hills. The views are extraordinary – 15 counties (using the old county boundaries) can be seen from here. A direction indicator, or toposcope, set on the peak to commemorate the reign of Queen Victoria, clearly confirms that the views stretch north from The Wrekin in Shropshire to the Mendips of Somerset in the south, beyond the Severn Estuary, and from Plynlimmon in Wales to Bardon Hill above Leicester to the northeast. From here, too, can be seen vividly the three great cathedrals of Gloucester, Hereford and Worcester, as well as six battlefields of England's warring past – Evesham (1265), where Simon de Montfort was defeated by Prince Edward, later Edward I; Shrewsbury (1403), the scene of the defeat of Henry Percy by Henry IV; Mortimer's Cross (1461) and Tewkesbury (1471) in the Wars of the Roses; and Edge Hill (1642) and Worcester (1651), where Parliamentarians and Royalists clashed in the Civil War.

Evidence of Bronze Age cremations more than 3500 years ago has been found on the summit, and it has been used as a beacon site for at least 400 years.

THE LAUGHING WOODPECKER

A cackling 'kew-kew-kew' that rings like laughter through the Wyre Forest is the signal that the green woodpecker is on the wing. It is the largest British woodpecker, brightly coloured and distinctively marked.

Yellow rump conspicuous in flight.

THE WREKIN

Shropshire
10 miles southeast of Shrewsbury

The sombre 1334ft whale-back hump of The Wrekin stands out like some giant geological pimple on the smooth face of the Severn Plain. It rises abruptly between the wild Shropshire hills to the south and the flat, northern lands, and is formed from some of the oldest rocks in Britain, lava, ashes and debris that were disgorged from a volcanic cleft 900 million years ago.

Although much trodden in summer and at weekends, The Wrekin still retains a special magic. Two thousand years ago, the earthworks on the summit were the ramparts of the tribal capital of the Cornovii. Now almost obliterated by time and weather, the Iron Age remains stand as a reminder of the fiercely fought resistance of the British tribes to the Roman expansion from the east. The fort is elongated and takes in most of the hill. It consists of a large central area of about 7 acres surrounded by a series of outer earthworks which enclose a total of $10\frac{1}{2}$ acres. Excavations have shown that the central area was probably a settlement before the 5th or 4th centuries BC. Hut floors have been found inside the main fort.

To tread the broad tracks and paths that wind up to the summit through oak, birch, holly, yew and upland bracken is to tread the paths that our ancestors followed. Nature's gently changing seasons add to the timeless character. Bluebells carpet the woods in spring, and on the lonelier southern slopes there are primroses; in summer, foxgloves and rosebay willowherb flourish. Green woodpeckers cackle in the woods and may be seen searching for ants on the ground; treecreepers dart up the oak trunks and tits flock among the branches.

Though it is now crowned by a television transmission mast, the wild and windy summit is magnificent with panoramic views all round.

WROXETER

Shropshire
5 miles southeast of Shrewsbury

The Romans established a fort at Wroxeter during the 1st century, and when the legions left to go to Chester it became the fourth largest town in Roman Britain – Viroconium. The town covered some 200 acres and excavations have exposed a market hall and a swimming pool.

The most impressive relic at Wroxeter is one wall of the exercise hall adjacent to the baths, known as The Old Work. This 20ft high wall contains a square entrance which had double doors leading to the frigidarium, or 'cooling off' room. A museum displays coins, pottery and painted plaster from the site.

WYRE FOREST

Hereford and Worcester/Shropshire Border
West of Bewdley

Fallow deer roam the 6000 acres of Wyre Forest, which is the remaining part of a vast Royal hunting forest mentioned in the Domesday Book. Walkers can wander for miles along three main tracks through the forest.

Large tracts of Wyre are natural oak woodlands, with plantations of larch and Douglas fir among them. Above the wild flowers that dot the forest floor in summer, silver-washed fritillary butterflies glide in and out of the trees' shade. Meadows among the woodlands are bright with flowers and scented by the delicate fragrance of wild thyme.

RIDGEWAY WALK *From Worcestershire Beacon a path follows the ridge of the Malvern Hills south to Herefordshire Beacon.*

INDEX

Page numbers in **bold** type refer to main entries in the book. Numbers in *italic* refer to illustrations.

A

Abberley, **8**
Abberley Hall, 8, 37
Abbey Dore, **8**, 47, 59
Abbots Bromley, **8–9**, *8*, *75*
Abdon Burf, 27
Abel, John, 8
Abraham, Robert, 11
Acton, Sir Edward, 89
Acton, Sir John, 89
Acton Beauchamp, 27
Acton Burnell, **9–10**, *9*
Acton Scott, **10**, *10*
Adam, Robert, 46
Addison, Joseph, 74
Alberbury, 86
Alcester, **10**
Aldenham Park, 89
Almeley, **10**
Alne, River, 10, 12, 56
Alrewas, **10**, *75*
Alton Towers, **10–11**, *11*
Alveley, **11**
Anson, Admiral, 114
Anson family, 114
Arbury Hall, **11–12**
Archer, Thomas, 19
Arden, Forest of, 56
Arden, Mary, 120, 146
Arderne, Thomas de, 50
Ariconium, 145
Arley, Upper, 136, *136–7*
Arrow, River, 10, 69, 102, 104
Arthur, King, 22, 85
Arthur, Prince, 16, 37, 79, 148
Arthur, Prince of Wales, 85
Arthur's Stone, 22, 47, 59
Ashes Hollow, 77
Ashmole, Elias, 74
Ashwin family, 22
Astley, **12**
Aston Cantlow, **12**
Aston on Clun, **12**
Aston Hall, 18
Aston Munslow, **12**, *92*
Atcham, **12**, *94–5*
Attingham Hall, 12
Augustine, St, 72
Avon, River, 20, 21, 32, 46, 52, 102, 119, 138, 140
Avoncroft Museum of Buildings, 26, 27
Axe Edge, 48, 108

B

Backbury Hill, 88
Bacon, Francis, 36
Bacton, 8
Baginton, **14**
Bagot family, 9, 20
Bagot goats, *75*
Balsall Common, 16
Barber Institute of Fine Arts, 18
Bardon Hill, 154
Bark House, 64
Barlaston, **14**
Barnard, Lady, 124
Baswich, 116
Batement, Viscount, 112
Batsford Park Arboretum, **14**
Bayton, **14–15**
Beauchamp, John, **50**
Beauchamp, Richard, 50, 139
Beauchamp family, 34
Beaudesert Castle, 56
The Beck, 72
Becket, Thomas, 47
Beecham, Sir Adrian, 65

Bellucci, Antonio, 55
Bennett, Arnold, 116, *116*, 117
Benthall Hall, 91
Berkswell, **15–16**, *45*
Berkswell Mill, *14*, 16
Berrington Hall, **16**
Berrow's Worcester Journal, 152
Berwick, Lord, 12
Berwyn mountains, 94
Bewdley, **16**, *16–17*
Biddulph, **18**
Bidford-on-Avon, 101
Binley, 46
Birch, Colonel John, 53, 144
Birmingham, **18–19**, *19*, 115, 126
Birmingham Canal, 18
Birmingham-Fazeley Canal, 18
Birtsmorton Court, 104
Bishop's Castle, **19–20**, *20*, 38
Black Death, 36, 98
Black Mountains, 22, 47, 48, 69
Blakesley Hall, 18
Blamyre, John, 8
Blists Hill, 40–1, 128, *128–9*
Blithfield, **20**
Blithfield Hall, 9, *75*
Blount, Sir George, 69
Blount, Lady, 69
Blount family, 69
Bodley, George Frederick, 63
Boeck, 63
The Bog, 116
Bollitree Castle, 145
Borrow, George, 116
Bosbury, **20**
Boscobel House, 133
Boswell, James, 74
Botticelli, Sandro, 18
Boudicca, 14
Boulton, Matthew, 18
Bourne, Hugh, 18
Bournville, **20**, *21*
Bradford, Earls of, 144
Bradford, Sir Francis Newport, 1st Earl of, 62
Bradnor Hill, 69
Brecon Brecons, 69
Bredon, *20–1*
Bredon Hill, 21, 24, 42, 51, 87
Bredon Tithe Barn, 21
Bredwardine, **21–2**, *59*
Bretforton, **22**
Breughel, Peter, 136
Bridestones, 18
Bridges, 116
Bridgewater, Duke of, 70
Bridgnorth, 16, **23**
Brindley, James, 18, 70
British Camp, 60–1
British Waterway Board, 56
Brito, Richard de, 47
Broad Down, **23**
Broadheath, 152
Broadmore, 147
Broadway, **24**, *25*
Broadway Beacon, 24
Broadway Tower, 24, *24*
Brockhampton-by-Ross, 147
Brockhampton Park, 27, *27*
Bromfield, **26**
Bromsgrove, **26–7**
Bromyard, **27**
Bronsil Castle, 50
Brookes, Dr William Penny, 90–1
Brown, Ford Madox, *19*
Brown, Lancelot 'Capability', 16, 133, 144
Brown Clee Forest Trail, 27
Brown Clee Hill, **27**, *28–9*
Browning, Elizabeth Barrett, *70*
Buckenhill, Lower, 147
Buckle Street, 24
Bucknell, **28**
Buildwas Abbey, **28**
Bulmers Steam Centre, 58
Bunster, 48
Burford, **28**, 129
Burford, Edmund Cornewall, 10th Baron of, 129
Burford, Richard Cornewall, 9th Baron of, 129
Burne-Jones, Sir Edward, 19, 24, 105, 147
Burnell, Sir Nicholas, 10
Burnell, Robert, 10
Burnell, William, 10
Burnell family, 10
Burritt, Elihu, 132

Burrow, 12
Burslem, 116, 117
Burton, 48
Burton Dassett, **28**
The Burway, 76
Bury Ditches, 38
Bushell, Thomas, 36
butterflies: comma, *49*
  common blue, *113*
  fritillaries, *72*
  peacock, *49*
Buxton, 130

C

Cadbury, George, 20, *21*
Cadbury, Richard, 20, *21*
Caer Caradoc, 12, *34–5*, 119, 126
Callow Hollow, 77
Cannock Chase, 30, **31**, *31*, *75*
Cantelupe, Thomas de, 12
Capler Wood, 53
Caractacus, 61
Caramanico, Prince, 89
Cardingmill Valley, 36, *76–7*, 77
Cardington, 31, *84*, 126
Castlemorton Common, **23**, *23*
Catherine of Aragon, 16, 42, 79
cattle, *144*
Chad, St, 73–4
Chaddesley Corbett, **31–2**
Chaddesley Wood, 32
Chandos, Duke of, 55
Charlecote, **32**
Charlecote Park, 32, 120
Charles I, King, 24, 32, 36, 44, 50, 53, 65, 115, 116, 138, *139*, 152
Charles II, King, 64, 89, 108, 133, *133*, 152
Charlett, Sara, 37
Charlton, 46
Chartley Castle, 144, *144–5*
Chase End Hill, **32**
Cheadle, **32–3**
Checkley, 33
Cheddleton, **33**
Cherrington, 94
Cherry Hill, 53
Cherwell, River, 138
Cheshire Plain, 108
Chester, 154
Childe family, 69
Childswickham, **34**
Chipping Campden, 62
Chirbury, **34**
Chirk Castle, 98
Cholmondeley, Sir Thomas, *43*
Church Stretton, **34–6**, 76, *113*, 126
Churnet Valley, 32
Civil War, 18, 23, 28, 32, 34, 36, 42, 43, 44, 50, 53, 56, 65, 67, 70, 78, 88, 98, 102, 110, 115, 118, 119, 138, 152, 154
Claverley, **36**
Clee Burf, 27
Clee Hills, 31, 119, 131
Clee St Margaret, 27
Cleeve Cloud, 24
Cleeve Prior, **36–7**
Clent Hills, 37
Cleobury Mortimer, **37**
Cleobury North, 27
Clifton upon Teme, **37**, *37*
Clinton, Roger de, Bishop of Coventry, 28
Clive, Robert, 85
Clopton, Hugh, 121, 125
Clopton, Joyce, 124
The Cloud, 108
Clows Top, 37
Clun, **38**, *38*, *113*
Clun, River, 38, *113*
Clun Forest, 19
Clun Forest sheep, *68*
Clungunford, **38**
Clutter's Cave, 23, 61
Coalbrookdale, **39–41**, *39*, *95*, 128
Coalport Canal, 128
Coalport Company, 40–1, *41*
Coalport Museum, 40–1, *95*
Cobridge, 117

Cockerell, Charles, 110
Cockshutford, 27
Colbrand, 138
Cole, River, 18
Colwall, **42**
The Combertons, **42**
Comley, 126
comma butterflies, *49*
common blue butterflies, *113*
Compton, William, 42
Compton Scorpion Manor, 65
Compton Wynyates, **42**
Condover, **42**, *43*, *113*
Congleton, 108
Congreve, William, 65
Constable, John, 18
Copeland ware, 116
Coppice Hill, 31
Corbet, Sir Andrew, 88
Cornewall family, 128–9
Corve, River, *92–3*
Cosford, 133
Cotswolds, 22, 24, 62, 65, 87, 104, 138
Cotton, Charles, 48
Coughton Court, **43**
Cound Brook, *113*
Coventry, 14, **44–6**, *45*
Coventry, Earl of, 24
Coventry Canal, 10
cows, *144*
Craven, Lord, 46
Craven Arms, *84*
Croeswylan Stone, 98
Croft Ambrey, 46
Croft Castle, **46**, *84*
Croft family, 46
Cromwell, Oliver, 18, 24, 28, 34, 47, 65, 88, 119, 138, 144, 152
Cropredy, 138
Cropthorne, **46**
Crowle, **46**
Croxden, 11
Curzon family, 134
Cut-thorn Hill, 130

D

Dane, River, 130
Darby, Abraham I, 39, *40*, 128
Darby, Abraham III, 40
Darwin, Charles, 112
Davies, Sir Walford, 98
De Cantelupe family, 12
De Say family, 118
Dean, Forest of, 145
Degas, Edgar, 18
Devil's Chair, *113*, 116
Devil's Mouth, 36
Dickens, Charles, 112, 133
Dickin, Nicholas, 78
Digbeth Branch Canal, 18
Dingley, Edward, 46
Dingley, Eleanor, 46
Domesday Book, 27, 49, 53, 68, 116, 144, 154
Donne, John, 110
Dore, River, 8, 138
Dore Abbey, 8
Dorstone, **47**, *59*
Dove, River, 47, 111
Dove Dale, **47–8**, *47*
Dove Holes, 48
Dovedale Castle, 48
Dover, Captain Robert, 48
Dover's Hill, **48**
Downton Castle, 26
Draycote Reservoir, **48**
Droitwich, **48**
Dudley, Ambrose, 139
Dudley Castle and Zoo, **48**
Dunsmore Heath, 126
Dyfrig, St, 85

E

Eardisland, **49**
Eardisley, **49**
Earl's Hill, **49**, *49*
East India Company, 110
Easthope, 141
Eastnor, **50**
Eastnor Castle, 50
Edge Hill, **50**, 53, 115, 138, 154
Edge Wood Nature Reserve, 141
Edmund, Lord, 12
Edward I, King, 154
Edward IV, King, 79, 85
Edward V, King, 79
Edward VI, King, 120
Edward VII, King, 54
Edwin Shakehead, 20, 82
Elder Bush Cave, 65
Elford, **50**
Elgar, Sir Edward, 152, *152*
Eliot, George, 12
Elizabeth I, Queen, 8, 22, 42, 67,
   95, 139
Elizabeth II, Queen, 135
Elkington brothers, 18
Ellesmere, **50–1**, *50*, *51*
Elmley Castle, **51**
emperor dragonflies, *27*
Etruria, 14
Evesham, **52**, 154
Evesham, Vale of, 22, 24, 34, 42,
   52
Evesham Abbey, 22, 46, *52*
Eye Manor, 16

F

fallow deer, *31*
Farnborough, **53**, *53*
Feckenham, **53**
Fenton, 116
Ferdinand IV, King of Naples, 89
Ferrers, Henry de, 134
Fetherston, John, 100
Fitzwarine, Fulke, 146
Fladbury, 46
Flaxman, John, 116–17
Foley, Lord, 55
Ford Green Hall, 117
Forest of Dean, 145
Forestry Commission, 12, 31,
   88, 147
Fosse Way, 126
Fownhope, **53**
Foxcote, 65
foxes, 75
Fradley Junction, 10
Fresian cattle, *144*
fritillaries, *72*
Furness Abbey, 28

G

Gainsborough, Thomas, 18
Garrick, David, 74, 124, 125
Garway, **54**
George II, King, 112
German, Sir Edward, 146
Giant's Cave, 23
Gibbons, Grinling, 37, 103
Gibbs, James, 104
Giffard, John, 133
Gladestry, **54**
Gladstone Pottery, *117*
Gloucester, 152, 154
glow-worms, *87*
Gnosall, **54**
goats, Bagot, *75*
Godiva, Lady, 44, *44*, 90, 147
Golden Valleys, 22, 47, 103, **104**,
   138
Goodere, Sir Edward, 46
Goodrich Castle, **54**
Gorges, Ferdinando, 16
Gourden, Alexander, 138
Grafton Manor, 27
Grand Union Canal, 18, *45*, 56

Grandison, Lady, 90
Graveley Hill, 18
Great Comberton, 42
great crested grebes, *50*
Great Malvern, **85**, *85*, 96, *153*
Great Witley, **54–5**
Green Valley, 96
green woodpecker, *154*
Grinshill, **55**
Grinshill Hill, *54*
Grove, John, 11
Guild of the Holy Cross, 125
Gunpowder Plot, 43
Guy of Warwick, 138
Gwynne, John, 12
Gwynne, Nell, 58

H

Habberley valley, 49
Hall, Elizabeth, 121, 124
Hall, John, 124
Hall, Colonel Roger, 23
Hamilton, Duke of, 152
Hamps, River, 65
Hampton Bishop, **56**
Hampton family, 69
Hanbury Hall, **56**
Hanging Hill, 69
Hanley, 116, *117*
Hansom, Joseph, 18
Harley, Thomas, 16
Hartlebury Castle, **56**
Harton, 141
Hathaway, Anne, 120, 124
Hatton Locks, *45*, **56**
Haugh Wood, 88, *88*, 147
Haughmond Abbey, **56**, *95*
Hawksmoor, 33
Hay Inclined Plane, 40, *41*
Hazlitt, William, 141
Heber, Bishop Reginald, 64
Heber Percy family, 64
Hellen's, 90
Helyon, Walter de, 90
Hen Cloud, 108
Henley-in-Arden, **56**
Henry II, King, 37
Henry III, King, 67, 128
Henry IV, King, 154
Henry VII, King, 85, 112, 148
Henry VIII, King, 8, 16, 22, 26,
   42, 79, 90, 98
Hensborough Hill, 48
Herbert, Lord, 34
Hereford, **56–8**, *56–7*, *58*, 88,
   147, 152, 154
Hereford and Worcester
   County Museum, 56
Hereford cattle, *144*
Herefordshire Beacon, 23, 42,
   60–1, *60–1*, *153*, *154–5*
Hidcote Manor Garden, **62**, *62*,
   68
High Ercall, **62**
Highmeadow Woods, **62**
Hoar Cross, **62–3**
Hoarwithy, **63–4**, *63*, *64*
Hodnet, **64**
Hodnet Hall, 64, *95*
Holbache Museum of
   Childhood, 98
Holland, Henry, 16
Holling Hill, 147
Hollingsworth, Mrs, 24
Hollybush Hill, **87**
Holme Lacy, **64**
Holyhead Road, 128
Homme House, 90
Honington Hall, **64**
Hooke, Robert, 104
Hope End, *70*
Hopesay Common, 12, *13*
Horn Dance, *8*, *9*
Hosier, John, 82
Housman, A. E., 38, 82
How, William Walsham, 146
Howe, Sir Geoffrey, 8
Hulme, Upper, 108
Huntsham Hill, 126
Hurd, Bishop Richard, 56
Hurstway Common, 49

I

Ilam, **65**
Ilam Rock, 48
Ilmington, **65**, *65*
Ilmington Down, 65
Inkberrow, 65
Ippikin's Rock, 91, 141
Ironbridge, *39*, 128
Ironbridge Gorge, *39–40*, *41*,
   128
Irving, Sir Henry, 120, 125
Itchen, River, 115
Ivy Scar Rock, 96

J

James I, King, 34, 36, 124
Japanese maples, *110*
Jeffreyes family, 37
Jeffreys, Judge, *141*
Jephson, Dr, 109
Jervis, Admiral, 119
John, King, 34–6, 67, 148, *150–1*
John of Gaunt, 134
Johnson, Michael, 137
Johnson, Samuel, 65, 74, 137
Johnsonian Museum, Lichfield,
   74
Jones family, 8
Joseph of Arimathea, 42
Joyce, J. B., 145

K

Kenilworth, *45*, **66–7**, *66–7*
Kentchurch Court, 103
Kerry Hill sheep, 68
Kidderminster, 23
Kiftsgate Court Gardens, **68**
Kilpeck, *59*, **68**, *68*
Kilvert, Rev. Francis, 21, *58–9*
King Arthur's Cave, 62
King's Leap, 48
King's Men, 74
Kingswood Common, 69
Kington, *68*, **69**
Kinlet, **69**
Kinver, **69**
Kinver Edge, 69, *69*
Knapp and Papermill Nature
   Reserve, 72
Knight family, 26
Knighton, 98
Knights of St John, 58
Knights Templar, 54, 103
Knockin, **69**
Knowle, *45*, **69**
Kynaston, 'Wild Humphrey', 94
Kyrle, John, 108–9
Kyrle family, 90

L

Lacy, Roger de, 79
Langland, William, 37, 85
The Lawley, 126
Lawrence of Ludlow, 118
Lea & Perrins, 152
Leam, River, 48, 85, 109
Leamington Spa, 109
Ledbury, **70**, *70–1*, *153*
Lee, Richard Henry, 10
Lee, General Robert E., 10
Lee family, 10
Leebotwood, **70**
Leek, **70**, 130
Leicester, Robert Dudley, Earl
   of, 22, *45*, 67, 138
Leigh Brook, **72**, *72*
Leigh family, 119
Leighton, **72**, *73*
Leighton, Judge William, 31
Leighton family, 72
Leintwardine, **72**

Leofric, Earl of Mercia, 44, 90
Leominster, **72**
Lethaby, W. R., 147
Letocetum, 14
Lichfield, **73–4**, *73*
Lichfield, Earls of, 114
Light Spout, 77
Lilleshall, **74**
Lilleshall Abbey, 74
Lilleshall Quarry, 141
Lind, Jenny, 112
Little Comberton, 42
Little Malvern, **85**
Little Malvern Priory, 85, 104,
   153
Little Stretton, 34, 77, *113*
Llanyblodwel, **74**
Llanymynech, **74**
Llanymynech Rocks Nature
   Reserve, 74
Lloyd family, 98
Long Compton, **74**
The Long Mynd, 48, **76–7**, *76–7*,
   113, 116, 119, 126
Longton, 116, *117*
Loppington, **78**
Loppington Hall, 78
Lovers' Leap, 48
Low, David, *116*
Low Peak, 134
Lower Brockhampton Hall, 27
Lower Buckenhill, 147
Lower Rochford, **78**, *78*
Lucy, Sir Thomas, 32
Lucy family, 32
Ludlow, **79–82**, *79*, *80–1*, *82*, *84*,
   130
Ludstone Hall, 36
Lugg, River, 72, 88
'The Lunt', 14
Lutyens, Sir Edwin, 46
Lydbury North, **82**

M

Macclesfield, 130
Madley Court, 128
Madley, **85**
magnolia, *110*
Major's Leap, 141
Malvern, Great and Little, **85**,
   85, 96, *153*
Malvern Chase, 104
Malvern Hills, 23, 24, 32, 37, 42,
   60, *60–1*, 72, 85, 87, 96, 104,
   131, *153*, 154, *154–5*
Malvern Priory, 96
Manifold, River, 65
maples, Japanese, *110*
Mappestone, Godric, 54
Marie Antoinette, Queen of
   France, 138
Market Drayton, **85**
Marton, **85**
Mary, Queen of Scots, 134
Masefield, John, 61
Massey, General, 70
Meadowley Bank, 88
Mediolanum, 145
Melba, Dame Nellie, 64
Melverley, **86**, *86*
Mendips, 154
Merbach Hill, 22, 47
Merewald, King of Mercia, 90
Meriden, **87**
Meynell Ingram, Hugo, 62–3
Midland Air Museum, 14
Midsummer Hill, **87**, *87*
mignonette, *153*
Milburga, St, 90
Milford, **87**
Miller, Sanderson, 50
Milton, John, 79, *84*
Minsterley, **87**
Minton ware, 116
Mitchell, Reginald, 117
Moilliet family, 8
Mollington, 138
Monnow, River, 47, 115
Montfort, Simon de, 67, 154
Montgomery, Roger de, 36, 38
Montgomery Castle, 34
Moore, John, 21
Mordiford, **88**
More, **88**

Moreton Corbet, **88**, *89*
Morris, William, 24, 78
Morris & Co., 147
Mortimer, Hugh de, 37
Mortimer family, 37, 79
Mortimer's Cross, 154
Morville, **88–9**
Morville Hall, 88
Moseley Old Hall, **89**
Mow Cop, 18
Much Marcle, **89–90**
Much Wenlock, **90–1**, *90, 91*
Munslow, **92–3**
Museum of Buildings and
    Country Life, 12
Museum of Cider, Hereford, 58
Museum of Country Bygones,
    85
Myddelton, Sir Thomas, 98
Mytton, 'Mad Jack', 12

N

Napton on the Hill, **94**, *94*
Nash, John, 103, 109
Nash, Thomas, 121
National Agriculture Centre,
    119
National Trust:
    Attingham Hall, 12
    Berrington Hall, 16
    Bredon Tithe Barn, 21
    Broad Down, 23
    Cardingmill Valley, 36
    Charlecote Park, 32
    Farnborough Hall, 53
    The Fleece, Bretforton, 22
    Haugh Wood, 147
    Hawksmoor, 33
    Kinver Edge, 69
    The Long Mynd, 76–7
    Lower Brockhampton Hall, 27
    Midsummer and Hollybush
        Hills, 87
    Morville Hall, 88
    Shugborough, 114
    Skenfrith Castle, 115
    Upton House, 136
    Warren Wood, 27
    Wilderhope Manor, 141
Nature Conservancy Council,
    23, 116
Needwood Forest, 9, 62, *75*, 134
Nelson, Lord, 82, 126
Nesscliffe, **94**
Newburgh, Henry de, 138
Newdegate, Sir Roger, 12
Newdegate family, 11
Newport, **94**
Nordybank, 27
North Hill, **96**, *96–7*
nuthatches, *75*

O

Oakengates, 128
Offa, King of Mercia, 46, 98, *98*
Offa's Dyke, 38, 69, 74, **98**
Old Berry Hall, 115
Old Oswestry, 98, 99
Old Storridge Common, *72, 72*
Oldcastle, Sir John, 23
Ombersley, **98**, 99
Ombersley Court, 98
Onny, River, 26
Oswald, King, 98
Oswald, St, 148
Oswestry, 94, **98**
Ottley family, 102
Owain Glyndwr, 23, 60, 103
Owen, Judge Thomas, 42
Owen, Wilfred, 98
Oxford Canal, 94
Oxford Movement, 146

P

Packwood House, *45*, **100**,
    100–1
Paganini, Nicolo, 112
Parker, Sir Henry, 64
Parker, Rev. John, 74
Parr, Catherine, 42
Paxton, Sir Joseph, 134
peacock butterflies, *49*
Pebworth, **101–2**
Pembridge, **102**
Pembrugge, Lady Isabella de,
    132–3
Penda, King of Mercia, 98
Pennines, 108
Penyard Castle, 145
perch, *136*
Percy, Henry, 154
Percy, Thomas, Bishop of
    Dromore, 23
Perry, Blanche, 8
Perry, River, 109
Pershore, **102**
Pershore Abbey, 102
Peterchurch, 47
Philipps, Sir Thomas 24
Pickering Tor, 48
Pinsley Brook, 72
Piper, John, 44
Pitchford, **102–3**
Pitchford, Sir John de, 103
Pitchford Hall, 102–3, *102–3*
Plaish Hall, 31
Plowden family, 20, 82
Plynlimmon, 154
Pontrilas, 47, **103**
Pontrilas Court, 103
Poole, Rev. William, 64
poplars, *22–3*
The Port Way, 76
The Potteries, 116–17
Price, Cornell, 24
Pritchard, Thomas Farnolls, 40
Pugin, Augustus, 19, 20, 32
Pytel, Walenty, 147

Q

Quayle, Anthony, 8
Queen Stone, 126
Quiney, Judith, 125
Quiney, Thomas, 125

R

Radnor Forest, 54
Raggedstone Hill, **104**
Ragleth Hill, 126
Ragley Hall, **104**, *104–5*
Ramshaw Rocks, 108
Ravenshill Woodland Reserve,
    104–5
Raynalds, John, 90
Raynalds, Mary, 90
Raynalds' Mansion, Much
    Wenlock, 90, *90*
Redditch, 53
Redesdale, Lord, 14
Redlake, River, 28, 119
redpolls, *88*
Reeve, Robert, 106
Repton, Humphry, 110
Reynard's Cave, 48
Reynolds, William, 40
rhododendron, *94*
Ribbesford, 16, **105**
Richard II, King, 9
Richard III, King, 79
Richards Castle, *84*, **106**
ring ouzel, *77*
Ripple, **106**, *106–7*
The Roaches, **108**
Roberts, Richard, 74
Robin Hood, 87
Robinson, W. M., 87
Rochford, Lower, *78*, *78*
Rollright Stones, 74

Ross-on-Wye, **108–9**, *108–9*
Rossetti, Dante Gabriel, 24
Royal Brine Baths, Stafford, 116
Royal Leamington Spa, **109**
Royal Shakespeare Theatre, 125
Royal Warwickshire Regiment,
    140
Rubens, Sir Peter Paul, 18, 138
Rugby, 48
Rupert, Prince, 70, 116
Rushbury, 141
Russell, Gordon, 24
Ruyton-XI-Towns, **109**
Ryknild Street, 10
Ryland sheep, *84*

S

St John Coningsby Museum, 58
St Mary and St Anne School, 9
St Vincent, Earl, 119
St Weonards, **110**
Sandford, Rev. Holland, 36
Sandys, Samuel, Lord, 98
Sarehole Mill, 18
Sauner, Richard, 138
Say, Picot de, 38
Scott, Sir Gilbert, 53
Scott, Sir Walter, 38, 67, 120,
    138
Scudamore family, 64
Seddon, J. P., 64
Seven Sisters Rocks, 62
Severn, River, 11, 12, *16–17*, 23,
    39–40, 72, 105, 112, 119, 128,
    136, *136–7*, 137, 148, *148*
Severn Estuary, 154
Severn Plain, *96–7*, 154
Severn Valley, *54*, *94–5*, *153*
Severn Valley Railway, 11, 16,
    16, 23, 136, *136–7*
Seymour family, 104
Sezincote, **110**
Shakenhurst, 15
Shakespeare, John, 120
Shakespeare, Susanna, 121
Shakespeare, William, 12, 23,
    32, 42, 65, 101–2, 120–5,
    120–5, 146
Shakespeare Birthplace Trust,
    120, 124, 125
Shallowford, **110–11**
Shaw, R. Norman, 106
sheep: Clun Forest, *68*
    Kerry Hill, *68*
    Ryland, *84–5*
Shelsley Walsh, **111–12**, *111*
Shelve, 116
Sherratt, William, 24
Shifnal, **112**
Shipton Hall, 91
Shobdon, **112**
Shottery, 120
Shrewsbury, **112**, *112*, 154
Shrewsbury, Charles Talbot,
    15th Earl of, 10–11
Shrewsbury, John Talbot, 1st
    Earl of, 145
Shropshire Trust for Nature
    Conservation, 27, 49, 141
Shropshire Union Canal, 40, 54,
    85
Shugborough, **114**, *114–5*
Shugborough Park Farm, 114
Siddons, Sarah, 125
siskins, *88*
Skenfrith, **115**
Skenfrith Castle, 115
skylarks, *126*
Smallman, Major Thomas, 141
Smallthorne, 117
Smirke, Sir Robert, 50
Smith, Sarah (Hesba Stretton),
    36
Snailbeach, 116
Solihull, **115**
Solihull Hall, 115
Somers, 1st Earl, 50
Southam, **115**
Sow, River, 87, 114, 116, 119
Spence, Sir Basil, 44, *45*
Spetchley Park, **115**
spindle tree, *141*
Spode ware, 116
Spring, Tom, 53

Stafford, **116**
Stafford Castle, 116
Stafford family, 26
Staffordshire and
    Worcestershire Canal, 69, 119
Staffordshire County Museum,
    114
Staick House, 49
Stanton, William, 20
Steuart, George, 112
Stevens, Thomas, *44*
The Stiperstones, 76, *113*, **116**
Stoke-on-Trent, **116–17**, *116*
Stokesay, **118–19**
Stokesay Castle, 118–19,
    118–19
Stone, **119**
Stoneleigh, **119**
Stoneleigh Abbey, 119
Stour, River, 64, 69, 119
Stourport-on-Severn, **119**
Stourton Castle, 69
Stow Hill, **119**
Stratford-upon-Avon, **120–5**,
    120–5
Stretton Hills, **126**
Stretton-on-Dunsmore, **126**
Stretton Valley, 126
Stretton Westwood, 141
Stubbs, George, 136
Suck Stone, 62
Sutherland, 1st Duke of, 74
Sutherland, Graham, 44, *45*
Sutton Coldfield, **126**
Swynnerton, **126**
Symonds Yat, **126**
Symonds Yat Rock, 62, *127*

T

Talbot family, 26
Tame, River, 50
Tamworth pigs, *10*
Tanat, River, 74
Tar Tunnel, 41
Tarleton, General Sir Banastre,
    72
Tarlton, Richard, 42
Telford, **128**
Telford, Thomas, 16, *16–17*, 23,
    41, 128, *128–9*
Teme, River, 26, 28, 37, 72, 78,
    84, 105, *111*, 119, 129, *153*
Tenbury Museum, 128
Tenbury Wells, **128–9**, *129*
Tern, River, 85
Terry, Dame Ellen, 125
Tewkesbury, 154
Theatre Picture Gallery and
    Museum, Stratford-upon-
    Avon, 125
Thorpe Cloud, 48
Three Choirs Festival, 152
Three Shire Heads, **130**
Throckmorton family, 43, 46
thyme, *96*
Thynne family, 87
Tickenhill Manor, 16
Tims, George, 85
Titterstone Clee Hill, **130–1**,
    130–1
Tittesworth Reservoir, 108
Tomkins, Benjamin, *144*
Tong, **132–3**, *132–3*
Tong Castle, 133
Totnes, Earl of, 124
Treasure, John, 28
Trent, River, 18, 48, 114
Trent and Mersey Canal, 10
Trentham Gardens, **134**
Tresseck, 64
Trevithick, Richard, 39
tufted ducks, *50*
Tunstall, 116
Turn Edge, 130
Turnastone, 138
Tutbury, **134–5**, *134, 135*
Tutbury Castle, 134, *134*

U

Unk, River, 38
Upper Arley, **136**, *136–7*
Upper Hulme, 108
Upton House, **136**
Upton upon Severn, **137**, *153*
Uttoxeter, **137**

V

Van Dyck, Sir Anthony, 138, *139*
Van Gogh, Vincent, 18
Vernon, Lady Benedicta, 132
Vernon, Henry, 132
Vernon, Lady Margaret, 132
Vernon, Sir Richard, 132
Vernon, Sir William, 132
Vernon, family, 64, 132
Victoria, Queen, 46, 109, 154
Vienna (canal boat), 33, *33*
Viroconium, 112, 154
Vowchurch, **47**, *59*, 138
Vyrnwy, River, 86, *86*

W

Walcot family, 20
Wall, 74
Wall, Dr John, 152
Walm's Well, 23
Walpole, Horace, 112
Walton, Izaak, 48, *48*, 110–11,
   116
Warmington, **138**
Warndon, 115
Warren Wood, 27
Wart Hill, 12
Warwick, **138–40**
Warwick, Earls of, 138–9
Warwick, Roger, Earl of, 138–9
Warwick Castle, 138, *139*
Waterworks Museum, Hereford,
   58
Watling Street, 74, 128
Wat's Dyke, 98
Watt, James, 18
Waun Fach, 47
Wedgwood, Josiah, 14, 116–117
Wedgwood Company, 41
Wedgwood Memorial Institute,
   117
Wedgwood Museum Trust, 14
Welford-on-Avon, **140**, *140*
Wellington, 128
Wem, **141**, *141*
Wenlock Edge, 27, 72, *84*, 90,
   91, 92, **141**, *142–3*
Weobley, **144**
Weonard, St, 110
Wesley, John, 69
Wessington, 147
Wessington Court, 147
Westmacott, Sir Richard, 20
Weston, Henry, 89
Weston Park, **144**, *144–5*
Weston under Penyard, **145**
Whall, Christopher, 147
wheatears, *113*
Whispering Knights, 74
Whitchurch, **145–6**
White, Thomas, 37, 152
White House, Munslow, 92–3
Whiteleaved Oak, 32
Whitgreave family, 89
Whittington, **146**
Whittington, Dick, 146
Whittle, Sir Frank, 14
Wilbraham, Lady, 144
Wilbraham, Randle, 18
Wilderhope Manor, 141
Wilkinson, John, 40
William the Conqueror, King,
   134, 138
William Rufus, King, 85
William Salt Library, 116
Wilmcote, 120, **146**, *146–7*

windmills, *14*
Wint, Peter de, 63, 119
Winter, Thomas, 53
Witley Court, 54–5, *55*
Wolsey, Cardinal, 104
Wolverton Wood, 141
wood leopard moths, *23*
Woodmen of Arden, 87
woodpeckers, green, *154*
Woodseaves Cutting, 85
Woolhope, 88, **147**
Woolhope Dome, 147
Woolhope Naturalists' Field
   Club, 147
Worcester, 105, **148–52**,
   148–51, *153*, 154
Worcester-Birmingham Canal,
   18
Worcester Royal Porcelain
   Company, 152
Worcestershire Beacon, *60–1*,
   96, **154**, *154–5*
Worcestershire Nature
   Conservation Trust, 72, 104
Worcestershire Regiment, 152
The Wrekin, 72, 74, *94–5*, **154**
Wren, Sir Christopher, 56, 152
Wren's Nest Hill, 48
Wroxeter, 112, **154**
Wulstan, St, 148, 152
Wulviva, 147
Wyatt, James, 24, 104
Wyatt, Samuel, 114
Wye, River, 21, 53, 54, 56, *59*
   62, 64, 69, 88, 126
Wyre Forest, 16, 69, 104, **154**
Wysham, Ralph de, 37

Y

Yat Rock, 62, 126

ACKNOWLEDGMENTS

Photographs in this book were supplied by the following photographers and agencies. Work commissioned by Reader's Digest is shown in italics. Where more than one photographer contributed to a page the positions of the photographs are indicated by the letters: t (top), b (bottom), c (centre), l (left) and r (right).

7 *Richard Dudley-Smith*; **9** *Lucinda Lambton*; **13** *Nigel Cassidy*; **15** Neil Holmes; **16** *Andrew Lawson*; **17** *David Gallant*; **19** By permission of the Birmingham Museum & Art Gallery; **20** *David Gallant*; **21** *Ric Gemmell*; **22** *Colin Molyneux*; **24** *Lucinda Lambton*; **25** *Philip Llewellin*; **26** *Colin Molyneux*; **28–29** *Patrick Thurston*; **30** *Martyn F. Chillmaid*; **33** *Lucinda Lambton*; **35** *David Gallant*; **37–38** *Colin Molyneux*; **39** t *Phillip Evans*, b Robert Eames/Fotobank International; **40–41** *Patrick Thurston*; **43** *David Gallant*; **44** *Christopher Drew*; **45** t *Tony Howarth*, bl *Trevor Wood*, br *Philip Llewellin*, ctr National Portrait Gallery, London, cbr *Neil Holmes*; **47** *Nigel Cassidy*; **48** The Mansell Collection; **51–52** *Philip Llewellin*; **53** *Jon Wyand*; **54** *Colin Molyneux*; **55** *Andrew Lawson*; **57** *Philip Llewellin*; **58** *Penny Tweedie*; **59** Bredwardine *Colin Molyneux*, others *Neil Holmes*; **60–61** *Trevor Wood*; **63–64** *Jason Shenai*; **66–68** *Neil Holmes*; **69** *Patrick Thurston*; **70** The Mansell Collection; **71** *Jason Shenai*; **73** t *Martyn F. Chillmaid*, b *David Gallant*; **75** t *Colin Molyneux*; b *Martyn F. Chillmaid*; **76–77** *Neil Holmes*; **78** *Andrew Lawson*; **79** *David Gallant*; **80–82** *Nigel Cassidy*; **83** *David Gallant*; **84** cr The National Portrait Gallery, London, others *Nigel Cassidy*; **85** *Richard Dudley-Smith*; **86** t *Philip Llewellin*, b *Jon Wyand*; **89** *Philip Llewellin*; **90** *David Gallant*; **91** *Patrick Thurston*; **92–93** *Nigel Cassidy*; **94** *Neil Holmes*; **95** tr & bc *David Gallant*, bl & br *Philip Llewellin*; **96–97** *Patrick Thurston*; **98** Peter Clayton; **99** t *Philip Llewellin*, b *Colin Molyneux*; **100–101** *Neil Holmes*; **101** b *Philip Llewellin*; **102–103** *David Gallant*; **104–105** John Bethell; **106–107** *Patrick Thurston*; **108–109** *Jason Shenai*; **111** *Andrew Lawson*; **112** John Bulmer; **113** l *Patrick Thurston*, r *Colin Molyneux*; **114–115** *Colin Molyneux*; **116** The National Portrait Gallery, London; **117** *Malcolm Aird*; **118–119** *David Gallant*; **120–123**, **124** tl, bl *Philip Llewellin*; **124–125** *Julian Plowright*; **127** *Malcolm Aird*; **128–129** *Patrick Thurston*; **129** t & r *Patrick Thurston*, b The Mansell Collection; **130–131** *Nigel Cassidy*; **132–133** *David Gallant*; **133** br St Bride's Library; **134–135** *Jon Wyand*; **136–137** *David Gallant*; **139** Warwick Castle; **140** *Trevor Wood*; **141** The Mansell Collection; **142–143** *Nigel Cassidy*; **144–145** *Martyn F. Chillmaid*; **146–147** *Julian Plowright*; **148** *Richard Dudley-Smith*; **150–151** *Penny Tweedie*; **152** l & r John Bulmer, c John Sims; **153** *Richard Dudley-Smith*; **155** *Patrick Thurston*.

Artwork in this book was commissioned by Reader's Digest from the following artists.

8 *Peter Reddick*; **10** *Tim Hayward*; **11** *Derek Rodgers*; **14** *Brian Dell*; **27** *Richard Bonson*; **31** *Marjorie Saynor*; **48** *Colin Emberson*; **50** *John Francis/Robert Morton*; **59** *David Baird*; **66–67** *Ivan Lapper*; **68** *David Nockels*; **72** (top) *Richard Lewington*; **72** (centre) *Helen Senior*; **72** (bottom) *Leonora Box*; **75** (top left) *Eric Robson*; **75** (top right) *Ken Wood*; **75** (bottom right) *Peter Barratt*; **77** *Norman Arlott*; **84** *David Nockels*; **87** *Sandra Pond*; **88** *Ken Wood*; **94** *Nicholas Hall*; **96** *Brenda Katté*; **110** (top) *Nicholas Hall*; **110** (bottom) *Shirley Felts*; **113** (top) *Helen Senior*; **113** (bottom) *Norman Arlott*; **120** *Nick Hall*; **126** *Norman Arlott*.

The publishers would like to express their thanks to the local authorities, Tourist Boards and Tourist Information Centres for their help, and to Hilary Bird who compiled the index.

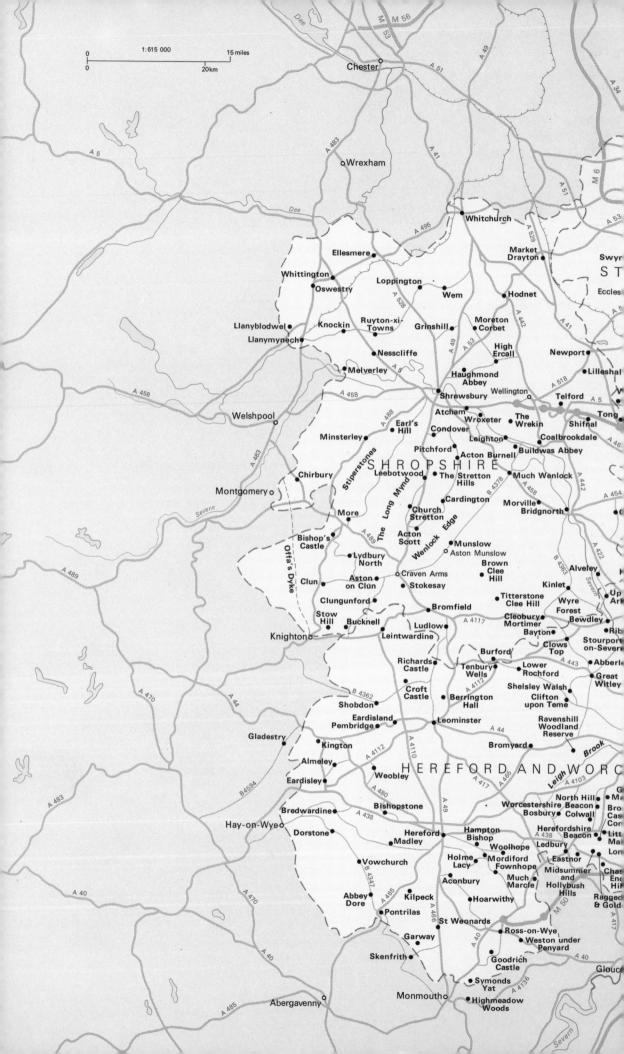